K

Nicaragua

Nicaragua

THE CHAMORRO YEARS

David Close

LYNNE
RIENNER
PUBLISHERS

BOULDER
LONDON

Published in the United States of America in 1999 by
Lynne Rienner Publishers, Inc.
1800 30th Street, Boulder, Colorado 80301

and in the United Kingdom by
Lynne Rienner Publishers, Inc.
3 Henrietta Street, Covent Garden, London WC2E 8LU

Library of Congress Cataloging-in-Publication Data
Close, David, 1945–
    Nicaragua : the Chamorro years /   David Close.
      p. cm.
    Includes bibliographical references and index.
    ISBN 1-55587-643-9 (hc : alk. paper)
     1. Nicaragua—Politics and government—1990–
    2. Nicaragua—Social conditions—1979–   3. Nicaragua—
Economic conditions—1979–   I. Title.
    F1528.C57   1999
    972.8505'4—dc21   98-27844
                                                CIP

British Cataloguing in Publication Data
A Cataloguing in Publication record for this book
is available from the British Library.

Printed and bound in the United States of America

 The paper used in this publication meets the requirements
of the American National Standard for Permanence of
Paper for Printed Library Materials Z39.48-1984.

5 4 3 2 1

Contents

Tables

Acknowledgments

Work on this project began in 1990, right after the election that pushed the Sandinista National Liberation Front from office in Nicaragua. The initial steps of the research were supported by a grant from the Social Sciences and Humanities Research Council of Canada. Later, salary-based research grants through the Memorial University of Newfoundland funded the work.

Having done research in and on Nicaragua since 1983, I have made many friends and acquaintances who have helped in innumerable ways. Listing them all would make the acknowledgments longer than the book, so I cannot name everyone. With that proviso, particular thanks go to David Dye, María Elena Martínez, Judy Butler, Luís Humberto Guzmán, Shelley McConnell, Felipe Rios, and many others whose assistance made my task easier and more enjoyable. Michael Wallack deserves more than a free book for having read the manuscript. Sherrill Pike gets special thanks for being a supportive friend, acute critic, good text editor, and able guardian of house and dogs while I was away. At Lynne Rienner Publishers, thanks are due, first, to Lynne Rienner, for taking an active interest in the project, and to Shena Redmond, senior project editor. With that much help there should be no errors left, but if there are, they are plainly mine alone.

David Close

Introduction: Sandinista to Post-Sandinista Nicaragua

For most of the more than 175 years that Nicaragua has been independent, it has been ruled by tyrants or oligarchs. Democracy—government in the interest of, chosen by, and accountable to all the people—did not figure into the country's politics. All of this was supposed to change when the Sandinistas overthrew the last ruling Somoza, General Anastasio Somoza Debayle, on 19 July 1979. Though the nation has become more democratic since the fall of the dictatorship, times have been anything but tranquil.

Since the start of the last big Sandinista push against the Somoza regime began in September 1978, Nicaragua has been in a constant state of political flux. The expulsion of the Somozas ushered in the "new Nicaragua," revolutionary, bold, and hopeful. This new Nicaragua was to make a transition to socialism different from all others in history, because it would permit a measure of political pluralism and would see the private sector coexisting with the state-centered economy.

By 1984, however, the new Nicaragua was already a part of history. The Sandinista National Liberation Front (FSLN) still governed but did so with different political institutions and distinct economic policies. More important, the Sandinista state had replaced revolutionary transformation with the institutionalization of the revolution as its principal political objective. In practice, this meant adapting the machinery of constitutional democracy (elections and representative government) to the needs of an embattled revolutionary state. In spite of its new state machinery and approach to governing, the FSLN had not given up the idea of building socialism in Nicaragua. Thus, its democracy was still a radically egalitarian one that aimed to limit the power of private wealth.

On 25 February 1990, this reformed Sandinista Nicaragua joined the original edition in the pages of history after the FSLN lost a general election to its conservative opponent, the National Union of the Opposition

1

(UNO).This marked the end of the revolutionary state. Nicaragua's government again embraced capitalism and promised that it would use the conventional political instruments in place to seek totally nonrevolutionary political ends. For the third time in just over a decade, Nicaragua's governors redefined their state, changing the ways politics would work and promising the nation a radically new path to its future.

The first (1979) and latest (1990) changes were especially profound, involving not just governing personnel, but the whole philosophy underlying the role and nature of government. Where before 1979, the state was often called on to protect the interests of the dictator's family and friends or of the established elites more generally, between 1979 and 1990, its purpose was to defend the poor and marginalized and make them "architects of their liberation."[1] After 1990, the Nicaraguan state would no longer be the defender of the workers and peasants and the architect of socialism, but rather would set about to dismantle the Sandinista legacy.

Where the Sandinista regime had been revolutionary, the post-Sandinista state would be counterrevolutionary. This was inevitable. The most resolutely anti-Sandinista politicians and political parties in Nicaragua made up the UNO. Their objective was to "de-Sandinize" the country, a process that went beyond ousting the FSLN from power to include thoroughly restructuring the system of economic, political, and social power that the revolution had nourished.

Not all counterrevolutionaries were reactionaries, however. To be a reactionary in Nicaragua in 1990 meant wanting a political system as close to what the Somozas had as one could get in a world intolerant of overt dictatorships. Although some UNO backers doubtless were reactionaries, many others sought constitutional democracy and the rule of law. Though no friends of either the Sandinistas or the revolution, they were very much on the side of open, accountable government. President Violeta Barrios de Chamorro, most of her cabinet, and a substantial number of legislative deputies actually belonged in this camp.[2] In fact, over the Chamorro administration's years in office, tensions within the UNO would contribute as much to making the country unstable and ungovernable as would relations between the FSLN and Nicaragua's new governors.

Whatever else this ceaseless change may mean, it certainly suggests that some substantial part of the country's citizens would really prefer one of the earlier political systems, Sandinista or Somocista, to the conventional constitutional democracy that arrived in 1990. Rapid and continuous political change works against consolidating and institutionalizing any system of rule. As a result, it is unlikely that there exists in Nicaragua a public philosophy—a view of what the state should do, at whose orders, and in what ways—that is acceptable to everyone. Without a common public philosophy to unite them, different factions see no need to tolerate one another. Indeed, holding contrasting notions of what a good state does to build a good society can impel opposing political blocs to view one another as enemies. Politics then becomes not a way to seek a necessarily shifting consensus, but an exercise in the arts of war.

Though Nicaragua's many recent political transformations have not produced an accord on the purposes of government, there is no disagreement that their price has been high. Besides the routine costs of significant political change (new departments and officials, new laws and regulations, new forms and procedures, and a different shade of red tape), Nicaragua's political reincarnations have been marked by conflict, much of it bloody. Each iteration of the revised Nicaraguan state was supposed to bring tranquillity and prosperity to the land. The two Sandinista variations failed to do this, though the revolutionaries left a substantial legacy. What can be said of the political system put in place by the politicians who defeated the FSLN at the polls, the administration of President Chamorro?

This book examines the Nicaraguan political system as it was from 1990 to 1996, presenting what happened during the Chamorro years. It is, first of all, a political history of the administration of Nicaragua's first female president, but it aims to be more than a mere recitation of facts and figures. When President Chamorro took up the reins of government on 25 April 1990, she inherited a country racked by war and worn by material hardship—and also a country whose political institutions and psyche had been profoundly changed by a decade of Sandinista rule. With a good dose of luck, Doña Violeta, as the president is universally known in her homeland, could have drawn out the positive from the revolutionary era and blended it with the merits of orthodox constitutionalism to give Nicaragua a political transition that would have astounded the world. Though this was not to be her fate, Chamorro did steer her nation through six difficult years, maintain a fundamentally constitutional regime, and turn power over to a legally elected successor from another party. The elements that led to this outcome and how Nicaragua's political system changed in the process are the central parts of this analysis.

Reaching beyond the immediate Nicaraguan context, the book is a detailed empirical study of the democratization of one political system. Since the mid-1970s, when the dictatorships in Greece, Portugal, and Spain fell, a great deal of intellectual energy has been expended on trying to understand how countries navigate the passage between authoritarianism and constitutional democracy. In fact, "transitology," to use Valerie Bunce's term,[3] has become an academic cottage industry. But in this exercise of trying to comprehend the dynamics of what Samuel Huntington labels "the third wave of democracy,"[4] Nicaragua has received surprisingly little notice.

Alone among the world's transitional systems, Nicaragua has gone from the unquestioned patrimonial praetorianism (a government run in the interest of the ruler and sustained by military force) of the Somoza state to the fundamentally orthodox electoral democracy of the Chamorro administration by way of revolutionary radicalism. This certainly merits attention, if only because remnants of both the Somoza system (Somocismo) and its Sandinista counterpart (Sandinismo) emerged to vex President Chamorro and her government. A country heir to two such dissimilar political traditions must pose different problems to its governors than one whose past is solely military authoritarian or Marxist-Leninist.

Nicaragua's path to democracy is notable for another reason as well. Of all the political systems that have embraced constitutional government in the last quarter of the twentieth century, Sandinista Nicaragua had the best claim to be called democratic itself. True to its radical, revolutionary democratic roots, the Sandinista government emphasized participation by the poor and introduced programs that built the social, economic, and cultural equality needed to offset the historic advantages of the wealthy and privileged. Further, the FSLN did this with a political order that was more pluralistic than any of its Central American neighbors, save Costa Rica. Democratic transition in Nicaragua was not about introducing democracy where none had existed before, but rather about moving from one form of democracy to another. The challenge facing the Chamorro administration was to assure that the exchange did not go wrong and leave the country with no democracy at all.

Equally important to understanding Nicaragua's transition is remembering that, although the country's political face changed dramatically after 1979, its social and economic structure retained far more of its prerevolutionary nature. In his analysis of Spain's democratic transformation, Victor Pérez-Díaz places great weight on that country's cultural, economic, and social evolution during the last twenty years of the Franco dictatorship.[5] That evolution left Spain a nation much more like the rest of western Europe than it had been in the fifties, and it made "Francoism-after-Franco" impossible. However, in Nicaragua, although real property was more equitably distributed than before the Sandinista revolution and the popular classes were better educated and more active politically, the country itself was as poor and underdeveloped in 1990 as it had been in 1979. Whether this socioeconomic foundation could sustain liberal constitutional democracy was very much an open question.

The study of contemporary democratization suggests that the process has two steps: transition proper and consolidation.[6] "Democratic transition" is the name applied to the business of choosing a constitutional democracy to replace an unconstitutional, authoritarian regime. In Nicaragua, unlike in most other countries,[7] transition has been a prolonged process, carried on in dissimilar ways by governments representing two very distinct ideologies.

Sandinista Nicaragua was unquestionably more democratic than its Somocista predecessor, but its vision of what made a state democratic (social and economic equality combined with high levels of political participation by the popular classes) had little in common with views espoused by the Chamorro administration (representative, constitutional government and the rule of law).[8]

Democratic consolidation comes after democratic transition. Democratic government is deemed to have been consolidated when no important political actors either wish to dispense with democracy entirely or depose a sitting, democratically installed government by unconstitutional means. In a consolidated democracy the conditions, practices, and machinery of democratic politics (effective protection for human rights, freedom of opposition, governmental accountability to citizens through elections, well-functioning representative organs, and independent judiciaries) are the regular institutions of rule. Institutions imply solidity. They function today much as they did yesterday and much as they will tomorrow. Institutions do change—they come into existence, evolve, and eventually are replaced or absorbed by other institutions—but they generally do not do so randomly.

Consolidating democracy, then, means that democratic institutions are the normal framework for winning control of and running the state. This, however, demands a consensus around not just the idea of democracy, a concept capable of being defined vaguely enough to please everyone, but a specific constitutional structure. In the United States this broad concurrence came only after the Civil War, three-quarters of a century after the Republic's founding. France took even longer, only arriving at a model of governance agreeable to all significant elements of society with the establishment of the Third Republic, eighty-two years after the French Revolution.[9]

Nicaragua shares some interesting, though troubling, ground with the two great pioneers of liberal constitutional democracy. In all three, the process of democratic consolidation is complicated by the existence of radically divergent public philosophies—all, save the French monarchists, claiming some affinity with democracy. In such a case, movement toward making constitutional democracy the only imaginable political system is perforce slow, because a lot of people have to be convinced that a specific democratic order will secure their aims, or at least not do them grave harm. Unfortunately, the U.S. and French precedents also suggest that cataclysmic violence has a part to play. For Nicaragua to avoid adding to its already long and sad history of violence, some way must be found to build confidence that democratic government actually works for everyone. Knowing how Nicaragua coped with its peculiar challenges between 1990 and 1996 will tell us how one actual government confronted concrete problems when building a new regime.

Nicaragua certainly offers an impressive array of problems and issues to consider. Since 1990, the country has experienced a significant revision of its state institutions and of most public policies, though it stopped short of the sort of total overhaul that took place in Central and Eastern Europe. The constitution adopted by the Sandinista state in 1987 has been substantially altered; although doing so almost brought government to a complete halt, much of the original document remains. The security forces shed their Sandinista labels, and a totally new law governing the military was adopted. Further, the state-centered Sandinista economic model was scrapped in favor of a free market approach. The new economic model brought in its train drastic reductions in the scope of welfare provisions, producing deep and widespread material distress.

Political restructuring of such magnitude necessarily generates opposition. Nicaragua's new political and economic order was contested both within the confines of governmental institutions, especially the legislature, and in the streets and mountains, where so much of the nation's recent history has been written. Besides the Chamorro administration and the Sandinistas, many others were involved in the process: organized labor; people whose property had been expropriated (*confiscados*); demobilized soldiers—both ex-contras (counterrevolutionaries) and Sandinista army veterans; the Catholic Church; the media; international financial institutions (IFIs); and the U.S. government. President Chamorro did not have an uninteresting term.

Obviously, it is impossible to give every aspect of the Chamorro administration equal attention. I have decided to emphasize factors touching partisan politics, the structure of the state and the operation of state institutions, and the effects of the redesigned economic policy. This clearly emphasizes the formal side of politics, as well as the political side of Nicaragua's recent history. Although some will find that such an approach leaves important things uncovered, or at best ill-covered, this method does make comparisons with other transitional polities easier. Several examples will help illustrate this.

As I have already implied, one of the distinguishing marks of the Chamorro administration was the continuous struggle among several contenders to define the nature of the post-Sandinista regime. The Sandinistas naturally wanted to minimize the change, while the most ardent anti-Sandinistas in the UNO sought to maximize it. Though it is misleading to think of President Chamorro as walking a tightrope between these extremes, because her administration did dismantle much of the old revolutionary system, she, her cabinet, and their agenda did not enjoy the support of the majority of Nicaragua's political establishment. As a result, Chamorro had to confront substantial political instability during the first five years of her term.

Analysts of democratic transition and consolidation argue that the most promising new democracies began life with an agreement about fundamental principles among the major players that guaranteed a measure of stability for a few years. This sort of interelite pact was either very limited or simply did not exist in Nicaragua. Still, the very survival of constitutional government in the country raises questions about how much consensus on basic values and institutional forms is needed. For instance, it may be that Nicaragua shows the absolute minimum level of concord among contending political elites needed for constitutional government to exist. Alternatively, the fact that the security forces, especially the army, stood with the administration (or against its rightist critics, to be more precise) throughout the six years may be the vital element. Whichever the case, President Chamorro's government had to confront profound and repeated conflicts over very basic issues. How she and her administration resolved these disputes will interest all students of democratic transition and consolidation.

Another aspect of the Chamorro years that merits attention concerns democratic strengthening: increasing the capacity of the everyday machinery of democracy to govern effectively. The usual targets for democratic strengthening are electoral administrations, legislatures, judiciaries, and political parties. The reasoning behind such projects is simply to make these key political institutions work the same way as their counterparts in established constitutional democracies. In Nicaragua the legislature did become stronger, though with unforeseen results, but the other featured players fared less well. The courts remained weak, parties stayed vehicles for personal promotion, and the electoral administration—once the pride of Nicaragua's public service—fell into disrepute because of its inefficiency. How this happened, why this happened, and what let the government survive this failure to enhance critical democratic machinery are matters of keen practical importance, as well as of substantial theoretical concern.

A further question emerging from the experience of the Chamorro administration is that of how a new constitutional democracy copes with potentially regime-threatening political problems. It was once held by students of political development that although established liberal democracies had confronted a series of predictable political crises one at a time, countries now democratizing faced a combination of crises simultaneously.[10] Russia, for example, has to build a capitalist economy at the same time that it adapts to new geographic boundaries, a changed international role, a totally novel constitution and political machinery, and new rules of political competition and standards of acceptable political conduct.

Nicaragua's challenges are a little less intimidating and fall into three categories: reorganizing the economy; settling claims for property expropriated by the revolutionary government; and addressing constitutional reform. The government's responses to these problems, as well as the degree of success it had in dealing with them, are important to know for two reasons. They are, first, essential parts of the story of the Chamorro years, the pith and substance of the administration's task. But beyond that, knowing how one government, poor in material resources and facing strong opponents, sought concrete policies to respond to grave political challenges will provide useful maps for others who have to cut through similar thickets. Though the problems of new constitutional democracies in the late twentieth century may be common to all, the solutions to these problems have to be found one country at a time.

This is not to suggest that Nicaragua is somehow a "typical" country in transition. Its recent history excludes it from typicality. I have studied Nicaragua actively now for some fifteen years, and in that time I have felt the hopefulness of a young revolutionary state, the determination of a nation at war, and the relief of a country sensing that it had found a path leading it away from its violent past. During these eventful years Nicaragua has grappled with economic chaos—some of it the product of faulty policies, natural disasters, bitter disputes over public issues, and of course war and instability. One thing I have learned is that every time it seems that Nicaragua is about to tumble irredeemably into the abyss, something good happens. Nicaraguans either have mastered better than other nationalities the art of conjuring hope from despair or they simply have done it so often that it is now a common political skill.

Though the Sandinista revolution did not fulfill the hopes of its architects, and even brought great pain to many Nicaraguans, the inauguration of Violeta Chamorro as president of the republic in April 1990 promised a chance to start over. By the end of her mandate Nicaraguans were again searching for new answers, having again seen a government fail to meet their expectations. Yet despite these disappointments, Nicaraguans continued to enjoy the freedom of constitutional, democratic government. Nearly two decades (1979–1996) of political change and innovation had added another war, continued political violence, and unrelieved economic hardship to the country's list of sorrows, but they had also brought glimmerings of justice and liberty.

The Plan of the Book

A central premise of this book is that the Chamorro years are best seen as a part of Nicaragua's long struggle to secure democratic government. Therefore, the first two chapters set out the historical context in which Violeta Chamorro became president. Chapter 1 presents an overview of the country's political history up to 1990. This not only sets the scene for

Chamorro's coming to power, but also reviews the principal trends, key events, and important names in Nicaraguan history. Chapter 2 examines the momentous election of February 1990 and the two-month period between it and Chamorro's inauguration. These sixty days would set much of the political tone of the next six years, as well as define the terms of the debate over expropriated property that dogged the administration until late 1995. This chapter also begins the work of putting Nicaragua's political transformation into comparative perspective.

The next four chapters look at the operation of politics during the Chamorro years. The institutional and legal framework is the subject of Chapter 3, which explores the 1987 constitution (in place until mid-1995), looks at the main players in national politics, and describes something of the administration's organization. Chapter 4 charts the operational dynamics of the political system between 1990 and 1996. Concretely, it presents a selection of the issues that made news and shaped Nicaragua's political universe: violence and ungovernability, executive-legislative conflict, and *cogobierno* (co-government)—the FSLN's support for the Chamorro cabinet. The economy is the subject of Chapter 5. It treats both the administration's relations with multilateral lenders (notably, the International Monetary Fund [IMF] and the World Bank) and the resulting structural adjustment program (SAP), as well as domestic policies aimed at reestablishing a more purely capitalist economy. Chapter 6 is dedicated to examining the two most serious crises of the Chamorro presidency: the constitutional conflict of 1993–1995 and the property question that remained contested throughout all of the period under review.

Nicaragua's troubled 1996 elections are featured in Chapter 7. Where the elections of 1984 and 1990 had been controversial because of suspicions that the Sandinistas would manipulate them, this latest vote was disputed due to administrative failings. These produced great confusion in the postelectoral period that, as in 1990, left a residue of distrust to haunt the newly elected president. Finally, Chapter 8 assesses Nicaragua's transition toward institutionalized democratic rule. Though it weighs the effects of both the Sandinista revolutionary government and the current administration of Arnoldo Alemán, it is principally concerned with evaluating how the country's democratic trajectory changed during the Chamorro years.

Notes

1. The term "architects of their liberation" comes from "Himno Sandinista," the Sandinista party anthem.

2. Though the legislators seemed at first to be among the hardest of the hard line, and thus part of the alliance's reactionary wing, within three years of taking office the majority of UNO deputies had abandoned the most right-wing of their

colleagues. This majority did not, however, back the president. Chapters 2, 3, 4, and 6 recount different parts of this story.

3. Valerie Bunce, "Should Transitologists Be Grounded?" *Slavic Review* 54:1 (1995): 111–127.

4. Samuel Huntington, *The Third Wave* (Norman: University of Oklahoma Press, 1991).

5. Victor M. Pérez-Díaz, *The Return of Civil Society* (Cambridge, MA: Harvard University Press, 1993), chap. 1.

6. Pérez-Díaz adds a third phase, institutionalization, to distinguish between the points at which there is no credible threat to the democratic regime (consolidation) and where representative democracy is recognized as legitimate and its rules internalized by most citizens (institutionalization) (*The Return of Civil Society,* pp. 3–4). This distinction is revisited in Chapter 8 herein.

7. The only countries in a situation truly similar to Nicaragua's are Angola, Mozambique, and perhaps Guinea-Bissau. Ethiopia shows some parallels, but it is my sense that the Dergue was less responsive and accountable and more repressive than were the Sandinistas.

8. Regardless of how many steps the process of democratization involves, contemporary political science overwhelmingly defines it as about *political* democracy—that is, accountable government, free and open politics, and respect for human rights. The possibility of using democracy to secure social, economic, and cultural equality and broaden the reach of democracy is seldom considered. To my mind, this reflects the sometimes unspoken assumptions that free government demands a free market and that a free market cannot be constrained to produce social and economic equality without compromising the entire democratic project. This could hardly be more different from the perspective of nineteenth-century North American and European democrats who saw democratic government as the means that would let the people use the power of their votes to break the power that aristocrats and capitalists obtained through birth and wealth. The class element in democracy has been well and deeply interred in contemporary political thinking.

9. One could even argue that the French did not settle on a model for constitutional government until the founding of the Fifth Republic in 1958, 169 years after the start of the Revolution.

10. Leonard Binder, et al., *Crises and Sequences in Political Development* (Princeton, NJ: Princeton University Press, 1971).

1

The (Not So Very) Old Regime: The Sandinista Legacy

Violeta Chamorro's years as president of Nicaragua should interest analysts for several reasons. First, she is the first woman elected president in a Latin American republic. Second, her electoral victory in 1990 marked the first time in the country's history that power had been transferred peacefully from one party to another. Third, Chamorro took the reins of power from the Sandinista National Liberation Front, which had seized power by a revolution in 1979 and was a self-proclaimed vanguard party committed to building socialism. Finally, Nicaragua was emotionally and materially drained by a decade spent fighting a counterrevolutionary civil war and coping with economic hardship.

President Chamorro faced daunting challenges. She had to reunite a nation torn by internal warfare and reconcile old enemies. Chamorro also had to restart the nation's economy. Further, her administration was determined to replace the statist, redistributive policies of the Sandinistas with more market-friendly ones. And she was heading a government that had to engineer a political transition from the radical populism of the FSLN, whose style was mobilizational and whose base was among the poor and working classes, to a more conservative representative democracy that shifted power back toward established elites.

Although many of Chamorro's colleagues in Latin America and elsewhere were similarly involved in charting a transition toward representative democracy, her task was at once easier and harder. It was harder than that faced by some, first because Nicaragua had to make an economic transition to reconvert to capitalist orthodoxy as it reoriented its politics and also because the old regime was not thoroughly repudiated—it won 41 percent of the vote in 1990. But the new president was heir to a political system that needed little reform to allow a conventional, Western-style democracy to function.

Western-style democracy is constitutional, representative democracy. It is identified by a number of characteristics: an essentially free opposition; regular, free elections with universal suffrage; the recognition and enforcement of human rights and civil liberties; a free judiciary; and a representative assembly that is not a cipher. This is a *political* democracy. Its objective is to let citizens make their government responsive and accountable to them. Constitutional, representative democracy does not prescribe any particular economic or social arrangements, beyond some form of capitalism, though at least moderate economic and social equality among citizens is needed if the system is to work.

Logically, the path a political transition follows to establish democracy must be related to the nature of the old regime. Elements of the old system incompatible with this new democracy have to be fixed. Some of these elements are institutional, such as government structures or the legal system. Others are processual, the way the old regime made policy and governed. Included here are the party system; how interests are represented, even which interests are represented; how opposition can be expressed and by whom; and the balance between persuasion and coercion employed to enforce policies. Further, there are behavioral elements: not just how citizens are permitted to express opinions, but the whole web of expectations that they develop about how governments and citizens normally act toward each other, the political culture.

The more closely the old regime resembles a constitutional democracy, everything else being equal, the easier the transition should be. There is less distance to travel, and equally important, both political activists and ordinary citizens have habits adapted to democratic politics. Following this logic, a country with a history of constitutional, representative government that was broken by a spell of dictatorship ought to have a good chance to consolidate democratic rule. Here the key is being able to restore the institutions and dynamics of democracy, instead of building them from scratch. And in both cases there is a domestic foundation, even if a limited one, on which to build the new regime.

On a more practical level, the politics of the old regime sets out the particular problem areas a new government will have to address if it is to craft a democracy. Is there a politicized military to be kept content? Do the police have to learn respect for human rights and legal procedures? If political opposition was illegal or licensed, how can a new regime foster the growth of responsible opposition among parties, the media, and interest groups? The gaps left by the old system define the challenges for the new.

Interpreting the legacy the Sandinista state left Nicaragua's new government in 1990 has partisan overtones. President Chamorro's electoral alliance, the National Union of the Opposition, liked to see its victory as the first democratic act in the country's history. In this they were joined by the U.S. government, which, since the Republicans took the White House in 1980, had branded the Sandinistas remorseless dictators. Yet these assertions overlook both the fact that the FSLN lost power in internationally observed elections and that the revolutionary regime had never been quite the totalitarian ogre its enemies claimed.

Because it is necessary to have a clear sense of the foundations on which President Chamorro would begin building her vision of Nicaraguan democracy, this chapter presents a capsule history of the Sandinista period. In particular, it emphasizes those parts of the FSLN's record that arguably either gave the Chamorro administration a head start on this project or presented the new government an extraordinary obstacle. Although the main focus is government and politics, the economic and social effects of a decade's rule by the FSLN also figure in this portrait. Though these elements all affect the construction of constitutional democracy in Nicaragua, consideration of theories of democratic transition and consolidation and their applicability to Nicaragua's experience will not be undertaken until the next chapter.

The FSLN's Revolutionary Era, 1979–1984

The Background to the Sandinista Revolution

Recalling Central America's political history summons up images of strife and turbulence. Though every country in the isthmus, even Costa Rica, has known more than its share of violence and instability, Nicaragua seems to have been especially unfortunate.[1] The first forty years of the country's independent life were marked by continuous civil war that ended only when the nation was captured by William Walker, a freebooting filibuster from New Orleans. Walker's design, to turn Nicaragua into a new slave state in the American Union, was frustrated by a pan–Central American armed force in 1857. Though the mercenary's fall opened the way to thirty years of peace, Nicaragua had not seen the last of either political unrest or armed intervention from the United States.

From 1889 to 1909, the Liberal dictator José Santos Zelaya ruled Nicaragua.[2] A hero to some at home, because he assured national dominion over the country's remote Atlantic coast where Britain had long held sway, Zelaya had some very important enemies. Domestically, the Nicaraguan Conservatives he had ousted from power by a coup in 1889 were constantly contriving revolutionary plots. Internationally, Washington disapproved of Zelaya's repeated interference in the affairs of other Central American states and took particular umbrage at his plan to invite Japanese and German capitalists to build a canal across Nicaragua to compete with the U.S. project in Panama. The two streams converged in 1909 when the U.S. government backed a Conservative revolution that toppled its nemesis.

Assisting in the overthrow of the Zelaya regime was but the beginning of a quarter century of direct U.S. political involvement in Nicaraguan politics. A serious threat to the newly installed Conservative government caused Washington to send a force of Marines to Nicaragua in 1912. Withdrawn in 1925, the US military returned in 1926 as civil war again threatened the country. This time the U.S. engagement lasted until 1933, and it was during this period that both Augusto César Sandino and Anastasio Somoza García arrived on Nicaragua's political scene.

Like many other Liberals, including Somoza, Sandino joined the rising against the ruling Conservatives in 1926. The conflict officially ended in 1927, with the U.S.-brokered Peace of Tipitapa giving the presidency to a Liberal general and calling for elections the next year. Sandino, however, did not lay down his arms. An ardent Nicaraguan nationalist and fierce anti-imperialist, he vowed to drive the Marines from his native soil. Over the next six years, Sandino and his Defending Army of National Sovereignty (Ejercito Defensor de la Soberanía Nacional) waged a successful guerrilla struggle against the Marines and the U.S.-trained Nicaraguan National Guard. Never defeated, "the General of Free Men" agreed to lay down his arms once the foreign occupiers withdrew.[3]

Somoza's role in the drama was starkly different.[4] Sent to Philadelphia to live with relatives after getting the family maid pregnant, Anastasio ("Tacho") Somoza returned home fluent in English. This and his affability landed him a job as translator for U.S. Secretary of War Henry Stimson, who was in Nicaragua negotiating the Tipitapa agreement. Somoza performed his task well, earning U.S. trust sufficiently to be the Marines' choice to command the National Guard when the United States withdrew.

Though the United States organized the Nicaraguan National Guard in a laudable effort to create a professional, nonpartisan military that would not meddle in civilian politics, that effort failed.[5] Putting Tacho Somoza in command of the guard indeed insured that it would become a political instrument. Within two months of the Marines' departure, the guard had captured and assassinated Sandino, who had come to the capital, Managua, to discuss peace plans. Within two years, it became the vehicle that let Somoza oust the legitimately elected president, his wife's uncle, from office, opening the way for the Somoza family to dominate Nicaragua for the next four decades.

The Somozas' control of the country stands as a remarkable feat of political engineering.[6] Not only did the two sons of Tacho Somoza—Luis and Anastasio Jr., another Tacho—inherit the presidential sash, the family was able to entrust the state to loyalists when political reasons forced it to vacate the presidency. The Somozas could do this because they always retained command of the National Guard, even when they left the chief executive's office in other hands. Assuring the National Guard's loyalty were two related policies. Enlisted men were recruited from the poorest parts of Nicaragua, taught to read and write, given a decent wage and some social benefits. Officers got all that plus lots of opportunities for graft. In both cases, the recipients knew that their benefactor was whichever Somoza commanded the Guard.

But it takes more than coercion to govern even a poor country for two generations. The first Somoza, Tacho Sr., was skilled at co-opting opponents when he chose that path. His handiwork was best seen in a pact he negotiated with the Conservatives in 1950 that assured the latter one-third of the legislative seats, judicial and diplomatic appointments, and representation on the boards of state-owned enterprises (SOEs) and international delegations; in return, the Conservatives accepted being perpetual also-rans. Beyond his political abilities, Tacho Sr. also promoted Nicaragua's economic modernization. Under his aegis the country developed into a substantial cotton producer in the 1950s, opening new opportunities for the nation's economic elite. None of this, however, was enough to spare Tacho a typical dictator's demise: assassination by a poet in 1956.

Luis succeeded to the presidency and, after imposing a short-lived reign of terror to root out supposed conspirators against the regime, continued his father's policy of mixing coercion with co-optation. What distinguished this second Somoza was his intention to remove the family from the daily chores of governing. He believed that the Nationalist Liberal Party (PLN), the Somozas' own, could govern successfully without a Somoza at the helm. To this end, he did not amend the constitution to give himself a second successive term in office but passed the baton to the reliable René Schick. The strategy might have worked had not both Luis and Schick died, allowing the younger Somoza brother to claim his patrimony.

Tacho Jr., or "Tachito," the last Somoza, was far more reckless and violent than his father or brother. These attributes would lead him to alienate the Nicaraguan establishment, the Catholic Church, and the upper classes, who should have been his supporters against the Sandinistas. This second Tacho's decline began after Managua's disastrous 1972 earthquake, when he and his allies pilfered relief supplies. It continued as Somoza-owned firms began to compete vigorously with the rest of the private sector, using their ties to the state to gain an unfair advantage. By 1978, support for the last Somoza shrank further as thugs, presumably in the pay of the dictator, assassinated newspaper publisher and leading opposition figure Pedro Joaquín Chamorro (Violeta's husband). From that point until the fall of the regime, an increasingly violent National Guard and Somoza's refusal to stand down to "save" Nicaragua from the revolutionaries convinced increasing numbers of even the upper classes that the dynasty was dispensable.

For all its travails, however, the Somoza clan would not have lost power had it not been for the Sandinistas. Over the years the family withstood numerous attempts to overthrow its regime by force, most of these mounted by its historic enemies, the Conservatives. Conventional legal politics offered no openings to the dynasty's foes. The Somozas' PLN had assured its lock on power through its 1950 pact with the Conservatives. The dynasty renewed the deal in 1974, increasing its opponents' share of state positions to 40 percent from the earlier one-third; however, the increased representation reflected Tachito's judgment of what it took to keep the Conservatives on his side, not their growing strength. Less tractable opponents, like the Independent Liberal Party (PLI), the Nicaraguan Socialist Party (PSN), and the Social Christian Party (PSC) were excluded from the deals, but they were not significant political players at the end of the seventies.

Things were not much different outside the realm of party politics. Associational life was not well developed in pre-Sandinista Nicaragua. The agro-export economy allowed little room for the development of labor unions, and before the 1972 earthquake, the possessing classes were willing to acknowledge the Somozas' command over the state that made their wealth secure.[7] Neither had the Catholic Church been a significant political actor before the 1970s. Civil politics, then, offered no possibilities to change the regime, leaving revolutionary violence the only immediate alternative.

The Sandinista National Liberation Front was a politico-military guerrilla organization with significant Marxist roots.[8] Formed in 1961, and inspired by the example of Fidel Castro's Cuban revolution, the FSLN had little success in its early years. In this it differed little from Fidelista offshoots elsewhere in Latin America. Sandinista luck began to change with a dramatic 27 December 1974 raid on the home of a prominent Somoza supporter who was hosting a reception for the U.S. ambassador. Though the guerrillas missed the diplomat, they did capture President Somoza's brother-in-law and cousin. The National Guard surrounded the house in one of the capital's plushest suburbs, and the archbishop of Managua, Miguel Obando y Bravo, was asked to mediate an end to the standoff. The deal Obando negotiated saw fourteen Sandinista prisoners released from jail, a plane readied to fly the guerrillas and their released comrades to Cuba, a payment of $1 million in ransom, and a communiqué to be read on radio and published in Pedro Joaquín Chamorro's newspaper, *La Prensa*.

The Sandinistas, however, could not build on this good fortune. Within two years, the National Guard had reclaimed its military edge over the guerrillas, killing Carlos Fonseca, one of the movement's founders and its leading theoretician. After Fonseca's death, the FSLN entered a downward spiral, splitting into three factions (tendencies), each committed to a different revolutionary strategy. The Prolonged People's War (GPP) faction favored continuing the FSLN's historic strategy of rural guerrilla warfare and the slow "accumulation of forces" in the countryside, even though this tactic had a fifteen-year record of failure. Arguing for emphasizing the cities and organized workers was the Proletarian Tendency (TP), despite Nicaragua having only a shadow of an industrial proletariat. Rounding out the triad was the Insurrectional Tendency, or the Terceristas, who supported forming a broad, multiclass movement to oust the Somozas.

It was the Tercerista outlook that carried the day and became the basis for the Sandinista position adopted in 1979. But this ideological victory did not bring the insurrectionists immediate organizational dominance. Rather, the unification scheme brought representatives of all three tendencies into a National Directorate (DN), the soon-to-be-famous nine "Comandantes of the Revolution" who would chart Nicaragua's fortunes throughout the 1980s. The GPP contributed Tomás Borge, Bayardo Arce, and Henry Ruíz; the TP sent Carlos Nuñez, Jaime Wheelock, and Luis Carrión; and the Terceristas were represented by Victor Tirado, Humberto Ortega, and Daniel Ortega.

Once unity was achieved, things began moving the Sandinistas' way. Not only was the increasingly violent and obdurate Somoza government rapidly losing supporters, but the newly elected Carter administration in Washington was pushing a human rights agenda that meant that Tacho Somoza Jr. could not count on unconditional U.S. support. By early 1978, civilian opposition to Somoza was growing. Businesspeople and professionals organized a Broad Opposition Front (FAO). Fourteen left-wing organizations (mainly parties, unions, and student groups) formed the United People's Movement (MPU), which was linked to the Sandinistas. Also linked to the FSLN, though less closely, were "the Twelve," a dozen intellectuals and executives who had come together in late 1977 to call for a popular insurrection to overthrow the dynasty. As time passed, the relatively moderate FAO lost ground and members (including the Twelve) to the more radical MPU.

The actual military phase of the insurrection lasted from October 1978 to 19 July 1979, with the final offensive beginning in early June. Throughout the country people in working-class neighborhoods tore paving blocks (made in Somoza's cement plant) from the streets to build barricades. When a last-minute effort by Washington to get the Organization of American States (OAS) to send a peacekeeping force to keep the revolutionaries out of power failed, nothing could stand in the way of a Sandinista victory. Somoza decamped for Guatemala on 17 July 1979; two days later the FSLN entered Managua.

Sandinista Rule: The Radical Phase

Where the Somoza regime was built to assure the comfort of a privileged few, Sandinista Nicaragua would be built around the "logic of the majority." This emphasized social, economic, and political reforms that favored the country's underprivileged and marginalized: labor, rural workers and smallholders, women, and the poor. The new policies would be part of a transition to socialism that would forever break with the past. And since the Sandinistas were revolutionaries who had fought the old regime for eighteen years, they wanted to move the transition along smartly. To this end, they installed political machinery that would facilitate change.[9]

Formally heading the revolutionary state was the Governing Junta for National Reconstruction (JGRN). Though this body always had members from outside the FSLN, the Sandinistas always held a majority. In fact, it was the DN, the nine Comandantes of the Revolution who led the FSLN, that actually exercised final authority. This was understandable since the FSLN was a self-proclaimed vanguard party, and a vanguard cannot cede responsibility for directing its revolution.

Besides the DN, the Sandinistas made their presence felt in other parts of the newly restructured state. Where orthodox, bourgeois democracies expected citizens to form pressure groups and political parties to advance their special concerns, revolutionary democracy in Nicaragua was to be built around Sandinista mass organizations. Perhaps more important, the Sandinistas formed the foundation of the revamped military (centered on the Sandinista Popular Army [EPS]) and police force (formally, the Sandinista Police).

A new Nicaragua was to evolve as part of a transition to socialism. It was an article of faith that only a system that restrained the power of private wealth and redistributed resources to the majority could be truly democratic. For in the new Nicaragua, democracy was more than formal rules of the sort found in North American textbooks. Anyone could proclaim a constitution and declare themselves democratic, then happily continue governing by force and fraud. To assure that this did not happen, the FSLN sought a more radical democracy based on substantive material and social equality.

Realizing this aim required more than political transformation, however; economic and social change also had to occur to assure success. Bringing this part of the new Nicaragua into being called for land reform—implying expropriation and expanded rights for organized labor, making it easier to confront capital—the extension of health and education benefits to the poor, and the imposition of a formerly unimagined equality between rich and poor, city dwellers and country folk, men and women.

Promising change of this magnitude strikes fear into conservative hearts. It resonates of Bolshevism, Castroism, and Maoism. It conjures up images of turning the world upside down overnight, to the tune of rolling tumbrels and cries of *"Al paredón!"*—"To the wall!" Yet the new Nicaraguan revolutionary government generally avoided the terror and carnage that had marked previous socialist revolutions. The Sandinistas were able to do this because there was an intellectual commitment, and even more important a moral one, to a limited but real pluralism. This outlook became the distinguishing mark of early Sandinista political practice.

Whether the result of careful calculation or the product of applying the FSLN's democratic principles, Sandinista Nicaragua began life as a more open, tolerant, and pluralistic system than any prior socialist revolutionary state. This is not meant to overlook the new system's failings—notably, a politicized justice system—but it is important to stress that Nicaragua was never Cuba or Czechoslovakia. First, there were functioning opposition parties that eventually carved out enough political space to turn the FSLN out of office. Originally included in the revolutionary regime because of their roles in the struggle against Somoza, these parties were weak and ill-organized, and the most antirevolutionary of them were occasionally harassed by the government. Still, the only permanent legal limitation on them was that they could not promote a return to Somocismo. On the whole, the opposition parties stayed within the law, making it easier for the Sandinistas to tolerate these marginal political forces than to repress them.

Beyond this, a private sector with large, medium, small, and micro-entrepreneurs existed in Nicaragua throughout the revolutionary government's tenure. Though often the bane of the Sandinistas' existence, the private sector retained its independence and was instrumental in the electoral defeat of the revolutionaries. By committing itself at the outset to a mixed economy (meaning here one with a functioning private sector that was rigorously controlled and monitored by the state), the revolutionary government made the private sector a key part of the national economy, one that could occasionally demand preferential treatment.

Finally, the Sandinista era witnessed not just the emergence of mass organizations as policy actors, it also saw new oppositional forces surface. For example, though the Catholic Church hierarchy showed some signs of political initiative in the last days of the Somoza era, it reached maturity as a political agent only through its resolute opposition to the Sandinistas. More interesting, at least one of the mass organizations, the National Union of Farmers and Ranchers (UNAG), had made itself into a relatively independent and effective pressure group by the late eighties.

Though the government's care not to offend Washington, or Nicaragua's generous aid to donors, too grievously explains a lot of the Sandinistas' patience with their opponents, the FSLN did make political pluralism and a mixed economy two of its founding principles for the new regime. Even if it read these principles in ways foreign to North American centrists, the revolutionary state was starting off in a novel and tolerant direction.[10] A useful way to highlight this novelty is to look more closely at the Sandinistas' governmental machinery and the policies they implemented with it.

Sandinista Politics, 1979–1984

It is helpful to think of early Sandinista Nicaragua as having an unwritten constitution. That is, like Britain, it did not have a single document that laid out the regime's governing philosophy and described the structure and idealized operation of government. Thus, in looking at the governmental institutions with which the Sandinista state started life, we are constructing a picture of the revolutionaries' political values and aims. The central agency of the new regime was the revolutionary vanguard, the FSLN.[11] Though the revolutionaries did not seek to monopolize state power, they did want to effectively dominate the operations of government. Stephen Gorman describes how, during its first year in power, the FSLN managed to consolidate control over the state apparatus.[12] Though the new regime initially had many top officials who were nonrevolutionary opponents of the Somozas, most of these soon left government, opening the way for those more committed to radical change. Curiously, however, it was only after moving the state in a more liberal direction in 1984 that the FSLN formally ruled totally alone.

Perhaps the most public example of the Sandinistas' belief that this was their revolution and their government came with the dispute over the Council of State, the new representative assembly created in 1980. Unlike liberal democratic legislatures, the Council of State represented corporate entities (from political parties to an ecumenical council, by way of unions, business groups, and the EPS) and did so with members named by the constituent organizations. Though there is some dispute over what the exact allocation of seats in the chamber was to have been, observers agree that the distribution made before the July 1979 triumph would have left the FSLN without a reliable majority.[13] Thus when the Sandinistas announced a recomposed council that included Sandinista mass organizations that had not existed before the triumph, and that incidentally gave the revolutionaries their assured majority, conservative anti-Somoza elements smelled a Marxist coup. However one evaluates the Sandinistas' actions here, it is clear that they wanted a political system that would advance revolutionary change.[14]

Policies as well as institutions reflected the nature of this new Nicaragua. Agrarian reform is an integral part of Third World revolutions, both because the landless and the land-poor have usually taken important roles in the struggle and because agrarian capitalists make inviting targets for revolutionary justice. The Sandinistas got a head start on the process when the Somoza entourage fled the country, leaving fully one-fifth of Nicaragua's arable land ownerless. This let the new government limit head-on conflicts with the remainder of the landowning classes for a few years while still setting out a new agricultural model for the country.

Early Sandinista agrarian policy revealed the transformational direction of the government. It used the former Somoza holdings for large-scale state farms (fundamentally, state-owned agribusinesses) and cooperatives. Though the FSLN government acknowledged that North American–style co-ops, which build up numbers to create market strength in both buying inputs and marketing outputs, might exist, these were discouraged in favor of a model that emphasized collective ownership and management. Distributing land to individual owners was not part of the original scheme: peasant agriculture was the past, not the future. Despite the accent on constructing a socialist agriculture, however, the Sandinistas did not encourage the rural poor to seize land and confront the wealthy. Unlike their counterparts in the Chinese revolutions, Nicaraguan peasants were not invited to "speak bitterness" against their old oppressors. It was important to the new state to keep agrarian capitalists producing, and that meant keeping them secure in their property, at least for the time being.[15]

An equally important policy direction in the new Nicaragua was mobilizing volunteers for great national projects.[16] The most famous of these was the Literacy Crusade of 1980, but there were also national mobilizations to vaccinate children against polio and animals against rabies, as well as campaigns to clean up pools of stagnant water as part of a broader anti-malaria prophylaxis. Further, the volunteer neighborhood patrols, "revolutionary vigilance," deterred common criminals as well as political enemies and made the country a safer place to live.

Another element of politics in the new Nicaragua that we need to note is the rise of new political forces. The most obvious examples are the Sandinista mass organizations[17] and the FSLN's own evolution from guerrilla front to political party, but players that became active in the last years of the dictatorship kept growing, too. The Roman Catholic hierarchy, led by Archbishop (later Cardinal) Obando y Bravo, and organized big business (the Superior Council of Private Enterprise [COSEP]) became the leaders of conservative, civic opposition to the FSLN and the revolution. Though relations between the government and these spokespeople of the right were amiable at first, it did not take long for both sides to discover many areas where their interests differed.[18]

That these last two actors persisted signifies the advent of an age in Nicaraguan public life that made room for legal political opposition. But why did the FSLN leave its opponents room to operate? In the case of COSEP, the revolutionary government's initial commitment to build a

mixed economy (by which the Sandinistas meant one where a tightly regulated private sector was allowed to exist but not expand) gave private enterprise the weight to greatly influence the country's economic health. This
role grew as the war against the contras expanded and the state's need for
revenues expanded. As for the Church hierarchy, it not only enjoyed substantial popular legitimacy in this heavily Catholic country, but Cardinal
Obando y Bravo evolved into an international figure able to command the
attention of the world's media. Finally, we cannot forget that both COSEP
and the Catholic Church received the patronage of the Reagan administration, meaning that any too-spirited attempts to stifle their activity might
provoke reprisals from Washington.

There remain two factors to consider: social programs and the war. The
Sandinistas sought to create as extensive a welfare state as their resources
allowed, but it was a welfare state with some new twists. Some of the inno-
vations were negative, such as the state's attempts to control food prices to
the consumer.[19] Though this policy did make some limited array of basic
foods more securely available, it also impoverished the peasants and turned
the revolution into their enemy—a superb example of the "unanticipated
consequences of purposive action."[20] Less often noted was the revolution's
policy on higher education. This did not impose political criteria on entry to
Nicaragua's universities, but it did set political performance standards for
admission to accelerated remedial programs. Again we see the mix of liberal and radical philosophies that is the real characteristic of Sandinista
administration.

Important as all of the above are, the defining event of the Sandinistas'
tenure was the contra war. All revolutions should expect counterrevolutionary action. The displaced rulers and their foreign supporters will try to
restore the ancien régime or, failing that, make the new system's life as
miserable as possible. But the war with the contras (short for *contrarevolu-
cionarios*) went beyond that. Perhaps it started as just the latest installment
of the fratricidal wars that have been Nicaragua's lot since independence,
but the obsession of U.S. president Ronald Reagan with the FSLN made it
inevitable that this would be a particularly bitter and bloody war. The war,
which gets greater attention in the next section, took more than lives and
wealth; it also pushed many Sandinista social and economic programs off
the agenda. The road that led to revolutionary government being associated
with war, hunger, pain, and death began with the first contra attack.[21]

The FSLN's Electoral Era, 1985–1990

National elections held in November 1984 marked the end of the Sandinistas' experiment in radical transformation and the birth of a new model
of Nicaraguan revolution. The second edition of the revolutionary state

differed from the first in that it placed less emphasis on transformation and more on consolidation. This made sense, viewed from either of two perspectives. On the one hand, the Sandinistas could claim that they had made significant progress in their first five years and needed to take a breather and revise their plans and policies before continuing toward further socialist construction. A less sanguine reading of the same record would have seen the first five years of Sandinista rule producing serious problems that needed correction. Neither version is absolutely true or totally false.

What most obviously set the revised system off from its parent was an increased reliance on the machinery and rhetoric of formal, liberal, constitutional democracy. The mobilizational politics of the first five years became a memory as political action came to be the preserve of parties whose raison d'être was winning elections.[22] The mass organizations of the early days still existed and were important parts of Sandinista politics, but they lost their standing in official state institutions, and those that best represented their constituents were those that, like UNAG—the Sandinista farmers' organization—acted most like liberal democratic pressure groups. Despite these changes, the FSLN still thought of itself as the vanguard of the revolution and could not conceive of being repudiated by the Nicaraguan people.

Another factor that distinguished the second installment of Sandinista Nicaragua from the first was the introduction of austerity politics. Elsewhere in Central America (e.g., Costa Rica), austerity came with World Bank structural adjustment programs, bringing loans from the Bank to dampen the shock. In Nicaragua, however, there was no outside relief, for the conditions IFIs typically imposed on those seeking loans would have been anathema to the revolutionary government. Besides, the U.S. government would probably have stopped any financial institution in which it participated from extending loans to Nicaragua.[23]

Not only did Nicaraguans have to bear the pain of austerity (layoffs in the public sector, cutbacks in services, generally rising unemployment), they also had to shoulder the rising costs of the contra war. Nevertheless, the FSLN never resorted to dictatorship. When compared to the rightist regimes then ruling El Salvador and Guatemala, the Sandinista record looks good. There were no death squads, few arbitrary imprisonments, and political life functioned remarkably normally. The result of these efforts, however, was the FSLN's loss of power by constitutional means.

The New Political Machinery

The changes in political institutions and the constitutional framework of Nicaraguan politics that produced a reformed Sandinista state obviously had to begin before 1984. The process started with the government's 1982

Political Parties Law. The bill had two objectives: (1) to set up a framework for recognizing legal parties; and (2) to lay down ground rules for future elections. The first goal was essentially uncontroversial. By the 1980s, most liberal democracies had in place some rules governing the legal status of parties, their financing, and their eligibility for access to public funds for electoral campaigns. The second was more controversial, for it went beyond saying what criteria a party must meet to get on the ballot to state what elections would be about in Sandinista Nicaragua.

A famous 1980 speech by Comandante Humberto Ortega showed the initial Sandinista position on elections: there would be no lottery to decide who exercised power; the people had decided that in the revolution.[24] The first draft of the parties law reaffirmed this, noting that parties other than the FSLN would have to content themselves with "participating in public administration," accepting the roles the vanguard offered them. Nicaragua's other political parties, small and poorly organized though they were, rejected this, lobbied aggressively for changes, and eventually got a law recognizing that elections are about getting the right to run the state. Though the final version of the bill, passed over a year after its introduction, excluded parties proposing a return to the sort of regime the Somozas maintained from running in elections, the Sandinistas had formally abandoned an important part of Leninism by conceding that they could be voted out of power.[25]

Though it is doubtful that the FSLN really believed that it was jeopardizing its control over the state by transforming itself from a hegemonic party that legally could not lose elections into a dominant one that did not lose them in practice, it still took a huge step away from its original principles. From there the revolutionary state went on to draft an elections act that again had two goals. First, the Electoral Law (1984) governed the conduct of elections, setting out the electoral system and the mechanisms by which voters would register, the vote held, and results tallied and reported. But it also had to define the posts to be elected, and in so doing it prescribed a new constitutional order for the country. Nicaraguans were to elect a president and vice president, and a legislature whose members ran on party lists in geographically defined constituencies. The mass organizations lost their official place in the machinery of government, and the Sandinistas bet that their organizational strength and residual legitimacy as architects of the revolution would keep them at the helm.

The 1984 elections themselves were controversial because the main anti-Sandinista coalition declined to stand. Few, however, were surprised when it was later revealed that it had never intended to contest the election but only made noises about running so it could withdraw and embarrass the FSLN.[26] The results (see Table 1.1) strongly favored the incumbents, who captured the presidency with 67 percent of the vote and took sixty-one of

Table 1.1   Nicaraguan Election Results, 1984

Party	Presidential Vote (%)	National Assembly Vote (%)	National Assembly Seats[a]
FSLN	67.0	66.8	61
Democratic Conservative Party	14.0	14.0	14
PLI	9.6	9.7	9
Popular Social Christian Party (PPSC)	5.6	5.6	6
Communist Party of Nicaragua (PCN)	1.5	1.5	2
PSN	1.3	1.4	2
Marxist-Leninist Popular Action Movement (MAP)	1.0	1.0	2
Totals	100	100	96

Source: Adapted from Close, *Nicaragua,* p. 136.

a. Includes defeated presidential candidates who received over one-ninetieth of the total vote.

ninety-six seats in the new National Assembly.[27] More important, the Sandinistas had indissolubly linked the legitimate exercise of power to electoral victory.

Once in office, the electoral Sandinistas, led by Daniel Ortega, Comandante of the Revolution and elected president of Nicaragua, set about to institutionalize their revolution. Their main tool would be a constitution, the country's seventh of the century. Adopted in 1987, the document was significant as much for how it was put together as its content. Great public meetings (*cabildos abiertos*) were held to let organized interests, not least the Sandinista mass organizations, expound on what belonged in a constitution that embodied the aims and entrenched the forms of the Sandinista revolution. Once these were completed, the scene shifted to the National Assembly for debate and passage. Involving the Assembly was an interesting touch; one would have expected a more plebiscitary approach from the participation-minded FSLN, but perhaps this was part of institutionalizing an active legislature. In any event, there were at least some opposition victories on the floor over small matters, for example, recognizing the right to establish private schools (Article 123).

Political science texts note that constitutions reflect the values of a society's political elites. Read in that light, Nicaragua's 1987 constitution[28] suggests that the Sandinistas wanted a system that would use predominantly liberal democratic governmental machinery to preserve and advance broadly revolutionary aims. Title IV ("Rights, Duties, and Guarantees of the Nicaraguan People"), for instance, contains sixty-eight articles that are conventional enough, though North American conservatives would not want to see the right of collective bargaining constitutionally enshrined. Title VI ("National Economy, Agrarian Reform, and Public Finances"), however, would not be at home in liberal democratic constitutions. Articles 98 and 99 show why:

> Article 98   The principal function of the state in the economy is to develop the country materially, abolish inherited backwardness and dependence, improve the standard of living of the people, and create a more just distribution of wealth.
>
> Article 99   The state directs and plans the national economy in order to guarantee the defense of the interests of the majority and guides it to serve the goals of socioeconomic progress. The Central Bank, the National Financial System, Insurance and Reinsurance, and Foreign Commerce, as instruments of the economic system, are irrevocable responsibilities of the state.

One other aspect of the 1987 constitution merits attention. Latin America has historically favored executive-centered polities, and the newer Nicaragua was no exception. For example, besides a veto, the Nicaraguan president could "enact decrees with the force of law in fiscal and administrative matters" (Article 151.4) and "administer the economy of the country, determine its socio-economic policy and progress" (151.13). Beyond these, the chief executive could "decree and put into effect a State of Emergency . . . and forward the decree to the National Assembly for ratification within . . . forty-five days" (151.9; cf. 185 and 186). The new National Assembly did get an easy veto override (50 percent plus one of all deputies; Article 143) and finally received normal budget-making authority (138.6). Though these mark substantial improvements in the legislature's status, this is still a "presidential" constitution.

Beyond the constitution, the Sandinistas produced one other fundamental piece of legislation in their second term, the Autonomy Statute for the Regions of the Atlantic Coast of Nicaragua.[29] Adopted in 1987, the act was the government's political response to the participation of the *Costeños* (the people of the Atlantic coast) in the contra war. After spending their entire preelectoral term trying to fit the *Costeños,* who are culturally and ethnically different from Nicaraguans living in the mountains or on the Pacific slope, into a pan-Nicaraguan mold, the FSLN finally acknowledged the coast's uniqueness. This it did both in the constitution (Articles 89–91, 180–181) and in this statute. Though it in no way established a federal system, it did devolve substantial administrative powers to the coastal regions, including the right to establish regional administrations (Articles 15–31) and to recognize the communal rights of the indigenous inhabitants of the area (Articles 10–14).

Though not all the political history of Nicaragua under electoral Sandinismo pointed toward growing pluralism—there was a notorious case of
government meddling with a Supreme Court decision to restore an expropriated property to its original owner that prompted the resignation of several justices—the general direction was clear. What is most interesting, and
most important for countries now navigating a democratic transition, is that
this all occurred in conditions of material distress and escalating insurgency.

Nicaragua's New Economic Reality: Austerity with Hyperinflation

Governments that embark on austerity programs are not supposed to run
into hyperinflation afterward. Austerity packages always include a specific
program to stabilize prices and the value of a nation's currency. This is an
indispensable first step, without which later reforms are pointless. So how
did Nicaragua go from its first austerity policy in 1985, just after the 1984
elections of course, to an annual inflation rate of some 30,000 percent in
four years?

The main culprit was the contra war. It took people out of productive
activities and put them into the front lines, so less was grown or made for
sale. This naturally cut supplies to civilians who bid up prices. Though the
Sandinistas imposed rationing, Nicaragua in the late 1980s was not the
United States or Canada during World War II, and neither price controls nor
rationing proved effective.

There were other suspects, however; there had to be, otherwise the collapse of the Nicaraguan economy would not have been so great. Between
1981 and 1990, the Nicaraguan economy shrank by 14 percent—the worst
performance in Latin America—and inflation reached 33,500 percent in
1987.[30] The principal contributors were a generalized slump throughout
Latin America (except in the Central American nations that received lots of
U.S. aid in Washington's war against the Sandinistas), a U.S. embargo
against Nicaragua after 1985, and the FSLN's own policies. When mixed
together, these elements heightened poverty, created new domestic tensions, and undid much of the material good achieved by the first five years
of Sandinista rule.

Yet the most telling commentary on the economy is found not in figures, but in a 1988 strike. Construction workers struck to protest wage
restrictions that came with the 1988 Sandinista austerity package. The government broke off negotiations, sparking a hunger strike by the workers to
which the response was blockading the strikers in their union offices, turning off the lights and water, and starving them out.[31] True, the strike was
called by the union affiliated with the PSN (for Sandinista unions were too

tightly controlled to strike), but this was nevertheless unusual behavior for a government that claimed to represent workers and peasants. There could hardly have been a more dramatic illustration of tensions brought on by economic decay and war.

This period also brought renewed conflict with the bourgeoisie. At the root of the conflict was the need to find land for people fleeing the war zones, a need that could only be met by expropriations.[32] All the same, the revolutionary government strove to maintain correct working relations with the wealthy. Summits among the state, the big private sector, and labor (*concertaciones*)[33] were regular, if ineffective, occurrences. The Sandinistas were plainly trying to minimize open conflict with the bourgeoisie, even when they could no longer avoid it. But the economy had escaped the hands of the state, whose constitutional duty it was to control it. Instead of being able to point to rising living standards and correct relations with business, by the end of the 1980s the Sandinistas faced an economic disaster.

The Contra War

Fighting the contras cost lives and money[34]. According to Paul Oquist, 30,865 Nicaraguans died and twice that many were injured.[35] Destruction of property and harm done to the economy was similarly startling.

> The material damage and damage to productive forces resulting from the war totalled US$1,998 million; the financial blockade meant for Nicaragua a loss of US$642 million, and the commercial embargo another US $459 million; the added costs for defense and security (in excess of the average 1980–1982 defense expenditure) in the period 1983–1989 totalled US$1,933 million, for a total of US$5,032 million. The aggregate effect of these on the gross national product was US$4,055 million, for a grand total of US$9,087 million.[36]

To combat the contras, the Sandinista government waged an exemplary counterinsurgent war.[37] That is, it adopted the proper military tactics and responded appropriately to the political demands of its opponents. The clearest examples of reforms made to satisfy actual or potential insurgents were the autonomy statute for Nicaragua's Atlantic coast and the new land reform policy granting individual title, but the entire constitutional structure of this newer Nicaragua should be seen at least partly as an effort to keep dissidents from becoming defectors. Yet all this went for naught because there were too many forces, from the contras themselves to the intractable civic opposition, who neither wanted nor needed to make peace. Assured of the Reagan administration's support, they could resist where others would have had to compromise.

Though the Sandinistas spoke of "the strategic defeat of the contras" throughout this period, the facts of the matter led them to sign the Esquipulas Accords (also known as the Arias Plan) in 1987. These accords bound all Central American governments to open their political systems to competition and strive for peace with their insurgent enemies. By 1988, the FSLN was holding formal talks with the contras, already having lifted the restrictions on public life brought by successive states of emergency. Had the Sandinista state been able to conclude a durable peace with the contras, the FSLN might still be governing Nicaragua. Being unable to do so doubtless cost the revolutionaries power.

Elections, 1990

Accepting the loss of the 1990 elections may have been the most important thing the Sandinistas did in their years in power. Admittedly, they had little choice. They had been routed at the polls in a vote that was overseen by the United Nations and the OAS and scrutinized by teams of official and volunteer electoral observers from around the world. Still, the FSLN lost as gracefully as any political party, stunned by an unexpected reversal at the polls, could have. There was no rioting or even vandalism. There were, it is true, individual Sandinista supporters who wanted to settle accounts, but this stayed at the level of talk. Overall, the behavior of the FSLN and its followers in defeat showed a political maturity and tolerance that was not found in Nicaragua before the revolution.

Because the results were so dramatic (see Table 1.2), it is easy to overlook the more subtle ways the 1990 elections affected Nicaraguan politics. Consider, for example, the Electoral Law that was in place. The Electoral

Table 1.2   Nicaraguan Election Results, 1990

	Presidential Vote (%)	National Assembly Seats
UNO	54.7	51
FSLN	40.8	39[a]
Others	4.2	2[b]

Source: Adapted from Close, "Central American Elections, 1989–90," *Electoral Studies* 10:1 (1991): 73.

a. One assembly seat was awarded to the defeated FSLN presidential candidate because the party received over one-ninetieth of the national vote.

b. One seat went to a defeated presidential candidate of the Unified Revolution Movement (MUR) for receiving over one-ninetieth of the national vote; and one seat was officially held by the PSC, though occupied by Yatama, the Miskito Indian party, which provided the PSC slate in the region where the seat was won. Both deputies sat with the UNO caucus in the National Assembly.

Law introduced for the first Sandinista elections, in 1984, was designed to favor the participation of small parties. It gave any party winning one-ninetieth (1.1 percent) of the national vote a National Assembly seat for its presidential candidate. This gave defeated ticket leaders a continuing place in national politics, but it did so at the cost of encouraging miniparties. In 1984, this made sense, as the Sandinistas wanted as many participants as possible to lend legitimacy to the contest. By 1988, however, the government wanted to set a higher threshold for entry to the assembly to encourage the formation of larger, stronger parties. Opposition parties objected strenuously, and the old system was restored with minor modifications. The consequence has been to sustain "vanity" parties that are instruments for political self-promotion and to maintain conditions encouraging personality-based politics.

A happier side effect of the 1990 elections was that Nicaraguans gained confidence in their electoral system. Traveling to different polling stations in 1984, I heard several people comment that they were voting only so the government would know that they had turned out. They were not particularly concerned about the authorities knowing how they voted, having confidence in that part of the process, but feared that abstention, though legal, would bring reprisals. In 1990, by contrast, the only comment I heard about the entire electoral mechanism was *"Tu voto es secreto"* ("Your vote is secret"), the slogan used by the Supreme Electoral Council (CSE) in its "get out the vote" drive.

In fact, the CSE itself was another big, if indirect, winner in 1990. Recognized for its good work in 1984,[38] the first elections it administered, the CSE faced substantial challenges in 1990. It was charged with organizing and administering an election in wartime conditions, in an impoverished country, and under intense international scrutiny. If the CSE had a problem in its first elections, it was that results were announced slowly. In 1990, this was corrected, partly because the United Nations and the Organization of American States observation teams were doing "quick counts": samples that would be used to verify the accuracy of the official counts. By carrying out its mandate well, the CSE showed Nicaraguans that elections can be honestly run and counted on to reflect the public's will.

The last point to note about these elections was how wrong the polls were. Though 54 percent of Nicaraguans supported Chamorro's UNO, pre-electoral polls showed the FSLN winning comfortably.[39] Respondents apparently misled pollsters, as the Nicaraguan folk figure, the *Güegüense,* double-talked his way around colonial governors. But the real question is why the Sandinistas would have believed polls showing them leading. The economy was in ruins; there was a war that showed no signs of ending; and the FSLN itself was showing increasing signs of "verticalism," the tendency to command instead of lead. Only the weakness of the UNO, an alliance of fourteen parties united solely by their opposition to the Sandinistas, gave the incumbents a chance. That a feeble opponent dealt the revolutionary government such a massive defeat shows clearly how badly Nicaraguans wanted change. The wave of revolutionary enthusiasm of July 1979 had ebbed, and the Sandinista government was carried out on the tides of history.

Ten Years of Sandinista Rule in Retrospect

Though the Sandinistas failed to institutionalize their revolution, they did leave a country very different from the one they found in 1979. The damage from a decade of war was the most obvious change but the least relevant one. Far more important was an unintentional and often invisible political change. During the decade the FSLN ruled, Nicaragua saw the beginnings of legitimate oppositional politics. The limited pluralism of the early revolutionary state grew with the 1984 elections and expanded again with Esquipulas. By 25 February 1990, the process had advanced far enough to let the opposition win a fair, open election and see a self-proclaimed vanguard leave power, defeated by ballots instead of bullets.

Two further parts of the Sandinista legacy merit mention: the politicization of the marginalized and dramatic changes in rural society. A key element in Sandinista political strategy was converting the lower classes and historically excluded sectors of society, like women, into effective political actors. Though most Sandinista mass organizations had little autonomy at the time the revolutionaries lost power, these institutions did offer many people their first taste of political action. Neither the organizations nor the people who belonged to them would cease making their claims on the state just because a new party held office. This democratized the Nicaraguan political system by injecting new forces into the fray.

Democratization also resulted from Sandinista agrarian reform in the countryside. Breaking up even the Somozas' holdings (20 percent of Nicaragua's arable land) meant that the balance of political power in rural areas changed radically. As the Sandinista decade wore on, the government leaned increasingly toward private producers in UNAG, creating a new voice in the making of agricultural policy. Finally, after 1985, the government began distributing private land titles to ordinary peasants, giving the country a class of small, independent farmers for the first time. As a result, rural Nicaragua presented a more varied and democratic face than ever before.

Weighed against this positive, democratizing legacy of the Sandinista era is the aftermath of the contra war. Beyond material destruction, the war created refugees and left a society deeply divided between those who had supported the revolution and those whose aim was to destroy it. When added to the broader economic losses the country suffered during the 1980s, this debit side of FSLN's balance sheet is impressive.

Overall, though, I believe the Sandinistas left Nicaragua better off than they found it. It is difficult to conceive of the Somozas leaving office voluntarily. Those who argue that eventually Nicaragua's dictatorial dynasty would have had to follow the Duvaliers into exile forget that it was the need to legitimize Washington's war against the Sandinistas that pushed the U.S. government into abandoning its erstwhile strongman allies. Chamorro began her term in office with a country better suited to democratization than ever before in its history. Her problem was whether even that would be enough to let her govern effectively.

Notes

1. There is no standard history of Nicaragua in either English or Spanish, but Ralph Lee Woodward, *Central America* (New York: Oxford University Press, 1973), and the appropriate volumes of Leslie Bethel, ed., *The Cambridge History of Latin America* (Cambridge: Cambridge University Press, various dates), contain sections on Nicaragua and place the country in its regional context. James Dunkerly, *Power in the Isthmus* (London: Verso, 1988); is a very useful comparative work, though its focus is more on modern Central America. With respect to Nicaragua specifically, E. Bradford Burns, *Patriarch and Folk* (Cambridge, MA: Harvard University Press, 1991), is very good on the early national period. José Dolores Gamez, *Historia de Nicaragua* (Managua: Banco de America, 1975 [1889]), is both venerable and a useful introduction to Nicaraguan historiography. The standard work on the Walker episode is still William O. Scroggs, *Filibusters and Financiers* (New York: Macmillan, 1916), which is written in a lively, muckraking style. A history of the *trentenio*—the thirty years of stable Conservative government in the late nineteenth century—remains to be written.

2. Benjamin Teplitz, *The Political and Economic Foundations of Modernization in Nicaragua: The Administration of José Santos Zelaya,* unpublished Ph.D. diss., Howard University, Washington, DC, 1973, is the only thorough and balanced treatment of Zelaya. An equally good and more easily encountered introduction to Zelaya is Charles Stansifer, "José Santos Zelaya: A New Look at Nicaragua's Liberal Dictator," *Revista Interamericana* 7:4 (1977): 468–485. Nicaragua's relations with the United States are very well chronicled. To get a sense of the varying interpretations of these relations before the Sandinista era, one might consult Dana Munro, *The Five Republics of Central America* (New York: Russell & Russell, 1967 [1918]), and *The U.S. and the Caribbean* (New York: Johnson Reprints, 1966 [1934]); Thomas Dodd, *Managing Democracy in Central America* (New Brunswick, NJ: Transaction Publishers, 1992); Neil Macauley, *The Sandino Affair* (Durham, NC: Duke University Press, 1985); and Karl Berman, *Under the Big Stick* (Boston: South End Press, 1986).

3. Besides Macauley's *Sandiso Affair,* readers interested in Sandino should see Gregorio Selser, *Sandino* (New York: Monthly Review Press, 1980); Edelberto Torres Rivas, *Sandino* (Mexico City: Katun, 1984); Carlos Fonseca, *Sandino:*

Guerrillero proletario (Managua: Departamento de Propaganda y Educación Política del FSLN, 1984), and *Ideario político de Agusto Cesar Sandino* (Managua: Departamento de Propaganda y Educación Política del FSLN, 1984); Sergio Ramírez, ed., *El pensamiento vivo de Sandino* (San José, Costa Rica: EDUCA, 1980); and Donald Hodges, *Ideological Foundations of the Nicaraguan Revolution* (Austin: University of Texas Press, 1986). This is rather partisan literature, for all of the above are friendly to Sandino, and it will probably be some time before a detached appraisal of the greatest Latin American guerrilla of the twentieth century can be produced.

4. The literature on the Somoza period is sketchy, but two works stand out. Bernard Diederich's *Somoza* (New York: Dutton, 1981) is the work of a longtime observer of Latin American dictatorships that lays bare the cruelty and corruption that brought the dynasty down. Different in tone is the recent book by Salvadoran historian Knut Walter, *The Regime of Anastasio Somoza, 1936–1956* (Chapel Hill: University of North Carolina Press, 1993). Pedro Joaquín Chamorro, *Estripe Sangriente: Los Somozas* (Mexico City: Diógenes, 1979), is a personal account by one of the dictatorship's fiercest opponents.

5. The essential work on the Nicaraguan National Guard remains Richard Millett, *Guardians of the Dynasty* (Maryknoll, NY: Orbis Books, 1977).

6. Besides the Somozas, only two families in the Western Hemisphere have managed to maintain a dictatorship for two generations: the Duvaliers of Haiti, roughly contemporaries of the Somozas, and the López family of mid-nineteenth-century Paraguay.

7. The usual, facetious reason given why Nicaragua's wealthy tolerated the dynasty's dictatorship was that the Somozas had already stolen enough to keep themselves happy. More seriously, the rich recognized that the Somozas did keep order and suspected that a more open politics might bring serious disruption.

8. Material on the origins and development of the Sandinistas is now easily available. Among the works providing useful introductions to the FSLN are George Black, *Triumph of the People* (London: Zed Books, 1981); John Booth, *The End and the Beginning,* 2d ed. (Boulder, CO: Westview Press, 1988); David Close, *Nicaragua: Politics, Economics, and Society* (London: Pinter Publishers, 1988); and Thomas Walker, *Nicaragua: Land of Sandino* (Boulder, CO: Westview Press, 1991). All have bibliographies to guide the reader to more specialized sources.

9. The material in this section is drawn from Close, *Nicaragua,* unless otherwise noted.

10. For example, a Sandinista mixed economy placed the state sector in the dominant position *and* consciously aimed at reducing the scope and power of private capital. As well, the initial version of Sandinista political pluralism made no provision for power to be exercised by anyone but the FSLN. When placed against the backdrop of Nicaraguan history, the first seems almost tolerant (it did permit alternative economic systems to exist without great restraint) and the second merely a continuation of the principles that guided most of the nation's governments throughout history.

11. The Sandinistas' views on vanguardism are discussed by Dennis Gilbert, *Sandinistas* (Oxford: Blackwell, 1988); cf. David Nolan, *The Ideology of the Sandinistas and the Nicaraguan Revolution* (Coral Gables, FL: Institute of Interamerican Studies, Graduate School of International Studies, University of Miami, 1984).

12. Stephen Gorman, "Power and Consolidation in the Nicaraguan Revolution," *Journal of Latin American Studies* 13:1 (1981): 133–149.

13. Cf. Black, *The Triumph of the People,* pp. 198–199; and Shirley Christian, *Revolution in the Family* (New York: Vintage Books, 1986), pp. 171–173.

14. The FSLN's action was not without justification: many of the organizations slated for inclusion in the Council of State before July 1979 had dissolved by 1980. Moreover, the Sandinistas had been actively assembling the marginalized into mass organizations to offer the majority its first taste of effective, formal political action. Excluding these organization would have made the council unrepresentative and probably would have led the Sandinista-controlled JGRN, the executive, to ignore the chamber completely. Some details on the council's operations are found in David Close, "Nicaragua: The Legislature as Seedbed of Conflict," in *Legislatures and the New Democracies in Latin America,* ed. David Close (Boulder, CO: Lynne Rienner Publishers, 1995), pp. 49–69.

15. Laura Enriquez, *Harvesting Change* (Chapel Hill: University of North Carolina Press, 1991), is a handy scholarly analysis of Nicaragua's agrarian reform process.

16. Besides the general works cited in note 8 above, see Joe Collins, *What Difference Could a Revolution Make?* (San Francisco: Food First, 1982).

17. Gary Ruchwarger's *The People in Power* (South Hadley, MA: Bergin & Garvey, 1987) is the best introduction to the Sandinista mass organizations.

18. Although there is an extensive journal literature on Sandinista relations with both the Roman Catholic hierarchy and the representatives of big business, there are several monographs on each topic that offer the interested nonspecialist good starting points. On the Church, see Philip Williams, *The Catholic Church and Politics in Nicaragua and Costa Rica* (London: Macmillan, 1989); Michael Dodson and Laura O'Shauhhnessy, *Nicaragua's Other Revolution* (Chapel Hill: University of North Carolina Press, 1990); and John Kirk, *Politics and the Catholic Church in Nicaragua* (Gainesville: University Press of Florida, 1992). Regarding the private sector, see Rose Spalding, *Capitalists and Revolution in Nicaragua* (Chapel Hill: University of North Carolina Press, 1995); and Phil Ryan, *The Fall and Rise of the Market in Sandinista Nicaragua* (Montreal: McGill-Queen's University Press, 1995).

19. Brizio N. Biondi-Morra, *Revolucion y política alimentaria: Un análisis crítico de Nicaragua* (Mexico City: Siglo Ventiuno, 1990), discusses not just the food policy of the Sandinistas, but also that policy's impact on the government's wage, credit, and foreign policies.

20. Robert Merton, "The Unanticipated Consequences of Purposive Social Action," *American Sociological Review* 1 (1936): 894–904.

21. Curiously, the FSLN was never able to make its nonviolent opposition responsible for the contra war. I have not seen anything that directly addresses this question, but it may be that the links between the contras and Washington were so clear that even the Sandinistas' strongest supporters realized that fellow Nicaraguans who cheered Reagan on were not essential to U.S. policy. Though speaking to a different issue, Roberto Cajina suggests that the army's policy of sending draftees to fight in frontline counterinsurgency units was so well known that the revolutionary government could not escape the blame for the war's human costs. See Roberto J. Cajina, *Transición política y reconversión militar in Nicaragua, 1990–1995* (Managua: CRIES, 1997), pp. 19–41.

22. Wayne Cornelius, "The Nicaraguan Elections of 1984: A Reassessment of the Domestic and International Significance," in *Elections and Democratization in Latin America, 1981–1985,* ed. Paul Drake and Eduardo Silva (San Diego: Center for Iberian and Latin American Studies, University of California at San Diego, 1986).

23. In fact, a 1982 World Bank report "included the tacit admission that the United States had, by that date, blocked all loans and grants to Nicaragua from the International Development Association [the Bank's soft loan facility]" (Michael Conroy, "Economic Aggression as an Instrument of Low-Intensity Warfare," in *Reagan Versus the Sandinistas,* ed. Thomas Walker [Boulder, CO: Westview Press, 1987], p. 68).

24. The speech is quoted in Black, *Triumph of the People,* pp. 255–256.

25. An extended treatment of the Political Parties Law is found in Close, *Nicaragua,* pp. 123–124. That the FSLN gave up the Leninist principle that only the vanguard could govern so much more easily than did, say, the Soviets is, I think, more evidence that they were Marxists unlike the others. Throughout the 1980s, the party was sufficiently pluralistic that there would have been many voices counseling accommodation on topics that did not seem to threaten its hold on power. And the Sandinistas were very good at convincing themselves that the people of Nicaragua would never vote "their vanguard" from power. However, the FSLN has been much slower to rid itself of another Leninist attribute, namely, the suppression of dissent within party ranks.

26. LASA (Latin American Studies Association), "Report of the Latin American Studies Association Delegation to Observe the Nicaraguan General Election of November 4, 1984," *LASA Forum* 15:4 (1984): 9–43. A shorter treatment is David Close, "The Nicaraguan Election of 1984," *Electoral Studies* 5:2 (1985): 152–158.

27. I shall relegate to an endnote the matter of the honesty and openness of the 1984 elections. This evaluation turns on (1) whether the presence of Arturo Cruz, heading the list of the Coordinadora Democrática (Democratic Coordinator)—the most important anti-Sandinista bloc—would have made a difference, and (2) whether a 66 percent vote for the FSLN was plausible. My own view is that a Coordinadora ticket would have had some impact, but that it probably would not have reversed the electoral outcome. I hold this position because the Coordinadora's platform was advanced by two parties (the PLI and the Democratic Conservatives) who ran and did rather better than Managua's many pundits predicted. The conservative, antirevolutionary position was available to those who wanted to support it. There is no apparent reason to think that a different party running on the same platform would have done dramatically better.

Where Cruz's candidacy would have made a difference, because it would have been better financed and higher profile, is in the total vote going to the Sandinistas. A Coordinadora ticket very likely would have pulled this down below two-thirds and well toward 60 percent, perhaps even slightly lower. This would have been a psychological blow to the Sandinistas, but it might have shown them where they most needed to work to shore up their support and maybe even let them avoid the even harsher beating they took from the voters in 1990.

28. All subsequent references to the constitution are to the version published in *La Gaceta: Diario Oficial* (the Nicaraguan Official Gazette), 9 January 1987; the translations are the author's.

29. A copy of the law is found in *Monexico* 13 (1989): 45–64. Useful secondary sources on issues of the Atlantic coast include Ronnie Vernoy, "Starting All Over Again," unpublished Ph.D. diss., Agricultural University of Wageningen, Netherlands, 1992; and Carlos Vilas, *State, Class, and Ethnicity in Nicaragua* (Boulder, CO: Lynne Rienner Publishers, 1989).

30. ECAC (Economic Commission for Latin America and the Caribbean/ Comisión Económica para América Latina y el Caribe), *Anuario Estadístico de América Latina y el Caribe, 1993* (New York: United Nations, 1993), pp. 753, 757.

31. The best account of this scandalous episode is Ricardo Avila, "Hunger Strike in Nicaragua," *Nicaragua Through Our Eyes* 3:4 (1988).

32. Background information can be found in Close, *Nicaragua,* pp. 93–99; a conjunctural analysis is in *Envio* 8:97 (1989): 16–19.

33. *Concertaciones* in Sandinista Nicaragua (a practice continued under the Chamorro administration) saw the state try to broker deals with big business to induce it to maintain production and to keep some political doors open. Spalding, *Capitalists and Revolution,* treats this subject well.

34. The literature on the counterrevolution is quite extensive. I cite only a few of the more significant monographs and edited collections, giving the interested reader a starting point from which to pursue the matter independently: Christopher Dickey, *With the Contras* (New York: Touchstone, 1987); Sam Dillon, *Commandos* (New York: Henry Holt, 1991); Peter Kornbluth, *Nicaragua: The Price of Intervention* (Washington, DC: Institute for Policy Studies, 1987); William I. Robinson and Kent Norsworthy, *David and Goliath: The U.S. War Against Nicaragua* (New York: Monthly Review Press, 1987); Holly Sklar, *Washington's War on Nicaragua* (Toronto: Between the Lines, 1988); Thomas Walker, ed., *Reagan Versus the Sandinistas* (Boulder, CO: Westview Press, 1987), and *Revolution and Counterrevolution in Nicaragua* (Boulder, CO: Westview Press, 1991). Though not specifically on the contra war, the following should also be noted: Thomas Carothers, *In the Name of Democracy* (Berkeley: University of California Press, 1991); Saul Landau, *Guerrilla Wars of Central America* (New York: St. Martin's Press, 1993); William Robinson, *A Faustian Bargain* (Boulder, CO: Westview Press, 1993).

35. Paul Oquist, "The Sociopolitical Dynamics of the 1990 Nicaraguan Elections," in *The 1990 Elections in Nicaragua and Their Aftermath,* ed. Vanessa Castro and Gary Prevost (Lanham, MD: Rowman & Littlefield, 1992), pp. 1–40, esp. 7–10.

36. Ibid., p. 8.

37. David Close, "Counterinsurgency in Nicaragua," *New Political Science,* nos. 18–19 (fall/winter 1990): 5–19.

38. LASA, *Report of the LASA Delegation to Observe the Nicaraguan General Elections of February 25, 1990* (Pittsburgh: LASA, 1990).

39. William A. Barnes, "Rereading the Nicaraguan Pre-Election Polls," in *The 1990 Elections,* ed. Castro and Prevost, pp. 41–128.

2

Changing Governments, Changing Regimes

By electing Violeta Chamorro president on 25 February 1990, Nicaraguans committed their country to a double political transition. One involved a change of government. Though routine in established democracies, Nicaragua had never had a party lose power electorally, so the Sandinistas had no guidelines for how to hand the government over to its new masters. Neither did they have any precedents for how to behave during the two months before inauguration when they were lame ducks. All of this would be learned on the fly.

The other transition involved the political regime.[1] Transforming a regime means changing fundamental aspects of the composition and operation of political authority. When the regime changes, the following elements of the political system are altered:

1. the bases of a system's legitimacy;
2. the manner by which and to whom government is held accountable;
3. patterns of influence over and access to the governors;
4. the relationship among the state, civil society, and private citizens.

Though the list could be longer, it is clear that bringing in a new regime profoundly transforms a nation's public life. It is what happened when the Sandinistas replaced the Somozas; thus, for the second time in just over ten years, Nicaraguans would be learning to play by new political rules.

However, this regime change promised to be less traumatic than the last. The final five years of Sandinista rule saw the introduction of many of the forms and structures of constitutional government.[2] President-elect Chamorro would not, then, have to invent an entirely novel set of governmental machinery. Moreover, as elections had figured prominently in Sandinista politics since 1984, at least some of the fundamental processes

37

of constitutional liberal democracy were familiar to Nicaraguans. Nevertheless, Chamorro's administration really was part of a new regime.

Where the FSLN claimed legitimacy from both its 1984 electoral win and, far more important in Sandinista eyes, the 1979 revolution, the new UNO administration counted solely on its victory at the polls to justify its right to govern. Though the new government did not seek to obliterate the Sandinista revolution from the nation's memory, the works and styles of the revolutionary era were turned into historical data—good to know, but not terribly relevant to getting along now.[3] The Sandinista revolution stopped defining the nature of Nicaraguan politics with the 1990 election.

With President Chamorro came a political system rather more like the liberal democratic norm.[4] Not only was it purely electoral in origin, but it promised to be more accountable. Vanguards, of which the Sandinistas were a mild example, are accountable only to the cause that they pursue. Just as absolute monarchs answered only to God, vanguards, in theory, need only be concerned about how history judges their pursuit of their objective. Constitutional democracies, however, are constrained both by law and by the need to periodically obtain fresh mandates from their citizens.

Though the FSLN had committed itself to honor electoral results, something unprecedented in the history of socialist revolutionary states, by still claiming to be the vanguard of the Nicaraguan revolution, the Sandinistas suggested that they had not totally abandoned the idea that their regime might be above the law. Until they renounced the principle of vanguardism, a Sandinista government could still substitute revolutionary objectives for the rule of law.

At a homelier level, a new regime brings a new band of political influentials. Though this happens with any change in government, the shift is more marked when the regime changes. For example, the Sandinistas were generally better disposed toward the "majority," the poor and marginalized, than toward the wealthy. All other things being equal, then, representatives of labor, the urban or rural poor, women's groups, and indigenous communities were the most likely to get a serious hearing from the Sandinista government. As this was part of the root ideology of the FSLN, it was unlikely to be altered. These interests would not be forgotten by Chamorro, but those linked to big business would find a far warmer welcome than they had in the past. Patterns of access to government and influence within government were sure to change with the new regime.

Finally, a new regime reforms relations among the state, civil society, and private citizens. The revolutionary state was strongly interventionist and did not formally exclude any part of society from its purview. This is perfectly consistent with being a revolutionary vanguard, charged by history with effecting great and lasting social transformation. Liberal constitutional regimes, of course, mark off a distinct private sphere where the state does not normally trespass. Even though the Sandinistas permitted private organizations and individuals far more autonomy than did either other revolutionary systems or the old Somoza regime, the revolution's opponents were never convinced that this tolerance was not simply tactical. The Chamorro administration would leave greater parts of civic life in private hands. The state would shrink, and civil society, families, and individuals would have to fill the resulting gaps.

Such dramatic alterations do not come about easily or quickly. Difficult to achieve under the best of circumstances, President Chamorro would have to implement these changes in a politically divided and economically devastated country. This was a task calling for an adept and experienced political engineer. Nicaragua got some sense of how well the new president and her advisers would do in the two months separating electoral victory and accession to office.

A Difficult Two Months

Very early on the morning of 26 February, the Sandinistas knew that they had lost. They had only two months before Mrs. Chamorro's inauguration, but they still controlled the levers of government. They would use their remaining time to shore up what they thought were the most valuable yet vulnerable parts of the revolution's accomplishments, all the while organizing themselves as a powerful opposition.

The UNO faced a different, but no less daunting, challenge. Though the winners had policies and plans, it was not clear that they had a very sure sense of how to run a government. Potentially worse, now that victory was in hand, the UNO coalition had to find more common ground than simply opposing the Sandinistas.

The potential for divisions in the UNO went back to the alliance's search for a presidential candidate in 1989.[5] Two veteran anti-Sandinistas, Enrique Bolaños, head of the private-sector pressure group COSEP, and Virgilio Godoy, former minister of labor and leader of the PLI, saw themselves as the main contenders for the nomination. Each had a long history of opposing the revolutionary government, and both were recognized leaders of the intransigent anti-Sandinista forces. Mrs. Chamorro was recruited as a candidate as well. The alliance's Political Council, the leaders of the fourteen parties who composed the UNO, would choose the leader, who needed to carry ten votes to win. It took three ballots, and when Doña Violeta emerged the winner, not everyone was happy. First, there was a sense that the U.S. embassy was applying pressure on her behalf, having decided that she was the most electable of the top contenders. Second, and perhaps more important, while the leaders of the member parties had been active in oppositional politics throughout the 1980s, Chamorro effectively retired from active public life when she quit the JERN in 1980. She was an outsider who really had not paid her dues, yet she would lead the UNO to victory and become the nation's chief executive.

Reading the Results

With 54.1 percent of the vote and fifty-one of the ninety-two legislative seats, Mrs. Chamorro and the UNO were plainly Nicaragua's choice. But just what had Nicaraguans chosen? Two things made matters unclear. First, the 1990 elections were very much an exercise in turning the rascals out and bringing in anybody but the FSLN. Surprisingly, this sort of election leaves a new government with an ambiguous mandate. Should it press forward to implement its platform as rapidly as possible, reading its landslide victory as a clear vote of confidence? Or does prudence dictate reading a resounding win as indicating only that the electorate was tired of the defeated administration? In the latter case, treading lightly was in order. Second, the UNO itself presented voters mixed signals during the campaign. Doña Violeta stressed reconciliation and the need to achieve peace, but her party had a more ambitious and potentially confrontational agenda. Not only did the UNO platform demand far-reaching economic and administrative reforms,[6] but the party's legislative and municipal candidates built their campaigns around these themes to a far greater extent than did their leader.[7]

No one expected the National Union of the Opposition to weld its fourteen member parties, running the gamut from Conservatives to Communists, into a model of unity. Despite their obvious programmatic differences, however, the parties shared a sufficiently high level of animus toward the FSLN to bring them together for the short run. Because activists in these parties, few of which had memberships extending far beyond their leadership cadres, had experienced repeated run-ins with the revolutionary government over the years, they injected a note of venom into the election.

Mrs. Chamorro, on the other hand, spent most of the Sandinista era on the sidelines of active politics. Though she belonged to the first revolutionary JGRN, she left that post within a year and returned to private life. Attached to Nicaragua's Conservatives by family traditions, Chamorro nevertheless remained aloof from party politics during the 1980s. Her nonpartisanship was best seen in her team of campaign advisers, overwhelmingly drawn from among her family and friends. Violeta's men (her daughter Cristina was the only other woman involved at a high level), shared a technocratic outlook, as well as high social status. They were more interested in making Nicaragua work right than in settling scores with the FSLN.[8] The difference between the outlooks of the two sides came through clearly in their views of the administration of the electoral process.

Nicaragua's 1990 elections must have been the most closely supervised and scrutinized ever held anywhere in the world. Both the United Nations and the OAS had substantial delegations of full-time electoral observers on site throughout the campaign. Other organizations, such as the Carter Center, the National Democratic Institute, and the National Republican Institute, all from the United States, maintained smaller operations for the duration of the electoral process, and a myriad of groups dispatched their own volunteers to oversee the last weeks of the campaign. In light of this, Iqbal Riza, chief of the UN's team, declared that fraud would be very difficult.[9]

Not everyone agreed with Riza, however. Both UNO vice presidential candidate Virgilio Godoy and Alfredo César, who headed the party's legislative slate in Managua, gave interviews to the foreign press indicating they expected fraud from the Sandinistas. Godoy, interviewed by Spain's largest daily, *Diario 16,* claimed that the FSLN could not win cleanly: "They can win if they have Violeta Chamorro assassinated, if they have me assassinated, if they decapitate the UNO, maybe they could win."[10] César told the *Miami Herald* that he planned to have people take to the streets in protest if official counts did not match UNO samples.[11] Antonio Lacayo, UNO campaign chief and Doña Violeta's son-in-law, quickly made clear that neither Godoy nor César spoke for the party or its presidential candidate,[12] but the gap between Chamorro and some of her supposed backers was plain to see.

Had running a "good cop, bad cop" campaign, stressing both reconciliation and getting tough with the Sandinistas, been just an electoral tactic, Nicaragua would have been spared much conflict over the next six years. Unfortunately, each side of the UNO understandably read the landslide victory as endorsing its preferred line. The president's advisers would soon see the UNO legislative caucus and municipal governments as little more than people seeking revenge for having property expropriated by the Sandinistas.[13] The legislative and municipal wings of the UNO were quickly convinced that the administration had sold out the party's electoral victory to enter a marriage of convenience with the hated FSLN. As Managua's wags put it, the UNO (one entity) became *dos* (two). A more prudent and nuanced reading of the votes cast on 25 February 1990 might have led to a different outcome.

Although the UNO was understandably proud of having vanquished the mighty FSLN, a moment's reflection would have suggested that the conquest was not complete. True, the Sandinistas won only 41 percent of the vote, but they remained the largest single party, as opposed to an electoral alliance, in Nicaragua. To a rather greater extent than the UNO, the

FSLN in February 1990 was a unified political force. It had also shown great, if misguided and poorly used, organizational capacity in the campaign. After the election, the party rallied behind its leaders and found a new purpose in the defense of the redistributive programs and egalitarian policies it had pioneered.

Further, though this was not obvious at the time, the Sandinistas did not fare badly when compared to Eastern Europe's ex-Communists (see Table 2.1). Only the renamed Communists of Bulgaria, Romania, and Albania, who actually retained power after their countries' transitional elections, recorded higher levels of support than did the FSLN; and even these did less well than the Nicaraguans in their second run at power. In fact, the revolutionaries did not do appreciably worse than the defeated incumbents in Costa Rica, where the National Liberation Party received 47.3 percent of the vote in 1990, and they did rather better than El Salvador's Christian Democrats, who fell to 36 percent in 1989.[14] This was not a political organization about to vanish without a trace.

Besides the FSLN as a political party, there were the many organizations affiliated with the Sandinistas. Though most of these had been unobtrusive politically while the FSLN held power—only the National Union of

Table 2.1   FSLN Versus Eastern Europe's Ex-Communists, 1984–1993

Country	Year	Vote (%)	Rank Among Parties
Nicaragua	1984	66.3	1
	1990	40.7	2
Albania	1991	56.7	1
	1992	25.0	2
Bulgaria	1990	47.1	1
	1991	33.1	2
Czech Republic	1990	13.3[a]	2
	1992	14.1[a]	2
Slovakia	1990	13.9[a]	3
	1992	14.7[a]	2
Estonia	1992	1.6	7
Hungary	1990	10.9	4
Latvia	1993	5.8	5
Lithuania	1992	42.6	1
Poland	1991	12.0	2
	1993	20.4	1
Romania	1990	66.3	1
	1992	27.7	1

Sources: Adapted from John T. Ishiyama, "Communist Parties in Transition," *Comparative Politics* 27:1 (January 1995): 157.
a. Elections for Czech and Slovak National Councils.

Farmers and Ranchers was truly active and vocal—nothing but the greatest naivete could have led the UNO to believe that things would not change. Either the Sandinista leadership would mold these groups into an extra-parliamentary oppositional movement, or the once-docile groups, particularly the unions, would find their own voices and make their own demands on government. The actual roles taken by these groups is discussed in Chapter 4.

Moreover, the electoral system installed by the Sandinista government before the 1984 elections worked to the detriment of the majority party.[15] As a result, the FSLN turned not quite 41 percent of the votes cast into almost 45 percent of the seats in the National Assembly. This was critical, because the 1987 Nicaraguan constitution (Articles 192 and 194) provided that a "super majority" of 60 percent of the entire house was needed in two successive annual legislatures to amend the constitution. Unless four members of the Sandinista caucus defected, no constitutional change was possible. The FSLN was well positioned to defend the system it had put in place, and the UNO's prospects for even a partial overhaul were dim.

A further reason for a cautious interpretation of the election's outcome was the UNO's own campaign. This was built around two slogans: *Qué se vayan!* (Get rid of 'em!) and *Tuvieron diez años y no pudieron. La UNO si puede!* (They had ten years and couldn't do anything. Well, the UNO sure can!). These are two wonderful examples of the "turn the rascals out" school of campaigning. The challenger focuses the public's attention on the incumbent's woeful record and says little about its own plans. The UNO's nationwide sweep[16] showed that Nicaraguans plainly felt it was time for a change, but they did not make clear what kind of change they wanted.

Soon after the election, information about what the people meant by their vote began to appear. The data used here to analyze these motives are drawn from postelection surveys conducted by the Instituto de Estudios Nicaraguenses (IEN).[17] Though the sample in the main survey was quite large (N=1037), it had a strong urban bias, something not uncommon in Nicaraguan polling of that era. Nonetheless, the results are clear enough to permit reasonable speculation about the concerns voters carried into the polls.

Table 2.2 shows that UNO voters most liked their party's promise to end the military draft. When combined with those choosing "peace," over two-thirds of reported UNO voters named the alliance's stand on war-related issues as their favorite part of the program. A similar pattern emerges from what voters reported disliking about the Sandinista government. The most unpopular feature of the revolutionary government was the draft (*Servicio Militar Patriótico*), named by 33 percent of all respondents; among declared UNO voters the proportion was 34.4 percent, while 26.4 percent of self-identified FSLN voters made the same comment. In a sense,

Table 2.2   Favored Parts of UNO Platform, 1990 (*N* = 1037)

Platform Promise	UNO	FSLN
Peace	10.1	8.6
End draft	57.3	22.5
Change, generally	20.0	10.7
Other	5.4	1.6
Don't know/no answer/nothing	7.2	56.5

Source: IEN, *Encuesta socio-política nacional, #1.*

then, the 1990 election was a referendum on Sandinista foreign and defense policy. It was certainly far from evident that the Nicaraguan electorate was ready for another bout of wholesale economic, political, and social reconstruction.

None of the above evidence gainsays the existence of very real and deeply felt animus against the Sandinistas. Marvin Ortega, the head of a left-wing think tank, argued that the vote reflected accrued resentment toward what people saw as characteristic Sandinista behavior.[18] In war zones, those who were not committed Sandinistas took exception to the high-handedness with which the military and police regularly operated. Throughout rural Nicaragua, the policy of requiring grain sales to the state at concessionary prices, though abandoned by the time of the elections, still rankled. Urban Nicaraguans who were not part of the FSLN remembered bitterly the early days of the revolutions when gangs of Sandinista supporters (*turbas*) defaced people's houses with graffiti reading "Keep an eye on me, I'm a Somocista." Though all of these practices had changed or were changing, voters could hardly be blamed for taking the opportunity to exact a measure of revenge or to ensure that history did not repeat itself. And this list of complaints does not even include those from people whose property was confiscated, or who suffered arbitrary justice at the hands of the state, or, above all, who lost a loved one to a war in which they did not fully believe.

There was certainly no shortage of reasons to want to punish the Sandinistas. But even had the 54 percent of voters who backed the UNO uniformly done so to seek retribution against the revolutionary state, they still constituted a small majority. President-elect Chamorro, her cabinet, and her advisers viewed their mandate in this light and moved cautiously,[19] knowing that they had until late 1996 to do their work. Other important UNO leaders, led by Vice President–elect Godoy, wanted to erase every trace of Sandinista rule from the country as quickly as possible. Thus, a poor country, with a war-racked economy and fragile society, comes to have a government at odds with itself.

Negotiating the Handover

Real conflict began between the two camps of the newly elected government when the UNO sat down with the FSLN to work out the transfer of power. Before 1990, Nicaraguans had never worried about the mechanics of how one administration handed the reins of government over to its successor, so Nicaraguan politicians were about to learn a new skill. Interestingly, the defeated Sandinistas had an advantage in this enterprise. They knew the machinery of government, and they had a clear command structure that was accepted by most of the party. Moreover, once past the shock of losing, the FSLN quickly decided to use the handover talks to protect its loyalists from partisan reprisals. So the FSLN had clear objectives.

The UNO was in a more difficult spot. Not only were most of its leaders unfamiliar with the inner workings of the revolutionary state, but the party's internal divisions posed a delicate political problem for the president-elect as well. If Chamorro gave the outspoken anti-Sandinistas an important role in the talks, she faced the specter of breakdown, walkout, and possibly even armed conflict. Yet if she marginalized them, she risked creating an intransigent opposition within her own party. She chose the latter path.

Both incumbent President Ortega and President-elect Chamorro entrusted negotiating the transition of power to close relatives. The FSLN team was led by General Humberto Ortega, the president's brother and Nicaragua's chief of defense staff. The other Sandinistas were Jaime Wheelock, former agrarian reform minister and member of the FSLN's National Directorate, and Major General Joaquín Cuadra, the military's second in command. Antonio Lacayo, Chamorro's son-in-law, headed the UNO side, much to the dismay of the more committed anti-Sandinistas. His team included Carlos Hurtado and Luis Sanchez, both associated at that time with the alliance's accommodationist wing. The more conservative wing of the winning side saw itself being pushed to the margins.

Viewing the contents of the Protocal of Agreement, also called the Transition Accords, gives a good sense of what was at stake. This protocol was signed on 27 March 1990, at the midway point between the elections and the inauguration. There were four key elements of the pact: disarming the contras; assuring the integrity of the military; recognizing the need to equitably settle competing property claims; and acknowledging the need to protect public employees from political dismissals. The actual Protocol of Agreement is short enough to allow the full reproduction of its

"Stipulations for the Transfer of Executive Power of the Republic of Nicaragua":[20]

1.   Implementation of the Toncontín Agreement signed on March 23, 1990, in Tegucigalpa, Honduras, for the demobilization of the Resistance forces before April 25, 1990, which constitutes an essential element form creating the climate of peace, stability and tranquillity necessary for the transfer of government.[21]

2.   The Defense and Public Order forces of the nation will be subordinated to the civilian power of the President of the Republic in accordance with the Constitution and the Laws of the Republic. Their characteristics and size will be revised in relation to the economic capacity and social needs of the country in keeping with the Contadora and Regional Peace Accords.

     The Armed Forces will have a professional character and will not belong to any political party. Its members in active service will not be able to hold leadership positions in political parties. Political campaigns with the Armed Forces will be permitted only with the framework of the country's Electoral Law. Respect for the integrity and professionalism of the Sandinista Popular Army and the forces of public order, as well as for their ranks, chain of command and specific duties in accordance to the Constitution and the Laws of the Republic, in itself constitutes the fundamental basis for the orderly transfer of government.

3.   Similarly, as an essential part of the process of democratic consolidation, the integrity and independence of the Branches of Government must be strengthened with the proper application of the Constitution and of the Laws.

4.   There is agreement on the need to provide peace of mind and legal security to those Nicaraguan families who have received the benefit of urban or rural property through State assignment before February 25, 1990, reconciling this with the legitimate legal property rights of other Nicaraguans, all procedures to be conducted with the framework of the Law. Adequate forms of compensation will be established for those who have suffered any damage.

5.   The orderly transfer of the Executive Power must take place within a framework of mutual security and trust wherein any act of vindictiveness, reprisal or revenge will not have a place, and in a climate of respect for people's physical and moral integrity. In this respect, both transition teams support the initiatives of the public authorities to create a climate of National Reconciliation and Amnesty in benefit of the Nicaraguan family, and express the need to assure that arms and combat equipment are only in the hands of the armed institutions of the Republic.

     It is also understood that existing associations and labor and community organizations in the country will enjoy the guarantees established by the Constitution and the Law.

     Similarly, monuments dedicated to Heroes and Martyrs who died in the struggle against Somocismo and in defense of the Homeland will be respected.

6. The guarantee of job stability for government officeholders—based on efficiency, administrative honesty and years of service—is also supported by both transition teams.
7. Both teams agree they should join forces to obtain international resources during the transition stage in order to promote stability and economic growth.

Reading this protocol some years after its drafting leaves one with the sense of how utterly normal it is. This pact that permitted the first peaceful, interparty transferral of government in Nicaragua's history attempted to establish a legal basis for what would be accepted unthinkingly as standard practice in Britain, Canada, or the United States. That the protocol *had* to be drafted, and that it was the result of several weeks' work, speaks volumes about the political tension prevailing in Nicaragua in early 1990. Even more ominous for the nation's future tranquillity, this was the strongest statement that could emerge from talks from which anti-Sandinista hard-liners were absent. So the document was a pact not among all Nicaragua's political elites, but only about three-quarters of them. Time would prove that this was not enough to solidify a new order.

Getting the Transition Accords in place did not end the president-elect's travails. She still had to confront a two-sided military problem. One side of the issue was how to reduce the military's size. After ten years of war Nicaragua's military establishment counted at least 63,000 soldiers.[22] Not only would many of these troops be redundant in peacetime, but the nation's economy could not support them and still recover.

But this was not an ordinary military the new administration had to restructure. The Sandinista Popular Army, the EPS's name (per Article 95), was highly politicized and strongly committed to the goals of the revolution. For it to be reorganized by an administration with members who had supported that army's enemy would be very hard to accept. Accordingly, Chamorro's second task was to find a way to make the army more economical without losing its confidence. The most obvious way to do this was to assure the continuity of its chain of command by leaving General Humberto Ortega as chief of staff. The UNO right wing and the contra forces were both loathe to accept this.

Many of the "resistance fighters," the label the contras themselves had adopted, had visions of becoming the new Nicaraguan army or, at a minimum, of displacing the Sandinista officer corps. Further, much of the UNO found the notion of any serving EPS officer continuing to command the forces unpalatable, and General Ortega was not just any officer. Besides being President Daniel Ortega's brother, the general was a member of the nine-man DN, the FSLN's governing body. Worse, from the perspective of many Unistas (UNO members), it was he who in 1980 said that "our elections will be held to perfect revolutionary power, not to hold a raffle among those who seek to hold power."[23] Moreover, in 1989, during the U.S. invasion of Panama, he declared that Nicaraguan security forces might have to execute "traitors" who aided the Yankees.[24] Finally, it was his armed, mobile escort that shot and killed a teenager, Jean Paul Genie, who had tried to pass the general's unmarked caravan. However, Chamorro opted to appease not her caucus but the military—a gesture later repaid through the military's acceptance of massive troop cuts—by retaining Ortega as top commander, though he did have to renounce his position on the FSLN's National Directorate.

When she announced this decision on 25 April, her inauguration day, it was the last straw for those who were fast becoming the UNO hard-liners. Two members of the cabinet associated with that tendency, Jaime Cuadra and Gilberto Cuadra, resigned, leaving the cabinet in the hands of technocrats, the majority of whom had spent the Sandinista years outside the country. The fourteen UNO party leaders had entertained visions of ministerial portfolios for themselves and their closest allies, but they got scarcely a nod.

What began on 25 February as a famous victory for the UNO had taken a curious turn by 25 April. In just two months a successful electoral alliance had fallen to infighting and showed signs of fragmenting, because the executive and legislative parts of the new UNO administration had conflicting agendas and appeared incapable of devising mechanisms to reconcile their differences. Even before taking office, Violeta Chamorro had to confront crisis and make hard decisions.[25] Unfortunately, she would have to do the same thing many times over her six-year presidency.

Sandinista Lame Ducks

As did the UNO, the FSLN made decisions in the transition period that would fundamentally affect Nicaraguan politics for the next six years. The Sandinistas' main concern was to tie up legal loose ends to protect programs they had implemented during their decade in office. Never expecting that the people would vote their vanguard into opposition, and not as attentive to detail as a governing party in a competitive constitutional democracy should be, the Sandinistas had left a surprising number of important policies without proper legal foundations. Unless this was corrected, the UNO would not even have to repeal Sandinista laws favoring the majority, paying the political costs that would entail; it could simply legislate in the vacuum left by the previous administration.

Before the FSLN could address this problem, however, it had to reanimate its supporters and find a new political purpose for itself. The first step was President Ortega's "governing from below" speech, given the Tuesday after the election, 27 February, in the Plaza of the Nonaligned in Managua:

> We were not born at the top, we were born at the bottom and we are used to fighting from below. We are used to struggling, to fighting from below . . . in the face of our executioners and torturers. We are used to fighting and struggling from prisons. So now that people's power, revolutionary power exists in this country, we have much better conditions in the short term to return to governing the country from above.
>
> I tell you that the day will come when we return to governing from above, because the Sandinista National Liberation Front, with the Nicaraguan people, will continue governing from below. We will continue governing from below . . . insisting on respect for our rights.[26]

At the very least, this implied an active extraparliamentary opposition. Hence, politics would not be confined to the National Assembly, the courts, and bureaucratic channels. Ortega's words also served as a warning that the government should expect pressure from all quarters and should not interpret its victory as a mandate for total change. The president-elect dismissed the whole notion of governing from below the next day, answering Ortega by declaring, "My dear, I'm the one who governs here!"[27] It was a good sound bite, but the Sandinistas set quickly to work to assure that their rights were respected.

Because it enjoyed a two-to-one majority in the National Assembly, the FSLN was able to push through a lot of lame-duck legislation before handing over the state to its new managers. In a session running from 2 March to 19 April, the Assembly approved twenty-six measures.[28] Six of these are especially noteworthy:

1. The General Amnesty and National Reconciliation Law was enacted, covering the period from 19 July 1979 to 13 March 1990, the day it passed.
2. The Civil Service and Administrative Careers Law was enacted, strengthening the rights of public-sector workers and the guarantees and protections afforded them.
3. Labor code revisions were enacted, the first significant amendments to the code since 1945.
4. The Media and Social Communications Law was repealed, ending the state's monopoly over television.
5. The University Autonomy Act was enacted, increasing universities' rights of self-management.
6. Three property laws were passed, granting title to those who had received urban and rural property from the revolutionary government.

All of this legislation was designed to protect Sandinista interests and Sandinistas themselves. The amnesty law gave "full and unconditional amnesty" to those who had committed crimes "against the public order and the internal or external security of the state."[29] This covered both Sandinistas and resistance fighters, and it was justified as a means of forestalling political reprisals. This reasoning was also used to explain the extension of the amnesty to those who had stolen state property. However, individuals already charged with crimes were excluded.

The two acts affecting labor were both to protect employees from political justice and to enhance labor's rights more generally. The civil service law set strict guidelines for dismissal; the labor code amendments, which were prepared by Sandinista Workers' Central (CST), the Sandinista union federation, did the same thing for private-sector workers. Danilo Aguirre, an FSLN deputy, said that "to leave [the workers] without a new labor code would not only be an irresponsible act, but, for a revolutionary, treason against the working class, and the FSLN can't do that."[30]

Although the University Autonomy Act might seem a strange inclusion in this package, the act provided that top university officials, from the rector down through deans and directors, would be elected by faculty, staff, and students.[31] This would make it harder for the new government to place its candidates in these positions. Abolishing the media law made privately owned TV stations legal. Though all expected the UNO administration to permit private television, repealing the act gave the FSLN a chance to get its application for a station in on the ground floor.

The most important of all these acts were the three property laws. As they figure prominently in a later chapter, for now it is enough to note that they gave everyone who had received property from the revolutionary state, including organizations, full legal title to that property. This measure would thus make it harder for those whose property had been confiscated, for whatever reason, to reclaim their former holdings. Though at the time the amnesty bill was seen as the most controversial, it was ultimately the property laws (numbers 85, 86, and 88) that caused the Chamorro administration and the country as a whole the most grief.

Opposition politicians were divided in their reactions to this breathless rush to fill legislative lacunae. Alan Zambrana, a Communist who had served as a representative since 1980, declared that "the most dramatic thing I've witnessed in all the legislatures [I've been part of] was representatives of opposition parties making a U-turn and latching on to the FSLN, turning themselves into a docile opposition."[32] But a Conservative, Eduardo Molina, saw things differently, saying, "we mounted an opposition with a high degree of responsibility and patriotic feeling; saying we made deals with the FSLN can't be taken seriously."[33] Even had the opposition wanted to stop the Sandinistas, it is unlikely that it could have. The FSLN was determined to protect itself, its followers, and its achievements.

The Theory of Transitions and Nicaraguan Practice

Regime transformation in Nicaragua coincided with a conventional change of government. A regularly scheduled election, conducted according to rules that had been in place for some time, was the instrument by which a new political order entered the country. There was no great and dramatic break with the past. No Berlin Wall fell. No Marcos or Duvalier fled the country on a U.S. Air Force transport. Rather, one group of politicians won more votes than another and duly took office. If the mechanics of handing over power had not needed to be negotiated, the transition would have left few traces in the official archives.

On the ground, however, things were different. People knew that something big had happened, something of great, if not quite revolutionary, proportion. The losers scrambled to protect themselves from future reprisals while the victors laid plans for their new order. The new government promised to use state power in ways very different from those of its predecessors. The regime had changed, but the meaning of this would be seen and felt clearly only after the new government had an opportunity to put its program into effect through legislation.

Political analysts and commentators since Plato have sought to explain how and why political change occurs. Some have had partisan interests, wanting to keep change at bay or hasten its arrival. Others have taken a more detached view, simply wanting to know how the process works. Since the mid-twentieth century, political science has studied several different examples of political change. Besides an abiding concern for revolutions, analysts have focused on the building of postcolonial polities in the 1950s and 1960s, the collapse of democracies and the rise of authoritarianism in the 1970s, and, since the mid-1970s, the failure of authoritarianism and the rise of democracy.

This latest installment in the saga of political change began in 1974 when two southern European dictatorships, the Greek junta and the Portuguese fascist government, were overthrown. A year later, Spain's Generalismo Francisco Franco died, unexpectedly taking with him the dictatorship he had founded in 1939. From those days until now, the world has been swept up in what Samuel Huntington calls "the third wave" of democratization.[34] Governments based on antidemocratic principles, or simply following antidemocratic practices, have fallen and been replaced by constitutional democrats in all four corners of the globe. Government analysts, journalists, and academic commentators have rushed to examine and explain this unexpected development. The result has been the emergence of theories of political transition and democratic consolidation. I shall not even try to summarize, much less review, this extensive literature,[35] but I shall select those elements that seem most pertinent to Nicaragua.

In his recent overview of the transitions literature, Doh Shull Shin remarked that there are four stages of democratization: decay of authoritarianism, transition, consolidation, and maturation.[36] Only the first two are relevant here, and the very first of these needs particular attention. Though no one would claim that the Sandinistas were constitutional liberal democrats, there is reason to ask if they were authoritarians in the ways that the Somozas, the Duvaliers, the Chilean or Argentine military regimes, or the Soviet Communists were. This is not a dilatory question, but rather one that may contribute to a better understanding of the workings of the Chamorro administration.

Though there is a substantial body of scholarly work on authoritarianism,[37] it is easier to work backward from a current definition of democracy in order to establish a standard by which to judge the FSLN's revolutionary state. Robert Dahl, the dean of American empirical liberal democratic theorists, has recently set forth what he sees as the distinguishing marks of modern democratic systems.[38] He specifies the simultaneous and effective existence of free and fair elections, extensive freedom of expression and association, and an extensive right to organize. By implication, a democratic government must be accountable to the governed *and* allow its citizens the freedom to organize and express themselves in ways that make them politically effective.

How well did the Sandinistas do this? For simplicity's sake, the hagiographic and "demonographic" extremes can be ignored. To accentuate the positive, one can stress the Sandinistas' renunciation of single-party rule in the 1982 Political Parties Law; the party's commitment to accept electoral outcomes in 1984 and 1990; and an increasing respect for political rights after signing the Esquipulas Accords in 1987. One could also add a slight but still clear increase in the power of the National Assembly. Emphasizing the negative, one can highlight the FSLN's continued commitment to vanguardism, the party's verticalism, the state's occasional disregard for legal forms, the rough justice that often comes in time of war, and even its general anticapitalist orientation.

Both positions are sustainable empirically, but choosing one over the other puts the transition of 1990 in a different light. If Sandinista Nicaragua was a socialist state with important liberal characteristics—more important, if it was not a party or military dictatorship—then the change in trajectory needed to achieve a conventional, even conservative, constitutional democracy is not daunting. But if one holds that the vanguardist, orthodox

Marxist side of the FSLN dominated, then the change needed is great indeed. Logically, the transition to orthodox Western democracy is easier where the old regime had important liberal, constitutional characteristics, because there are fewer antidemocratic, authoritarian residues to threaten the new order.

For the reasons I set out in the previous chapter, I endorse the more optimistic assessment of the Sandinista state, but rather than rehearse those arguments, I want to note that these themes are not often raised in discussions of Nicaragua's transition. In fact, Nicaragua's experience is usually ignored by transition theorists, who concentrate on Eastern Europe and the ex–Soviet Union, southern Europe, South America's Southern Cone (Argentina, Brazil, Chile, Uruguay), and now East Asia. Though scholarly work on the authoritarian backgrounds of transitions raises inherently important questions, it says little about this fascinating case, or about how the steady liberalization of the Sandinista state might have affected the prospects of a successful transition. Unlike her counterparts in former Communist states, President Chamorro did not have to scrap the existing constitution or tear down all the existing machinery of government before setting to work. That she and her followers might have preferred inheriting a more orthodox liberal democratic political system is understandable, but they were still able to maintain a semblance of order and implement significant parts of their agenda by using the instruments of the Sandinista state. As bad as things were, it is easy to imagine them having been much worse.

Nicaragua receives similar short shrift among the analyses of actual transitions, but once again, the questions asked and categories used are applicable to this case. Terry Lynn Karl and Philippe Schmitter identify four ideal types of transition:

> *pact:* when elites agree upon a multilateral compromise among themselves (e.g., Spain, Uruguay, Colombia, Venezuela);
> *impositions:* when elites use force unilaterally and effectively to bring about a regime change against the resistance of some incumbents (e.g., Brazil, Ecuador, Turkey, Soviet Union);
> *reform:* when masses mobilize from below and impose a compromised outcome without resorting to violence (e.g., Czechoslovakia, Poland, Yugoslavia, and Guatemala in 1946);
> *revolution:* when masses rise up in arms and defeat the previous authoritarian rulers militarily (e.g., Nicaragua [1979]).[39]

In a separate work, though, these same authors argue that pact making among elites offers the most successful path to democracy.[40] Two examples, Venezuela and Spain, show how transitional pacts can work. Venezuela's experience is the prototype for all pacted transitions.[41] The 1958 Pact of Punto Fijo designed governmental institutions and distributed political power in a way that quieted the fears of big landowners and business interests, satisfied the aspirations of the popular classes, assured the military that its interests were heard, and gave democratic politic forces the room they needed to operate. This deal among elites, both established (business, ranchers, and the military) and rising (democratic parties and labor unions), committed each and all of them to pursue political power solely within the limits of a democratic constitution. For conservatives this meant safeguards for their property and social privilege, while the reformers got guarantees that they would not face violent overthrow. All the country's politically significant elites had a hand in the pact, so all had a stake in its success.

The Spanish case is slightly different, because the actual deals struck were wholly the work of politicians.[42] This was possible because, aside from limited sectors of the military and the Guardia Civil,[43] there were no important antidemocratic sectors in society to oppose establishing a democratic government. By bringing in all interested players (including representatives of the long-repressed Basque, Catalan, and Galician regions), Adolfo Suárez, who took the lead in brokering the deals, laid the foundations for today's flourishing Spanish democracy.

Although it might be argued that it was the reform mode—that is, the vote—that brought the Sandinista state to an end, it is more prudent to focus on interelite deal making. Not only was the handover of state power the result of a negotiated protocol, but many significant changes in the Sandinista political system were the fruit of arrangements crafted by the nation's political elites.[44] In that case, if the theorists who emphasize the centrality of a transitional pact—the interelite deal—are correct, then Nicaragua started life as an orthodox constitutional democracy on a very unpromising note. Divisions within the winning alliance led to the marginalization of a significant portion of Nicaragua's political elite. That including these factions would probably have made an amicable transitional agreement impossible only throws the problem into sharper relief.

Nicaragua, then, faced a curious set of circumstances as the first female president in the republic's history took office. The ticket she headed had won a smashing victory in elections organized by the incumbents and intensively monitored by international observers; there was no doubt about the elections' probity or the validity of the UNO's triumph. Victory in hand, the winners fell to squabbling, not over the division of spoils, but over the meaning of their mandate and the character of state they should build. The now-defeated incumbents met with representatives of the executive-elect to organize the unprecedented handover of the reins of government. By meeting with the incoming executive, perfectly understandable in presidentialist Latin America, the losers effectively collaborated in minimizing the say that one segment of the winning party would have in setting the conditions for the transfer of power. This let Chamorro's faction profit most from the legitimacy of electoral victory and get a jump on its internal opponents in setting governmental priorities. But it also put part of the victorious alliance on the defensive and would eventually lead its members to seek extraconstitutional ways to enact their program.

This transition, which more than in most transformational settings really was about one government taking over from another, laid the foundations for many of the problems that Nicaragua would face throughout the Chamorro years. Unable to count on her fellow Unistas, President Chamorro soon found herself dependent on Sandinista votes to push through any of her policies. This alienated much of the UNO and compromised both the administration and the FSLN. The result was a dizzying spiral of increasing ungovernability that stabilized only in 1993, after the country had been more than once to the brink of civil war. The resultant relative equilibrium only made it easier to see the other questions that remain unresolved after six years of orthodox constitutional government.

Those two tough months, from the end of February to late April 1990, offered a preview of some of the challenges the Chamorro administration would face. The animus between the UNO and the FSLN, as well as within the UNO itself, was unmistakable. It made enemies where ordinary constitutional democratic politics has opponents, thus rendering productive political relationships between the two sides of the aisle extremely difficult. Moreover, this ill-feeling also underlay the legislative-executive wrangling that characterized the 1990–1996 period. Finally, and on a more speculative level, the UNO's internal divisions may have foreclosed the possibility of turning the UNO into Nicaragua's natural right-of-center party, thus opening the way for the 1996 victory of Arnoldo Alemán and costing UNO leaders a chance at real power.

More significant, the two-month interregnum showed that Nicaragua's governing elites did not share enough common ground to produce a vision of a proper political system that all could accept. The divisions within the political elite were deeply rooted, reflecting irreconcilable governing philosophies, and exacerbated by personal malice. Of course, this also helps explain why the Transition Accords did not become a full transitional pact and why a reasonably smooth handover of power between parties did not presage an era of goodwill and cooperation.

If there is a lesson in all this it must be that the business of crafting solutions, so vigorously emphasized by the theorists of pact making, is both very hard and absolutely crucial to new representative democracies. How this business is carried on and what results it yields are matters of primary importance. Analyzing these questions demands attention to the specific political matrix found in a country. Later chapters that trace the various policy disputes that consumed so much of the political energy of the Chamorro administration and its opponents will bear this out. We, the analysts of the ex post facto situation, know that negotiations to find satisfactory common ground matter greatly and that such negotiations will bear the marks of the context in which they are conducted. The next and truly important, though probably impossible, step is to discover ways to assure that the context lets the men and women trying to make the deals reach feasible, positive conclusions.

Notes

1. A useful starting point for inquiry into the classification of political regimes is Harry Eckstein and Ted Robert Gurr, *Patterns of Authority: A Structural Basis for Political Inquiry* (New York: Wiley, 1975); see also, Mark Lichbach, "Regime Change: A Test of Structuralist and Functionalist Explanations," *Comparative Political Studies* 14 (1981): 49–73. The extensive contemporary literature on democratic transitions, obviously treating regime transformation, is considered later in this chapter.

2. This is discussed in more detail in Chapter 1.

3. President Chamorro could hardly have buried the Sandinista past, even had she wanted to. She had been a member of the first JGRN, and two of her children were major players in Sandinista politics.

4. An introductory textbook offers this serviceable definition of liberal democracy: "A liberal democratic political system, then, is one in which, on the basis of universal adult suffrage, citizens select their governors (representatives); these representatives can be changed by the electorate through periodic elections; individual or group opinions can be discussed freely without fear of retaliation by public officials or private individuals; a legal opposition is free to criticize; and an independent judiciary resolves disputes between citizens, between citizens and government, and between levels of government" (Mark Dickerson and Thomas Flanagan, *An Introduction to Government and Politics,* 4th ed. [Scarborough, Ontario: Nelson Canada, 1994], p. 213).

5. This section draws on Guillermo Cortés, *La lucha por el poder* (Managua: Editorial Vanguardia, 1990), esp. pp. 157–224.

6. *Program of the National Opposition Union,* special supplement to *La Prensa,* 26 August 1989, Chaps. 4 and 5.

7. Unless otherwise noted, material on the campaign comes from Cortés, *La lucha por el poder.* This is a thorough and balanced account of the campaign by an editor of the Sandinista daily, *Barricada,* and is the best readily available source.

8. Carlos Vilas, "Family Affairs: Class, Lineage and Politics in Contemporary Nicaragua," *Journal of Latin American Studies* 24:2 (1992): 309–342, lays bare the family backgrounds of the two UNO camps and explains some of the reasons behind the conflicts within the new party.

9. *El Nuevo Diario,* 21 February 1990, p. 25.

10. Quoted in *Barricada,* 15 February 1990, p. 4.

11. Ibid., pp. 2, 5.

12. Ibid., 17 February 1990, p. 4. Lacayo had other run-ins with Godoy and his people, most notably in January when Godoy supporter Jaime Bonilla punched him during a rally.

13. In a November 1991 interview, Tomás Delaney, then the president's top

legal adviser, characterized the UNO caucus to me as being mainly *"confiscados o los abogados de confiscados,"* or people whose property had been confiscated or those people's lawyers. Interviews with other officials in the Chamorro government in 1991 and 1994 showed this to be a widely shared perception.

14. Data are from David Close, "Central American Elections, 1989–90: Costa Rica, El Salvador, Honduras, Nicaragua, Panama," *Electoral Studies* 10:1 (1991): 60–76.

15. Described in David Close, *Nicaragua: Politics, Economics, and Society* (London: Pinter Publishers, 1988), p. 135.

16. The victors took seven of Nicaragua's nine administrative regions, losing only in the thinly populated and remote Region I, near the Honduran border, and Region IX, on the Costa Rican border; the UNO also carried 81 percent (105 out of 129) of the country's municipalities, including the capital.

17. IEN, *Encuesta socio-politica nacional, #1* (Managua: IEN, 1990).

18. Marvin Ortega, interview, Managua, March 1990.

19. This was particularly true after attempts to make sweeping economic changes immediately upon taking office led to massive strikes that brought the country dangerously close to civil war. The specific incidents are treated in Chapter 4.

20. Carter Center, *Observing Nicaragua's Elections, 1989–1990: Report of the Council of Freely Elected Heads of Government* (Atlanta, GA: Carter Center, Emory University, 1990), pp. 113–114.

21. Negotiated between the incoming administration and the counterrevolutionary leadership, the Toncontín Agreement called for an immediate cease-fire, as well as the voluntary demobilization of contra fighters by 20 April 1990, five days before the inauguration. Beyond that, it was not very precise and was not enthusiastically endorsed by the contra leadership. For details, see *Central America Report* (hereafter *CAR*), 30 March 1990, pp. 89–90; and *Envio* 9:105 (May 1990): 5–6.

22. International Institute for Strategic Studies, *The Military Balance: 1991–92* (London: Brassey's, 1991), p. 200. The figure includes the active reserve and militia but not the estimated 140,000 inactive reservists.

23. Quoted in George Black, *The Triumph of the People* (London: Zed Books, 1981), p. 256.

24. Quoted in the *New York Times*, 28 December 1996.

25. In saying that Mrs. Chamorro made such decisions, I do not contest the generally accepted view that Lacayo, her son-in-law, minister of the presidency, and de facto prime minister, was the actual source of the policies.

26. Quoted in *Envio* 9:104 (March/April 1990): 41.

27. President-elect Violeta Chamorro, press conference, Managua, 28 February 1990.

28. *El Nuevo Diario,* 20 April 1990. Not everything proposed passed, either. A bill that would have set the minimum wage equal to the price of the *canasta básica*—the market basket of necessary goods—was defeated (*El Nuevo Diario,* 24 April 1990; *La Prensa,* 24 April 1990). Because many of the clippings from which this section is constructed do not bear page numbers, references will omit this datum.

29. *Envio* 9:104 (March/April 1990): 28. Some members of the opposition in the assembly wanted to grant an unconditional pardon instead of an amnesty so that the charges against an individual would remain a matter of record (*La Prensa,* 10 March 1990).

30. Quoted in *El Nuevo Diario,* 28 March 1990.

31. *Barricada,* 5 April 1990.

32. Quoted in *El Nuevo Diario,* 21 April 1990.

33. Ibid.

34. Samuel Huntington, *The Third Wave* (Norman: University of Oklahoma Press, 1991).

35. Useful starting points for further explorations into the question of late-twentieth-century transitions to and consolidations of democracy are: Dankwart Rustow, "Transitions to Democracy: Toward a Dynamic Model," *Comparative Politics* 2:3 (1970): 337–364; Guillermo O'Donnell, Philippe Schmitter, and Laurence Whitehead, eds., *Transition from Authoritarian Rule: Prospects for Democracy* (Baltimore: Johns Hopkins University Press, 1986); Giuseppe di Palma, *To Craft Democracies* (Berkeley: University of California Press, 1990); Diane Ethier, ed., *Democratic Transition and Consolidation in Southern Europe, Latin America, and Southeast Asia* (London: Macmillan, 1990); Scott Mainwaring, Guillermo O'Donnell, and J. Samuel Valenzuela, eds., *Issues in Democratic Consolidation* (Notre Dame, IN: University of Notre Dame Press, 1992); Dietrich Rueschemeyer, Evelyne Huber Stephens, and John D. Stephens, *Capitalist Development and Democracy* (Chicago: University of Chicago Press, 1993); Adam Przeworski, ed., *Sustainable Democracy* (Cambridge: Cambridge University Press, 1995); and Karen Remmer, "The Sustainability of Political Democracy: Lessons from South America," *Comparative Political Studies* 29:6 (1996): 611–634.

36. Doh Shull Shin, "On the Third Wave of Democratization," *World Politics* 47 (October 1994): 135–170.

37. See the extensive literature on authoritarian rule that appeared in the 1970s, for example, David Collier, ed., *The New Authoritarianism in Latin America* (Princeton, NJ: Princeton University Press, 1979).

38. Robert Dahl, "The Newer Democracies: From the Time of Triumph to the Time of Troubles," in *After Authoritarianism: Democracy or Disorder?* ed. Daniel N. Nelson (Westport, CT: Praeger Publishers, 1995), pp. 1–13.

39. Terry Lynn Karl and Philippe Schmitter, "Democratization Around the Globe: Opportunities and Risks," in *World Security: Challenges for a New Century,* 2d ed., ed. Michael T. Klare and Daniel C. Thomas (New York: St. Martin's Press, 1994), p. 50.

40. Terry Lynn Karl and Philippe Schmitter, "Modes of Transition in Latin America, Southern and Eastern Europe," *International Social Science Journal* 138 (May 1991): 268–284.

41. For an introduction to the Venezuelan case, see Terry Lynn Karl, "Petroleum and Political Pacts: The Transition to Democracy in Venezuela," *Latin American Research Review* 22:1 (1988): 63–94; and Richard S. Hillman, *Democracy for the Privileged: Crisis and Transition in Venezuela* (Boulder, CO: Lynne Rienner Publishers, 1994).

42. For Spain, see Victor M. Pérez-Díaz, *The Return of Civil Society* (Cambridge, MA: Harvard University Press, 1993); and Howard Wiarda, *Iberia and Latin America: New Democracies, New Policies, New Models* (Lanham, MD: Rowman & Littlefield, 1996), esp. chap. 6.

43. Besides the coup of 1981, we have learned that military radicals planned to assassinate King Juan Carlos and Prime Minister Felipe González on Armed Forces Day in 1985. See Miguel González, "Militares y civiles planearon asesinar al Rey y al presidente en el desfile de A Coruña de 1985," *El Pais* electronic ed. (9 December 1997), at: http://www.elpais.es/p/d/19971209/espana/coruna.html.

44. Close, *Nicaragua*, 124–126, offers a brief description of the interactions that underlay the 1982 Political Parties Law. The LASA reports on the 1984 and 1990 elections also contain examples of Sandinista deal making to get the elections on the rails and keep them there.

3

The New Political System: Framework, Actors, Institutions

President Chamorro set about to create in Nicaragua an *estado de derecho*, a fully constitutional regime in which the rule of law prevails. Since independence in 1821, whether Nicaragua had good government or bad depended, in the end, on the will of the governors themselves. A decent president brought humane rule. An abusive, dishonest president delivered corruption and malfeasance. Though the Sandinistas took some steps toward building an impersonal institutional framework for government, both their task (revolutionary transformation) and the conditions under which they worked (fighting a counterinsurgent war) meant that they had limited success.

Though faced with enormous challenges, Chamorro was not as badly placed as many other chief executives setting out to build constitutional democracies. Despite a decade's experiment with socialism, Nicaragua retained its capitalist memory, so the country did not have to master both a new economy and a new political system. More significantly, the new administration could use the 1987 constitution, though the Sandinistas' handiwork, as a basis for its government.

In the end, these apparent advantages were not enough to give Nicaragua a trouble-free transition. The country still had weak democratic institutions and values. Whatever the Sandinistas had done in ten years, they had not developed a sturdy foundation for constitutional democracy. Worse, their opponents convinced themselves that just pushing the FSLN from office would magically make Nicaragua a model democracy.

Looking at the status of Nicaragua's democracy, as it stood at the outset of the 1990s, reveals a system with troubling weaknesses. Institutionally, the 1987 constitution preserved the strong executive that had so often in the past fostered the growth of caudillos.[1] Though the National Assembly was beginning to take a more prominent role in policymaking, it had not yet learned to act independently. The courts were still weak, unprofessional, and politicized, making them an unreliable last line of defense for citizens' rights and constitutional propriety. However well or badly the bureaucracy may have worked, anti-Sandinistas viewed it with suspicion.

Looking beyond governmental machinery does not improve matters. Though the Sandinistas had a political organization that would become a reasonably successful conventional political party, their opponents were not as fortunate. There were enough parties: fourteen in the UNO; twenty-four before the campaign for the 1990 elections began; thirty-four by the time the 1996 campaign started. And some of them had long and admirable histories: the Socialists, Independent Liberals, and significant elements of the Conservatives had paid dearly for their opposition to the Somoza dictatorship. What they lacked, though, was a sense of what an effective party had to do in a constitutional democracy.

Neither Nicaragua's historic parties nor those that emerged more recently should be faulted for their failings. Certainly the Somozas never gave any encouragement to open organization or free competition. And though the Sandinistas were far more tolerant of opposition than their predecessors had been, the FSLN began governing with a vanguard's perspective on other political parties: they can exist, but they can never take power. These are not conditions that encourage building strong parties or permit individuals to make a career of service to a party, as a deputy or as a party bureaucrat. Parties simply were not what the nineteenth-century English journalist Walter Bagehot called "efficient parts of the political system"; they were not needed to make politics work.

To a degree, this was because many were "vanity parties," with little apparent purpose beyond advancing their leaders' careers. But vanity parties make political sense only where no real benefit comes from joining and working through larger, more impersonal organizations, or where there are none to join.[2] The bottom line is that neither the logic nor the practice of political organization in Nicaragua facilitated building the institutions associated with constitutional democracy. Political life was fractionalized and dominated by personalities looking to improve their place in the public hierarchy.

Beyond these structural constraints, the state of Nicaraguan political culture in 1990 impeded easy democratization. The worst problem was that the country faced a huge crisis of trust. Ten years of internal war had left few neutrals in Nicaragua: either you were for the FSLN or you were against it. President Chamorro had built her campaign around the theme of national reconciliation, unquestionably the country's greatest psychological need. But how Nicaraguans were to be brought together and healed, as well as what conditions had to be present to let this happen, remained unclear.

One thing, however, was certain: the new president would not be able to buy cooperation. In February 1990, Nicaragua's economy was a wreck, leaving the president unable to broker deals. The new Chamorro administration would lack the resources needed to soothe irritated spirits with the balm of government spending. And where material inducements are absent, contending interests can easily decide to ratchet up the stakes and play for unequivocal symbolic victory, giving no quarter and showing no regard for the consequences. Extremism carries no costs; moderation brings no benefits.

The conditions awaiting Chamorro after she received the presidential sash on 25 April were daunting. They would have challenged a politician far more experienced than the new president. Chamorro's background in government was limited. As noted earlier, she had briefly served in the first revolutionary government, the Governing Junta for National Reconstruction, resigning after less than a year, ostensibly due to ill health. Even then, she owed her place in the government not to her personal achievements, but to the fact that Somoza was behind the assassination of her husband, newspaper publisher Pedro Joaquín Chamorro. Aside from this one foray into active politics, Doña Violeta had a limited public role, exercised mainly through the editorial pages of the family's newspaper, La Prensa.[3]

When thinking about Mrs. Chamorro's emergence as a key political figure, it is tempting to speculate that the success of the Philippines' Mrs. Corazon Aquino, also widowed by a tyrant's assassin, raised the Nicaraguan's political stock. Though Chamorro lacked Aquino's obvious drive and energy, she, too, was a figure uniquely placed to rally all forces opposed to the government. Further, even though President Aquino's inexperience was already showing by 1989, when Chamorro took the UNO's nomination, it is also true that the Philippine chief executive had withstood a coup attempt, and her country's very fragile democracy remained intact.[4] That both presidents retained power and preserved constitutional government to the end of their respective terms is testimony to the political value of being a nonpartisan figure whose most obvious attribute is having a measure of good sense.

It may have been this nonpartisanship that led President Chamorro to gather around her a group of technocratic political neophytes to actually run her administration. The most important of the president's advisers was her son-in-law, Antonio Lacayo. Throughout the administration's six-year life, it was Lacayo who was engaged in the tough negotiations and who subsequently took most of the blame for harsh policies and bad decisions. By the end of 1996, all the members of the Chamorro administration were seasoned veterans, but they survived a rough apprenticeship to get there.

Having an administration of neophytes brought both costs and benefits. On the positive side, the amateurs did not bring with them the personal ideological baggage that would make bargaining with their opponents impossible. Had Lacayo been an active opposition politician in the 1980s, it likely would have been much harder for him to work productively with Daniel Ortega. On the negative side, Chamorro's neophyte advisers had an unshakable, though untested, belief in the efficacy of the free market and the virtues of free trade that ultimately caused needless economic hardship.[5] A more experienced team might have been more cautious in applying the rigorous laissez-faire strategies proposed by the IMF, the U.S. Agency for International Development (USAID), and the World Bank.

What was true of the administration was only slightly less true of the UNO caucus in the National Assembly. Though some had prior legislative experience, even from as far back as the Somoza congress, most were newcomers, and only a handful seemed to have any appreciation of the role representative institutions played in modern constitutional democracy. Though this greenness owed more to having had few chances to participate in government—the result of living under governments that discouraged opposition—than to disdain for public service, it still left the majority of the UNO at a disadvantage relative to the FSLN. Worse than their lack of government experience, however, was the uncompromisingly anti-Sandinista ideology characteristic of many members of the caucus. Though most would become more tolerant and pragmatic over time, there were still many zealots in 1990.

The 1987 Constitution

Politics in Nicaragua in 1990 operated within the legal framework of the 1987 constitution. This document was the product of an FSLN that was intent on giving the revolutionary state a permanent basis. It presented a mix of radical and liberal democratic themes, reflecting the state of political thought within the Sandinista Front. And enough conventional, democratic constitutionalism was included that this constitution did not, in the end, pose an impediment to any of President Chamorro's key policies. At different points throughout Chamorro's presidency, however, the Nicaraguan right wanted to scrap the constitution and draft a completely new one.[6] Examining the constitution's radical and orthodox parts separately is the best way to understand the document.

The Radical Elements

The more radical elements of the 1987 constitution[7] start with its preamble, which invokes the memory of, inter alia, "all the generations of Heroes and Martyrs who forged and developed the liberation struggle for national inde-

pendence" and "those who struggle and offer their lives in the face of impe-
rialist aggression to guarantee the happiness of future generations." This
section also notes the purpose of the constitution: "the institutionalization
of the conquests of the Revolution and the construction of a new society
that eliminates every form of exploitation and secures economic, political,
and social equality of Nicaraguans and the absolute respect for human
rights." This tone continues in Title I ("Fundamental Principles"). Article 4
states, in part, that "the State is the people's principal instrument for eliminating every form of submission and exploitation of human beings, for promoting the material and spiritual progress of the entire nation, and for guaranteeing that the interests and rights of the majority prevail." This is not a
recipe for building the limited state favored by constitutional democrats in
the 1990s.

Radically egalitarian notions of democracy also appear in the sections
concerned with social rights, the rights of the family, and those of labor.
For example, the 1987 constitution assured Nicaraguans of the right to
work (Article 57), to education (Article 58), to health care (Article 59), to
social security (Article 61), to shelter (Article 64), and to protection against
hunger (Article 63). It also established the absolute equality of rights and
responsibilities between men and women (Article 73), guaranteed workers
the right to participate in the management of their workplaces (Article 81),
and committed the state to providing full and productive employment
(Article 80).

With regard to the national economy and agrarian reform, the state
received a very significant role. Article 98 declared that the main economic
role of the state was to promote development, overcome backwardness,
improve the people's living conditions, and bring about an ever more just
distribution of wealth. Article 99 committed the state to "direct and plan the
national economy so as to guarantee and defend the interests of the majority," putting the control of the Central Bank, the banking system, insurance,
and foreign trade irrevocably in the state's hands to assure that this was
done. Agrarian reform, which the Sandinistas would defend fiercely
throughout their years in opposition, was to be an instrument to redistribute
land (Article 106), to abolish latifundia (Article 107), and to serve as a
strategic means for other revolutionary changes (Article 106).

The final radical element of the 1987 constitution dealt with the military. It created a constitutional duty for all Nicaraguans to bear arms "to
defend the homeland and the conquests of the people" (Article 96), and it
guaranteed that the state would "promote the massive incorporation of the
people in the task of defending the country" (Article 94). Particularly
galling to conservative opponents of the FSLN, the army was officially
styled the Sandinista Popular Army (Ejercito Popular Sandinista) and

defined as the military arm (*el brazo armado*) of the people (Article 95). This section, which simply entrenched the post-1979 status quo, gave rise to charges that the military was an instrument of the Sandinista party.

Despite the potential for mischief these radical parts of the constitution offered the FSLN, in the end they did not seriously hamper the Chamorro administration. Indeed, the Sandinistas paid little attention to symbols of revolutionary intent. Angel Saldomando suggests that this may have been because the Sandinista economic model was seen even by the FSLN to have failed and because the military had its autonomy guaranteed by the Transition Accords.[8] If Saldomando is right, the FSLN itself may have lost its faith in revolutionary change, and key elements of the revolutionary state were looking principally for sufficient quotas of power to save themselves.[9]

The Orthodox Elements

Some important aspects of the 1987 Nicaraguan constitution followed liberal democratic principles. The state itself was defined as a "democratic, participatory, and representative republic" (Article 7); and though some doubtless saw "participatory" as meaning "socialist," political forces as conventional as the Liberal Party of Canada had espoused the principles of participatory democracy in the 1960s and 1970s. More significantly, Article 13 specified that Nicaragua's patriotic symbols were the national anthem, the flag of the republic, and the Great Seal. No Sandinista symbols were included.

The individual civil liberties and legal rights recognized by the constitution (Articles 23–46) are similarly unexceptional. For example, every person has a right to individual liberty, security of person, and recognition of her or his civil and legal rights (Article 25). Guarantees of political rights are also basically conventional, with one exception: Article 49 recognized the right of workers, women, the young, farmers, artisans, professionals, intellectuals, and so on, to form organizations to "participate in the construction of a new society."

Besides setting out the principles on which a state is founded and describing the rights and duties of citizens, the 1987 constitution delineated the organization of the state in some detail. The machinery of government actually set out is generally conventional. Title VIII (Articles 129–195) provides for four branches of government. There are also sections treating emergency powers (Articles 185–186), municipal government and the autonomous regions of the Atlantic coast (175–181), and the procedures for amending the constitution (191–195). Whereas the elements included here are conventional in that they are not designed to expedite revolutionary transformation, they still were the source of many political conflicts between 1990 and 1996. It was the allocation of powers to the president that was a particular source of difficulty.

One of the great objectives of Latin American democracy has been to restrain the power of the executive. In many countries the president cannot serve two consecutive terms, and in some (Costa Rica, but also Mexico) the president can never be reelected. This is a reaction to decades, in some places centuries, of one-man rule. Nicaragua has had more than its quota of dictators and practitioners of *continuismo,* amending the constitution to permit the continuous rule of the same person, yet the 1987 constitution made no provision for limiting presidential succession and vested substantial power in the chief executive.[10]

Three articles of the constitution indicate the scope of the president's authority. First, Nicaragua's chief executive holds line-item veto power (Article 142), which permits rejecting only that part of a bill the president finds objectionable. Historically the U.S. president has not had this right.[11] A second very considerable capability is found in Article 150.9, which sets out the president's emergency powers. The executive need not send the decree declaring a state of emergency to the National Assembly for forty-five days, meaning that the legislature must wait over six weeks before getting the chance to debate the declaration.[12] Finally, though all executives have rule-making power delegated to them by their legislatures, the 1987 constitution let the Nicaraguan president issue fiscal decrees that changed taxes or affected spending. Such a provision would be found highly irregular in most constitutional democracies where fiscal powers are expressly and exclusively reserved to the representative assembly.

One reason the president received such extensive powers is that the constitution was drafted and debated during a war. National emergencies of a military character could appear quickly, and it would be inconvenient, even impossible, to refer the declaration to the legislature for consideration. Equally important was the Sandinistas' history. A guerrilla front turned political party might well have the same regard for strong, unencumbered leadership that any government issuing from military roots might hold. Then, too, there is a long-standing tendency among Latin American states to give the executive parts of their governments ample powers.[13]

Although all of this may have been acceptable under the revolutionary government, perceptions changed when President Chamorro came to office. Unlike her predecessor, Daniel Ortega, Chamorro did not have a unified legislative caucus behind her. Rather, the opposite was in fact true. The UNO bench in the National Assembly had been shut out of the politicking that occurred during the transition period (26 February to 24 April), saw that its exclusion produced policies it found unacceptable (e.g., naming General Humberto Ortega military chief of staff), and realized that it could use its control over the legislature to promote its own agenda. The UNO deputies were able to do this not only because the president and her cabinet lacked the partisan credentials needed to bring the legislators to heel, but also because the Assembly held real constitutional powers. The most notable of these was its power over the budget (Article 138.6), though this had not been exercised until the end of the Ortega government. In the new administration there would be legislators with an incentive to put these untested tools to work.

The problems the 1987 constitution posed for Nicaragua's democratic transition did not stem from the document's Sandinista origins. Its most obvious flaw was that it provided a highly executive-centered system with which an increasingly powerful legislature would repeatedly come into conflict. But there was an even more fundamental problem: Nicaragua had a constitutional document, but it had not developed the shared norms and expectations about how a legitimate government should act that underlie a constitutional regime. The country had not achieved a consensus about many basic political issues. Though everyone accepted that elections gave power to the winners, how that power should be used and who would make decisions about its use were still open questions.

The Structure of Nicaraguan Government: A Sketch

Nicaragua is a unitary state with four independent branches of government: executive, legislative, judicial, and electoral. These form the very broad boundaries of the arena in which the country's politics are played out. Though an extended analysis of the organization and operation of the formal machinery of the Nicaraguan state is impossible, some sense of how the government is structured is necessary. What is described here reflects the framework in place before the constitution was amended in 1995.[14] Because Nicaragua has a division-of-powers constitution, this outline highlights the attributes of each branch of government.

The Executive

Some of the powers of the president have already been noted, but a few comments about the composition of the cabinet and the range of executive powers of appointment are in order. The state's administrative apparatus is rather large, with sixteen ministries and thirty-five independent agencies having cabinet rank in 1996.[15] Particularly striking is the presence of two offices directly attached to the office of the president—the Ministry of the Presidency and the Private Secretary of the Presidency—among these. Of all the original ministers,[16] appointed in 1990, only one still held his post in 1996, Emilio Perreira of the Ministry of Finance, though Francisco Rosales only left his post at the Ministry of Labor in 1996 to join the Supreme Court.

The cabinet generally reflected the president's views, not those of her party. Portfolios went not to highly partisan veterans of a decade worth of struggles against the Sandinistas, but to technically proficient, frequently nonpartisan individuals who had spent much of the eighties overseas. Two of these, Antonio Lacayo, minister of the presidency from 1990 to 1995, and Carlos Hurtado, minister of government[17] from 1990 to 1993, were special targets of the UNO rightists for their alleged softness toward the Sandinistas. Other appointees were charged with corruption, most notoriously former vice minister of the presidency, Antonio Ibarra, who fled the country after allegedly stealing $2 million in aid funds in 1993.[18]

The appointive powers of the president were extensive. They extended to all ministers and vice ministers of state, minister delegates of the presidency, presidents and directors of parastatals (*entes autónomos*) and government institutions, and all other positions (*foncionarios*) whose nomination or dismissal is not otherwise specified by the constitution and the law (Article 150.6). There are, however, some interesting twists. Although the president chose the chief justice (*presidente*) of the Supreme Court, she did so from among puisne justices (*magistrados*) chosen by the National Assembly (Article 163). And although the president determined the three-person slates (*ternas*) from which magistrates of the Supreme Electoral Council had to be chosen, the assembly made that choice, selecting the council's president from among the magistrates (Article 170). These exceptions aside, Chamorro had plenty of legal scope to impose her mark on government during her term of office.

The National Assembly

In 1990, the National Assembly was composed of ninety members elected by proportional representation from nine administrative regions, plus the defeated presidential candidates of the two losing parties (Daniel Ortega, FSLN; Moises Hassan, MUR) that received over one-ninetieth of the vote.[19] The Assembly's most important powers were budgetary oversight (Article 138.6); the ability to summon the persons and papers of the president, ministers and vice ministers, and directors of government enterprises (Article 138.4); and its role in naming Supreme Court justices, magistrates of the CSE, and the controller general of the republic. The 1995 amendments to the constitution expanded these powers. Beyond its constitutionally assigned authority, the National Assembly also has an active system of standing and special committees. The chamber's greatest debility has been a lack of resources, which hobbles its operation.

The Assembly was becoming a more significant part of the political system during the Ortega administration, but a large and disciplined Sandinista majority meant that the house showed little independence.[20] Differences between the legislative and presidential wings of the UNO removed party discipline as an obstacle to the Assembly's autonomy, and the legislature began determining its own political course. As a result, conflict between the two main policy-initiating branches of government became one of the key elements shaping the course of the Chamorro administration. Later chapters describe these dynamics in several policy areas.

The Courts

Unlike Canada and the United States, Nicaragua does not have a history of politically important courts. This is partly explained, of course, by a past filled with dictators who had no use for the rule of law. Yet even a more democratic Nicaragua would not have had courts assuming the significant roles they held in its northern neighbors. As a unitary state it could not have the jurisdictional disputes between federal and state or provincial governments that U.S. and Canadian Supreme Courts confronted. Further, Latin America's civil law tradition gives a smaller role to courts in the political system.[21] Courts are to apply and interpret laws, not to make them, as do their North American peers.

Both the 1987 constitution and the 1995 amendments speak only of a Supreme Court, leaving the elaboration of the judicial system to ordinary legislation. In the 1987 document the Nicaraguan Supreme Court had seven magistrates, one of whom was the president (Article 163). In the immediate postelectoral period the Sandinistas looked to the courts as a bastion from which to defend the revolution's policies, because all of the magistrates had been appointed by the FSLN. Since a magistrate's term was six years, over the course of President Chamorro's term she was able to replace all the revolutionary state's appointees. This was of less lasting impact than amendments adopted in 1995. Now the Supreme Court has twelve magistrates and is organized into four *salas,* or divisions, each responsible for a specific realm of law: civil, criminal, constitutional, and administrative.[22]

Between 1990 and 1996, the courts, and not just the Supreme Court, were forced to make several politically sensitive decisions. This was unfamiliar terrain for the judicial branch, and it did not always perform well. For example, when former Minister of the Presidency Lacayo challenged the constitutionality of the 1995 amendment (Article 147.c) that forbade him to run for the presidency on the grounds of consanguinity, the Supreme Court referred the issue to the Supreme Electoral Council for a decision. At the very end of President Chamorro's term, however, the Court did act quickly to strike down laws passed by a lame-duck National Assembly that trenched on the president's powers of appointment.[23]

The Supreme Electoral Council

The fourth branch of government, the electoral branch, is intended to assure that electoral administration is nonpartisan. It is a common feature in Latin American constitutions, though it has not performed its advertised duties at all times or in all places. Nicaragua's Supreme Electoral Council was, however, an electoral authority that did its intended job. Established in 1983, it performed efficiently in the 1984 elections and received wide acclaim from international observers for its work in 1990. Headed until late 1995 by Mariano Fiallos, a Sandinista with a doctorate in political science from the University of Kansas and ex-rector of the Nicaraguan National University at Léon, the CSE was arguably the best working part of the Nicaraguan state. Effective and free of scandal, the electoral branch showed that administrative probity and competence were attainable in Nicaragua.

Though its original members were appointed by the FSLN, and presumably held Sandinista views, the council evolved into a highly professional and nonpartisan organization. Amendments to the Electoral Law passed in 1995, however, reorganized the CSE, made its membership subject to partisan appointment, and laid the groundwork for an ill-administered election in 1996 that brought the council into disrepute.

Political Actors: Those Who Make the System Work

Though the 1990 elections produced a change of government, they did not bring a complete turnover of Nicaragua's political elite. President Chamorro herself was a familiar figure. Many UNO leaders had made their names opposing the FSLN during the eighties. The Sandinistas crossed the aisle of the National Assembly to assume their new role as a minority party, but they remained one of the country's biggest political players. Similarly, many of the extragovernmental political forces active in the Sandinista era stayed on the stage: the Catholic Church, the unions, the employers' group COSEP, the military, even the contras and the U.S. embassy were still around.

There were, however, lots of newcomers, including people who had gone abroad during the period of revolutionary government. Among these were not a few of the technocrats who became the president's advisers. Families returning from overseas to claim their expropriated properties constituted another important group.

Key Individuals

A handful of people made a difference in how Nicaragua was governed between 1990 and 1996. The most obvious of these was the president herself, followed closely by Antonio Lacayo, her de facto prime minister. Daniel Ortega also remained in the public eye and shaped the country's emerging constitutional democracy. Two parliamentarians, Sergio Ramírez and Luís Humberto Guzmán, were instrumental both in shifting power toward the National Assembly and in spearheading reform of the constitution. Managua's mayor, Arnoldo Alemán, made the capital's city hall his springboard for a successful presidential campaign. Outside the ranks of professional politicians were Cardinal Miguel Obando y Bravo and General Humberto Ortega. There are many others who could be added—Vice President Godoy, the ever-resourceful Alfredo César, education minister and arch-conservative Catholic Humberto Belli, and public-service union leader Lucio Jiménez—but none of them was truly a formative force.

The administration.   President Chamorro came to office a political outsider, a trait she shared with her cabinet.[24] Though she was neither completely without political experience (having been swept up in Nicaragua's political turmoil for years), nor bereft of administrative skills (having taken an active interest in running her husband's newspaper after his death), she was nevertheless an amateur whose first serious governmental job was that of chief executive. Chamorro and her advisers and cabinet were not seasoned managers of public affairs. The president recognized her limitations and adopted an executive style more reminiscent of Ronald Reagan than Margaret Thatcher, as indicated in her 1995 autobiography:

> Like any executive, I have delegated to Antonio [Lacayo] and my cabinet the details of government. All of them without exception are excellent professionals who came from successful careers in the private sector. I picked them because they are smart, because they have demonstrated a sense of organization, and for their efficiency. I see myself as the person responsible for setting the agenda. . . . I provide the leadership and the inspiration. I sit in on all the big meetings, then turn to my advisors, get the consensus, and if it agrees with my views and principles, I tell them to proceed. . . . I simply say, "Work it out." They tell me what measures we need to implement and I say, "Okay, if you've studied all the alternatives and you think this is the way to go, let's do it." This is the way we work.[25]

Clearly this is not a president with a passion for policy. Though she held certain principles firmly—which judging by her record included a great respect for the Catholic Church, belief in the free market, and a desire for national unity—Chamorro was not an administrator.[26]

Actually running the government did, though, stay within the president's family, a task falling primarily to Lacayo. Assigning positions of trust to relatives is established practice in Latin America. The Somozas did it: Daniel Ortega gave his brother, Humberto, the toughest and most sensitive jobs; and even in historically democratic Costa Rica, Presidents Oscar Arias and Rafael Angel Calderón reserved special responsibilities for kin. Though Lacayo was a businessman with no previous direct political experience, he had been Chamorro's campaign manager in 1990, successfully steering her clear of the more confrontational parts of the UNO's platform. Once in office, Lacayo brought a technocratic, "government-as-business" outlook with him and recruited individuals with a similar perspective to the cabinet and president's staff.

Nicaraguan political observers often called Lacayo the prime minister, and the designation is apt. By taking the lead in most controversial matters, he let the president behave a little like a constitutional monarch, holding herself above the partisan fray. He began defining his role soon after the administration was sworn in, dealing directly with Daniel Ortega to reach a settlement of a public-service strike in May 1990.[27] Lacayo's willingness to work with the Sandinistas and his ability to strike deals with them made him a target for criticism from the UNO's hard-core anti-Sandinistas, who repeatedly called for his sacking.

For a while Lacayo appeared the logical successor to his mother-in-law, but these hopes were dashed by a constitutional amendment prohibiting close relatives from following one another to the presidency. A sensible precaution in light of Nicaragua's past, Lacayo sought to have the provision ruled unconstitutional. Although he was eventually unsuccessful in his quest, he resigned his portfolio in 1995, hoping that future developments would favor him.[28]

The Sandinistas. Heading the largest party in the country, blessed with a large legislative caucus, and at least the titular head of a range of Sandinista-allied organizations, Daniel Ortega was plainly the second most important politician in Nicaragua in 1990. Over time, however, he grew weaker as his party split and events showed that he followed rather than led the masses into political battle. But Daniel, as he is usually called, proved his resilience and took the FSLN to a respectable if unsatisfying second-place finish in 1996's election.

Most of the other members of the Sandinista DN moved out of active politics: former Interior Minister Tomás Borge, for example, went to head the Sandinista daily, *Barricada,* after purging its old editors; former Agrarian Reform Minister Jaime Wheelock did a stint at Harvard; and Humberto Ortega, longtime defense minister, left the party to retain command of the armed forces. This left Daniel the undisputed star of the FSLN and the logical leader of the opposition. In this role, Ortega would defend the social gains made by the revolutionary government against the incursions of the market-oriented new administration. Among these gains were agrarian reform, labor rights, and the right to retain properties redistributed by the revolutionary state—the *piñata* of March 1990.

Over the years of the Chamorro presidency, Daniel's oppositional program shifted from confrontational to cooperative and back again. At the outset, he stood squarely with public-sector union leaders and backed vigorous extraparliamentary protests against the administration's efforts at radical cost cutting. A little later, as the splits in the UNO caucus became more evident and the president's search for votes in the Assembly more desperate, Daniel and the Sandinistas moderated their attacks and sought benefits through legislation. When the FSLN's rank and file began demanding more forceful action to defend their interests in 1993, Daniel and the leadership abandoned cooperation. But when constitutional reformers, including Sandinista legislators, moved to undermine presidential powers, Ortega jumped to Chamorro's side and cast most of the deputies from the party. Daniel's pragmatism kept him at the head of his party, and his party visibly engaged in furthering the welfare of the FSLN's historic supporters.

Ortega's emergence as the unrivaled leader of the FSLN completed the concentration of power in his hands that began in 1985.[29] This power was visible in the deals he made with Lacayo. It also showed in how he drove Sergio Ramírez and the FSLN's right wing out of the party and the way he steamrollered other candidates to win the Sandinista presidential nomination. By 1996, he had taken on the persona of a political boss driving a strong party machine.

Other elected politicians.   Three individuals figure prominently here; two legislators, Sergio Ramírez and Luís Humberto Guzmán, and Arnoldo Alemán, who used the mayoralty of Managua to launch his successful 1996 bid for the presidency. Both Ramírez and Guzmán are important because they contributed to the strengthening of legislative institutions in Nicaragua. Ramírez was the FSLN's house leader, thus the Assembly minority leader, from April 1990 until the party relieved him of his duties in September 1994.[30] Guzmán presided over the chamber in 1994 and 1995, during the constitutional debates. While speaker, Guzmán took the unprecedented step of proclaiming as valid constitutional amendments to which President Chamorro refused her assent, leaving the country with competing constitutions.

What the two legislative leaders did that was most notable was to create an alliance favoring constitutional reform that crossed party lines in the chamber. At one level this is unexceptional: Nicaraguan parties, except the FSLN, were not disciplined organizations during the Chamorro administration. From a different angle, though, the alliance hinted at something more important: the formation of a political party based on a convergence of interests among legislators. Though the coming of elections in 1996 undid the unity wrought in the Assembly, the fact that the country's legislators could come together to pass important legislation in the face of strident opposition from the president marked an important step in Nicaragua's political evolution.

Both Ramírez and Guzmán left electoral politics after the 1996 elections. The Sandinista Reform Movement (MRS) that Ramírez founded after breaking with the FSLN did badly, winning only one seat in the chamber. Guzmán did even worse. He had tried to build an electoral coalition around Alvaro Robelo, a Nicaraguan who returned after a long sojourn in Italy with lots of money. The attempt failed when the CSE declared that Robelo had renounced his citizenship and was ineligible to run.

Arnoldo Alemán, however, continued riding a wave of success. Elected mayor of Managua after the UNO victory in 1990,[31] Alemán emerged as one of the leaders of the anti-Sandinista forces in national politics. He did this by using the mayor's office to build his national reputation. In so doing, he followed a pattern already established in El Salvador and Guatemala, both of which elected presidents in the early 1990s who had previously been mayors of their respective capitals. Moreover, Alemán's Liberal Constitutional Party (PLC) was well organized, the only party apart from the Sandinistas to have a grassroots presence throughout Nicaragua. The PLC first made its presence felt in elections held in 1994 to elect regional councils in the two semiautonomous departments of the Atlantic coast.

Much of the mayor's reputation rested on his program of civic improvements in Managua. Judiciously paving streets, curing long-standing traffic bottlenecks, and ensuring that aptly placed billboards pointed out to drivers exactly where the national Ministry of Construction was falling short on maintenance led Alemán to be seen as a doer. Combined with his florid speaking style and a considerable physical presence, this reputation made him an ideal populist *caudillo,* a leader who would look out for his followers and set the country straight. Sometimes Alemán's policies brought him close to conflict with the law, but he always managed to steer clear of serious trouble and keep his career on track.[32]

Cardinal Miguel Obando y Bravo.   Considered by many the most influential man in Nicaragua, Cardinal Obando y Bravo, archbishop of Managua, maintained a high public profile throughout the Chamorro years. Though personally close to President Chamorro, Obando was often ranked with the president's political enemies, siding with the most conservative elements of the UNO. Whether this reflected his own political preferences or simply his wish to see Nicaragua governed more rigorously is open to debate.

What is certain, however, is that the cardinal remained a central political figure. Yet he did come close to overstepping the bounds separating
church and state toward the end of the 1996 election campaign, when he
offered thinly veiled counsel to oppose the Sandinistas and gave Alemán a
prominent role in religious ceremonies on the eve of the vote. Perhaps
Cardinal Obando y Bravo simply suffered a lapse of judgment and cam-
paigned more openly for his personal choice than was appropriate. But if
the cardinal's actions reflected a desire for a more open and influential role
for the Catholic Church in national affairs, this could presage conflicts with
a growing Protestant community.[33] In fact, Pastor Guillermo Osorno, leader
of the Nicaraguan Christian Way (CCN), the country's third largest political
force after the 1996 elections, lashed out against Obando, saying the cardinal should keep his political preferences private and not proclaim them
from the pulpit.[34]

General Humberto Ortega.   Something of a bête noire among Nicaraguan
conservatives, Humberto Ortega played a crucial role in the politics of transition.[35] In the 1980s, the general was associated with the more intransigent
wing of the Sandinistas and of course commanded the Sandinista forces
against the contras. This made him the most controversial holdover from
the old regime, far outstripping in notoriety police chief René Vivas and the
seven Supreme Court justices who continued their terms into the new president's administration.

Yet Ortega occupied an absolutely critical place in the transition
process. As commanding general of the EPS, in name and in fact a
Sandinista army, he could make or break the government. Not only was he
the man who controlled the most guns, though the contras certainly were
well armed too, but his cooperation was essential if the new government
was to reduce the size and cost of Nicaragua's military establishment. At
least as important would be his attitude toward professionalization, that is,
how the EPS would adapt to no longer being the armed defender of the revolution. More bluntly, the question was whether the army would follow the
orders of a non-Sandinista.

Though the UNO right wing often complained that General Ortega and
his troops did not act with sufficient speed and vigor against strikers
(remember, though, that their model was the Somoza National Guard), the
Nicaraguan military proved far less a problem for President Chamorro than
the Chilean military was for Presidents Patricio Aylwin and Eduardo Frei,
and certainly less than the Argentine forces were for President Faul
Alfonsín. Not only were over 70,000 soldiers demobilized and the defense
budget slashed by 80 percent, but General Ortega also accepted President
Chamorro's decision to unilaterally announce his retirement with minimal
public fuss.[36] Any of these admittedly radical changes to the military's sta-

tus particularly interfering with its command structure could have brought about a crisis. That no tempest resulted and government, army, and country all survived intact reflects well on Ortega's statesmanship and comprehension of the rules of constitutional democracy.

Organized Interests

Though not wishing the responsibility of exercising power, numerous organized groups are regular actors in the political process. They try to influence legislation, persuade politicians in both government and opposition that some outlook is preferable to others, and maintain or improve their position in the hierarchy of those to whom the political elite listen. In Nicaragua it is best to distinguish between those of domestic origin and those of foreign provenance. This is a useful reminder of just how susceptible a small country like Nicaragua is to outside influences.

Domestic Pressure Groups

The most important domestic pressure groups during the Chamorro administration were big business, labor, the contras, and the *confiscados*.[37] Obviously, other groups had political claims to make and exerted pressure on the government: farmers, students, women, the unemployed. How the administration, or its opponents, dealt with the first four groups was critical, but the relations the country's first female president established with organized women's interests were the most intriguing.

Labor. Predictably, labor lost influence under the new government. Though the Sandinistas had kept a tight rein on the unions, if only to minimize economic costs, at least organized labor got substantial symbolic recognition as a pillar of the revolution and privileged access to top leaders.[38] To compensate for its lost status and to actually exercise its initiative for the first time in a decade, the Sandinista-affiliated union (the National Workers' Front [FNT]) was extremely combative. It organized, or was at least an active participant in, big strikes in May and July 1990; in March, April, and May 1991; in November 1992; in June and September 1993; and in August and November 1995. Several of these were quite violent, and all had the effect of delaying, though not derailing, the government's austerity plans.

Labor's aims were necessarily mainly defensive. It wanted to save jobs, especially in the public sector where the Sandinista unions were strongest, and block privatizations that looked like giveaways. It was in the realm of privatizations that the FNT was most effective, being able to negotiate important blocks of shares in privatized companies for workers, even if getting the government to deliver those shares posed yet another challenge.[39] At the end of six years of constant conflict, however, organized labor was worn out. Even if the Chamorro administration did not set out to disarticulate the labor movement, its austerity and adjustment policies produced that effect.

Reflecting on the administration's dealings with the unions raises an interesting question. In the context of Nicaraguan politics, the government's sustained attempts to weaken labor were plainly counterrevolutionary. If unions, especially Sandinista unions, were less able to influence government action and bargain effectively with the private sector, workers stood to lose any gains they had made between 1979 and 1990, and part of the Sandinista revolution's achievements would be undone. But the same sorts of policies were used by Prime Minister Thatcher in Britain and President Reagan in the United States, where they were part of an admittedly aggressive but fully constitutional democratic conservatism.[40] Whether this points up the moderation of Chamorro or the radicalism of Thatcher and Reagan is a question best left moot.

Business.   Where labor is marginalized, business should be pleased; but this was not the case in President Chamorro's Nicaragua.[41] Since the late 1970s, COSEP has spoken for organized big business in the country. It was an essential part of the anti-Sandinista coalition during the eighties, but it was unable to secure the 1990 UNO presidential nomination for its man, Enrique Bolaños. Relations between the government and COSEP worsened in the administration's early days. Not only did the president maintain open communication with the FSLN, but her government failed to restore expropriated property to its old owners and appeared to have no economic plan, save a general commitment to free enterprise.

At the outset, though, it looked as though COSEP would be influential in many areas of public policy. In 1990, following the first round of disruptive strikes attending the introduction of its austerity policy, the administration convened a *concertación*—a government-sponsored, politico-economic summit that brought together the representatives of organized business, labor, and agriculture to seek a basis for a common policy position on economic reorganization. Such summits had been a regular feature during the Sandinista era, so they were familiar to all players. Unfortunately, COSEP did not wish to compromise on the issues at hand. After a few more unsuccessful attempts at domestic summit diplomacy, the government abandoned this tactic, leaving big business without a formal role in the political process.

Closely associated with COSEP on the property issue were the *confiscados*. Though the details of the property question are treated later in this book, here it is important to note that those who lost property fell into two categories: those linked with the Somozas, whose property was seized under Decree 3 of 1979; and those who either later abandoned their property and left the country or who lost their land due to a politico-legal conflict with the state. Though both groups wanted their holdings restored, the former's case was more controversial, and the administration was hesitant to entertain claims from that quarter.

Armed groups. These actors might be thought of as coming from "uncivil society." A decade of war left plenty of ex-combatants from both the contras and the army. One of the administration's greatest failures was its inability to reintegrate these men into civilian life. Throughout the Chamorro years, and even into President Alemán's administration, armed groups of ex-combatants would roam the countryside in Nicaragua's north, sowing death and destruction. However, as the armed groups had no political agenda beyond getting material benefits for themselves, they did not become a substantial political force. The next chapter examines their role in more depth.

Women. A female president or prime minister frequently has not spelled good times for a country's women's movement. The most powerful and successful female heads of government in the twentieth century, Indira Gandhi of India and Margaret Thatcher of Great Britain, may have inspired other women to enter politics and certainly showed male politicians that they did not hold a monopoly on toughness and cunning, but neither could be styled a great defender of feminist values. Indeed, aside from Prime Minister Gro Harlem Brundtland of Norway and perhaps Prime Minister Tansu Çiller of Turkey, women political leaders have not been exceptionally strong defenders of women's rights. President Chamorro conformed to this general rule.

That Doña Violeta was no feminist should not have surprised anyone. During her presidential campaign, Chamorro presented herself as "the Mother of the Nicaraguans."[42] As well, her fervent, traditional Catholicism left her viscerally opposed to abortion and at least skeptically disposed toward contraception, divorce, and de facto unions. In fact, Chamorro and her administration took a strong stand promoting family values by, among other measures, ordering new school texts that emphasized women's traditional roles as wife and mother.[43] Further, the austerity that resulted from the SAPs her government enacted hit women especially hard.[44] Declining demand for labor forced increasing numbers of women into the informal sector—for example, as street vendors or selling food from their homes—where earnings were low and uncertain.

Despite these hardships, Karen Kampwirth found that "by 1992

Nicaragua had the largest, most pluralistic, and most feminist women's movement in Central America."[45] She explains this apparent contradiction by suggesting that the organizational experience gained by women during the 1980s, the Sandinista era, served them in good stead in the 1990s. Moreover, women deputies in the National Assembly occasionally crossed party lines to support questions of particular interest to women,[46] and the FSLN adopted a rule assuring women candidates 30 percent of the slots on the party's national electoral list. On the whole, however, women as a group did not fare well under the Chamorro administration. With few resources to interest a conservative government intent on slicing public services and keeping decisionmaking power in a few trustworthy hands, women in Nicaragua were doomed to fight a rearguard action after 1990.

Foreign Actors

In twentieth-century Central America, "foreign actors" generally means the U.S. government. This is only partly true of Nicaragua from 1990 to 1996. Perhaps the most important U.S. influence was not the government, per se, but Senator Jesse Helms of North Carolina, who led a crusade against the Chamorro administration for its failure to eradicate the Sandinistas as a political force and restore the status quo ante 1979. Senator Helms emerged as the champion of the Nicaraguan right. More responsive than the State Department or the White House to complaints that continuing Sandinista influence impeded the restoration of the rights of private property, Helms attempted to push the Chamorro administration toward the UNO hard-liners' position. Particularly striking was how leading figures of the Nicaraguan right, notably Alfredo César, lobbied Senator Helms on their repeated journeys to Washington. The details of this relationship are set out in Chapter 6, but the alliance between Washington and various sectors of the Nicaraguan political elite dates back to the Conservative revolution against Zelaya in 1909 and shows no signs of ending.

Besides the familiar U.S. actors came a new force: international financial institutions. The IMF and the World Bank became Nicaragua's bankers and very important shapers of its economic policies. In this Nicaragua differed little from other Third World countries with grave international debt and balance-of-payment problems. What the IFIs prescribed for the Chamorro administration receives a closer look in Chapter 5.

Overall, foreign actors and the international context more generally did not offer Nicaragua's still-unsteady constitutional democracy much help. Although it is true that President Chamorro fared far better than her Sandinista predecessors, she received notably less support from Washington than post-Franco Spain got from Europe. Madrid benefited from substantial financial transfers from the European Community (EC)

and was encouraged to boost spending to bring the country's social programs more in line with the Community's norms. Further, the EC's stipula-
tion that all its members be functioning representative democracies meant
that Spanish counterparts of the UNO hard-liners could not find respectable
foreign supporters. The government in Managua, in contrast, was encouraged, if not compelled, to impose economic austerity, with its potential to
undermine social peace, and saw its most dangerous and dedicated foes
succored by influential politicians in the world's most powerful country.
Generous foreign aid payments, most of which were dedicated to repaying
Nicaraguan foreign debt,[47] were poor compensation.

Political Parties

From the time of independence to that of the Sandinista revolution,
Nicaragua's politics were at least nominally bipartisan. Liberals ostensibly
found their roots in the Enlightenment values that existed in the old university town of León. Conservatives looked to Granada as the home of their
more traditionally Catholic beliefs. Though this is something of a caricature
of reality, conflict between the two parties was fierce and often escalated to
civil war between 1821 and 1928. The Somozas, though dispensing with
the reality of party competition, retained the identities: they were Liberals
who were opposed by Conservatives.

None of this dramatic history had provided Nicaragua with solidly
based, efficiently functioning political parties before the Sandinista revolution. Prior to the revolution genuinely honest elections had been held only
in 1928 and 1932, and then only under U.S. supervision. If parties form and
develop because ambitious politicians need them,[48] it is hardly surprising
that Nicaragua had weak parties. Power came not through organizing elec-
torates (though the results of elections were routinely organized), but from
closeness to a ruler or clique that got power by force. The Sandinistas simply continued this tradition in a different guise until 1982.

Nearing the end of its third year in power, the FSLN passed a political
parties law. Constitutionally this was significant, because it marked a turn
from official Leninism by recognizing the legal possibility of a Sandinista
defeat. However, stronger parties, able to generate alternative policies and
organize constituencies, did not appear. The state of parties actually worsened after the Central American peace accords of 1987 opened the way for
greater competition. Political "entrepreneurs" sought to make their mark by
founding parties that would promote their own candidacies.

The National Union of the Opposition had some of these parties among
its number, but it also featured some older parties whose names
Nicaraguans recognized. Parties of neither class, however, had many of the

marks of modern parties in established constitutional democracies. They were very small, had weak electoral organizations, and operated on a shoe-string. Some, like the Socialists and the Communists, had small unions affiliated with them, and all staked out their ideological ground as some variety of anti-Sandinista.

But theirs was not the logic of patient organization building character-istic of European socialist parties. Neither were these "brokerage parties" in the North American mold that swapped material favors to broad sectors of the electorate in return for votes. The parties served too much as vehicles for their leaders for that sort of organization and orientation. Elections were to be won with huge rallies that showed the leader to her or his maximum effect and brought the masses into the leader's van as all marched to victo-ry.[49]

On the Sandinista side there was organization, but the FSLN in 1990 showed many of the traits of a party grown old in office. Inflexible in its programs and increasingly isolated from its grassroots, the "people's van-guard," the political force whose raison d'être was "the logic of the majori-ty," was very much at sea. In such cases the best thing for the party is often to lose an election, see life from the opposition benches, find out what citi-zens really want, and reconfigure itself accordingly. Though the FSLN did start in this direction, its transformation was ultimately unsuccessful because the party split.

Over the course of Chamorro's six years, in fact, both big parties splin-tered. The UNO outdid the FSLN by splitting along two axes. Originally, the division was between the legislative and executive wings of the party, a breach that began during the election campaign. A schism within the caucus proper revealed itself in 1991, as a group of nine deputies began supporting the administration and not the legislative party on key issues, giving rise to a Center Bloc. There were no high-profile politicians in the bloc, suggest-ing that its members recognized that they owed their seats to the president's coattails and were willing to repay this debt with votes. Whatever its origin, this bloc evolved into a fairly solid political faction sustaining views more moderate than those proposed by the core of the UNO caucus. More impor-tant, the Center Bloc would join with the FSLN caucus to give Chamorro a legislative majority.[50]

The legislative wing suffered another, graver split in 1994 over consti-tutional reform. The right wing pressed for a constitutional convention but ended up a rump as increasing numbers of deputies defected to form an ad hoc alliance that pushed through a package of significant amendments. This effectively marked the end of the UNO as a functioning political party.

Though individual calculations were presumably at work in all of the processes that sundered the UNO, the underlying element was the incompatible policy agendas various parts of the alliance wanted to pursue. Ideological differences thus caused the UNO's breakup. Had it been a permanently established party instead of an ad hoc electoral coalition, leaders of the several factions might have resolved their differences before entering the campaign. They would have at least been aware of the need to keep the party from splintering. Maybe even just working in a political system where disciplined, unified parties were the rule would have inspired the UNO leaders to find a way around their doctrinal disagreements. But it is equally possible that the philosophical distance separating, first, the legislative and executive wings and, later, the hard-liners and the moderates, was too great to bridge. In a country struggling to find a constitutional identity and a generally acceptable formula for governance, irreconcilable visions of the proper role of the state may be unavoidable.

Ideology also divided the Sandinistas. This was not the FSLN's first experience with serious ideological conflict. Before the triumph of the revolution, the organization tore itself into three contending factions, each with its own view of how best to beat the Somozas. Eventually, the intervention of Fidel Castro helped knit the divergent tendencies back together, but in the 1990s there was no outside conciliator with enough weight to keep the Sandinistas united.[51]

At the root of the matter was the conflict between those who wanted to make the FSLN more of a conventional party and those who would keep its character as a revolutionary movement. The clash of "party versus movement" is not new, being familiar wherever grassroots movements evolve into professional political parties.[52] Nicaragua, however, was a particularly striking case, because the Sandinistas had led a successful revolution and now faced the challenge of defending the changes they had made from the constrained position of a constitutional opposition party. Though the revolutionary state had been substantially liberalized over its decade of existence, the revolutionary party had not changed as much.

The first signs of this incomplete adjustment appeared at the FSLN's postelection meeting, held in June 1990.[53] Although there was some self-criticism and promises made to move away from the top-down style that had characterized the FSLN's rule, there were also declarations blaming the United States for the party's defeat. Further, as the meeting took place in the midst of bitter protests led by Sandinista unions against the administration's economic policies, the FSLN would naturally be caught up in escalating social conflict.

It was the party's role in a number of serious, indeed violent, frays that sparked the publication in *Barricada* in late December 1990 of an article calling for a softer line. Written by Rafael Solís, a veteran of the insurrection who had served as a legislator until 1990 and was associated with the more conservative, constitutional side of the party, the article showed that some Sandinistas were ready to become an electoral party of the left. But they were not the FSLN's only unhappy members.

Sandinistas in the left or revolutionary wing also questioned the party's direction. First, the fact that it was Sandinista-aligned public-sector unions, and not the FSLN itself, that mobilized opposition to the UNO's austerity policies implied declining militance.[54] Worse, after UNO dissidents formed the Center Bloc and made it possible for the FSLN to become a silent ally of the president, the party's more conservative legislative caucus assumed greater importance.[55] If the Sandinistas' metamorphosis into a party was too slow for one wing, the FSLN's abandonment of its heritage as a revolutionary movement was too precipitate for the other.

Besides these ideological strains the FSLN also had to deal with matters of internal structure and party ethics. At their first-ever congress, in July 1991, the Sandinistas took some steps to broaden participation by expanding the role of internal elections and promised to listen more closely to the rank and file. As at the 1990 postmortem, the effects of *la piñata* were discussed. Yet no clear path toward a redefined FSLN emerged from the historic meeting.[56]

Crisis hit the FSLN in 1993. Responding to months of extreme instability, deputies from across the political spectrum united behind a package of radical constitutional amendments proposed by the Christian Democrats. Sergio Ramírez and the Sandinista parliamentary caucus were also prominent participants in the movement that aimed at limiting presidential power. However, the extraparliamentary FSLN, led by Secretary-General Daniel Ortega, took the president's side. The opening salvos were fired in early 1994 by two radical Sandinista radio journalists, Carlos Guadamuz (Radio Ya) and William Grigsby (Radio La Primerisima), who claimed that Ramírez was acting treasonably by pursuing constitutional reform.[57] Factions began forming: the Sandinistas for a Democratic Left around Ortega; the Sandinistas for a National Project (soon renamed the Sandinismo for the Majority) around Ramírez.

Personal differences between Ramírez and Ortega doubtless contributed to the fracture. Sergio was unlikely ever to become leader of the FSLN, because he had not been a combatant in the war against Somoza and would not, therefore, get the support of Sandinistas who had fought the dictator. His only route to the top was outside the FSLN. As for Daniel, since 1985 he had been centralizing power within the Sandinista leadership in his hands and showed no inclination to share it, let alone relinquish it.

By September 1994, Ramírez had been ousted from the FSLN's National Directorate and booted from the leadership of the parliamentary caucus where he was replaced by Daniel Ortega. But the decay did not stop there. That October, Carlos Fernando Chamorro, editor in chief of

Barricada, was dismissed from his post, and the paper again came under the direct control of the party. The new year saw Ramírez organize the MRS, splitting the FSLN legislative caucus and threatening the Sandinista hegemony over the left.[58]

Constitutional politics also affected the UNO, provoking its final fissure. The leaders of the reform faction, the Christian Democrats, came from the UNO. They were joined in defection by the Nicaraguan Democratic Movement and the Popular Conservative Alliance (APC). This last was a particularly painful loss, because its leader, Miriam Argüello, had been a stalwart of the UNO right.

Though the old parties were reeling, no newcomer emerged to deliver the knockout. There were signs of a center party forming in the National Assembly among the like-minded deputies supporting constitutional change. Some thirty deputies eventually coalesced into a solid bloc to push for reforms, but they did not carry on to form a party. There is certainly precedent for parties forming out of legislative alliances. Nicaragua's politicians, however, rejected union in favor of a strategy where individuals formed new parties or returned to their old parties, looking to get that little bit of extra bargaining power to ensure their future public careers.

Some might see this as a cultural tendency to *caudillo* politics, but it is also consistent with a reading of Nicaragua's history of two-party politics and a canny understanding of the country's electoral system. It is plausibly easier for an individual, as presidential candidate of a microparty, to win the one-ninetieth of the national vote required to get a seat in the legislature from which to do business than for the third person on a third party's Assembly slate to get back into power. The 1996 election would prove such calculations false, but in 1995 they must have been alluring.

Since 1979, Nicaragua's two "parties" have been the Sandinistas and the anti-Sandinistas; the latter group including violent counterrevolutionaries as well as conventional, constitutional opponents of the FSLN. This pattern probably will remain as long as the Sandinistas are a political force. But who will the anti-Sandinistas be? The replacement for the fractured UNO began revealing itself in the mid-1990s. It was not a new party, but one whose roots went back to the Somoza period: the Liberal Constitutional Party.

The PLC broke with the official Liberal party of the Somozas, the PLN, in the late 1960s over Anastasio Somoza's decision to assume the presidency in the 1967 elections. Its anti-Somocista credentials were good enough to land it a spot in the revolutionary state's first representative assembly, the appointed Council of State. But before the mid-1990s, the party was not a force to be reckoned with.

After the 1990 elections a small group of PLC faithfuls, including José

Rizo and Eusebio Núñez, began building an organization.[59] To do this they used what Núñez called "communist tactics," that is, building around small cells of activists. They also copied communists tactics by using the poor as the foundation for their party, even paying organizers from the lower social strata and making them party employees.[60] The party first made its presence felt nationally by winning the 1994 elections for the regional councils of Nicaragua's two semiautonomous Atlantic coast governments.[61]

Although Alemán was the party's star and became its leader and presidential candidate in 1996, he was not a founding member. Rather, the PLC recruited Alemán, seeing him as the sort of caudillo figure ordinary Nicaraguans had traditionally preferred as their leaders.[62] Combining a strong leader with a strong grassroots organization propelled the PLC to the front of the anti-Sandinista forces. Moreover, because it was a Liberal party, it could claim roots deep in the nation's past and perhaps draw even more adherents. The PLC would be what the UNO never was: a unified, organized party.

Though I have seen no formal analyses of the rise of the PLC, I think that there are two factors that explain the party's overnight appearance as a major force in Nicaraguan politics. First, as the UNO began showing itself incapable of delivering the anti-Sandinista agenda that it had promised and as President Chamorro showed herself capable of less-than-inspired leadership, the Nicaraguan right was looking for a new political vehicle. When they saw a party with organization and a vigorous leader, the most natural thing for them to do was to jump on board. But even if the entire Nicaraguan right had joined and voted for the party, the PLC would still be far from power. It also had to draw the politically nonaligned poor, a huge mass of people, into its ranks. This is where Alemán played a critical role, because he filled the part of an old-time, patronage-dispensing caudillo perfectly. I visited PLC headquarters a couple of times in late 1995, a year before the general elections, and saw lots of very poor people all busily seeking favors from PLC officials who were dressed in L. L. Bean buttondowns and neatly pressed Dockers. Whether those trying their hand at getting jobs in return for votes and political work had ever been Sandinista voters I cannot say, but it was clear that they had decided that material well-being was more likely to come from good personal relations with a powerful patron than from backing a party founded to advance their interests as a class.

Conclusion

This chapter has argued that President Chamorro began her tenure with a political framework (governmental machinery, parties, and groups) that did not seriously impede the consolidation of constitutional democracy, the *estado de derecho* that she sought. By 1996, however, whatever benefit she might have derived from that framework had long since disappeared with little advantage taken of it. In the interim, the political face of Nicaragua had changed dramatically. Though the FSLN remained the main party of the left, it was seriously weakened. And though the UNO still existed as a political alliance, it had suffered even more than the FSLN. The machinery of government had much the same form as it did at the outset of Doña Violeta's term, but constitutional amendments had reduced her authority and altered the relations among the branches of government.

What had not changed was the absence of a unifying governing philosophy, a theme that all major political players could accept, at least in principle. That President Chamorro was able to maintain a constitutional regime in the face of such discord must be counted her greatest accomplishment. That she was unable to lead Nicaraguans to discover a common set of principles will be reckoned her most serious failure.

Notes

1. *Caudillos* are strongman, boss-style political leaders. Their greatest asset is their personality that draws followers. Once in power, caudillos skip established channels, favoring direct, personal action. The nineteenth century was the era of the caudillo in Latin America, though rulers of this stripe persisted much longer in the less-developed countries than in the larger, wealthier ones.

2. Proliferating political parties is not a problem found only in Nicaragua or even Latin America. It is encountered in most of the democratizing world. Countries with limited histories of competitive, constitutional democracy apparently have to pass through a period of partisan anarchy while both voters and politicians get their bearings and develop preferences. There is, though, some evidence that having one solidly organized party can suffice, if that party is democratic and if the country has a strong democratic foundation. Costa Rica, Latin America's oldest democracy (dating from 1949), had only one strong, well-organized party until 1983, the National Liberation Party. Nevertheless, its opponents managed to sufficiently unite their several highly personalistic parties every four years to win three of the eight presidential elections held in that period. This may, however, say more about Costa Rican political culture than about strategies for personalized parties to win elections.

3. The president's personal perspective on this and other matters is found in Violeta Barrios de Chamorro, with Sonia Cruz de Baltadano and Guido Fernandez, *Dreams of the Heart: The Autobiography of President Violeta Barrios de Chamorro of Nicaragua* (New York: Simon & Schuster, 1996). Chapters 6–9 discuss how she came to be part of the first revolutionary government; chapters 10–12 cover the Sandinista period up to the start of the electoral campaign in 1989.

4. Lucy Komisar, *Corazon Aquino: The Story of a Revolution* (New York: George Braziller, 1987), is a useful place to start comparing Aquino and Chamorro.

5. These questions receive further treatment in Chapter 5.

6. Though at first this presumably was inspired by a desire to distinguish the new "democratic" state from the old "totalitarian" system, later there were occasions when calls for a constitutional convention were aimed at reducing the president's power, if not removing her from office altogether.

7. Unless otherwise noted, all constitutional references come from the official Spanish version of the document published in *La Gaceta: Diario Oficial,* 9 January 1987; translations are the author's.

8. Angel Saldomando, *Nicaragua con el futuro en juego* (Managua: CRIES, 1996), chaps. 1–3.

9. In this they differed substantially from Chilean supporters of the former military regime who have resisted attempts to amend the constitution designed by General Augusto Pinochet Ugarte.

10. Two Nicaraguan experts, Ada Esperanza Silva and Gustavo Vega, commented that the original 1987 constitution gave the president powers that could be used to rule "like a monarch." See *El Nuevo Diario,* 27 October 1996, p. 5.

11. In 1996, the U.S. Congress approved a line-item veto for the president, but in February 1998, a federal judge ruled it unconstitutional. As this is written, the matter is being appealed to the United States Supreme Court.

12. However, this is more restrictive than the corresponding article (Article 16) of the current French constitution, which does not require the president to submit his or her declaration of a national emergency to Parlement.

13. In 1985, the editor of the Sandinista magazine *Barricada International* indicated that the FSLN had briefly considered using a parliamentary system in its next constitution but abandoned the idea because it was too foreign. Nicaraguans expected a president, not a prime minister (Sergio de Castro, interview, Managua, November 1985).

14. The 1995 amendments significantly redistributed power among the branches of government; they are the subject of Chapter 7.

15. Ministerio de Relaciones Exteriores, press release, 10 January 1996. The cabinet was broken into subcabinets or cabinet committees to deal with specific themes, such as social or economic affairs. Unfortunately, not enough published information is available about either the structure of these subcabinets or their operation to make analysis possible.

16. Erwin Kruger was named the first minister of external cooperation later in 1990 and held his post until 1997; and William Baez, who became Minister of Social Action when the ministry was created in 1993, also remained in place to the end of the administration.

17. The Ministry of Government administers the National Police, the fire department, the prisons, and so forth.

18. *Nicaragua News Service* (hereafter *NNS),* 17 October 1993, p. 3.

19. Article 133 of the constitution provides an assembly seat for defeated candidates whose parties win votes "equal or superior to the regional electoral quotas," that is, one-ninetieth (1.1 percent) of the national total.

20. This material is drawn from David Close, "Nicaragua: The Legislature as Seedbed of Conflict," in *Legislatures and the New Democracies in Latin America,* ed. David Close (Boulder, CO: Lynne Rienner Publishers, 1995), pp. 49–70.

21. See John Henry Merryman, *The Civil Law Tradition* (Stanford, CA: Stanford University Press, 1969).

22. Article 163 was amended to reflect this new structure.

23. *La Nacion,* San José, Costa Rica, electronic ed. (8 January 1997), p. 1, at: http://www.nacionco.cr/08/nicaragua.html.

24. Chamorro also shared her outsider status with other presidents, for example, Aquino of the Philippines, Jean-Bertrand Aristide of Haiti, Vaclav Havel of Czechoslovakia, and Alberto Fujimori of Peru. Though her personal background is closest to Aquino's, the political conditions surrounding her rise to power have most in common with those that carried Fujimori to office.

25. Chamorro, *Dreams of the Heart*, p. 312.

26. This lack of administrative acumen extended to her staff: the president's press office gave so little attention to detail that it could not produce a list of cabinet changes made during the administration. In November 1995, I sought this information from various offices in the Ministry of the Presidency, the department that looked after both the partisan and technical aspects of the chief executive's operations, but the best anyone could do was direct me to the U.S. embassy, which they believed kept track of such matters. For the record, the embassy kept a record of cabinet changes, which it gave me.

27. The strike and Lacayo's role in economic issues receive fuller treatment in Chapters 4 and 5.

28. Details of the constitutional question are in Chapter 6; Chapter 7 touches on Lacayo's efforts to gain the presidency.

29. David Close, *Nicaragua: Politics, Economics, and Society* (London: Pinter Publishers, 1988), pp. 109–120.

30. *CAR*, 16 September 1994, pp. 1–2.

31. The Electoral Law in place in 1990 left municipal councils to elect the mayor. The law governing the 1996 elections had mayors directly elected.

32. On Alemán, see Mark Caster, "The Return of Somocism? The Rise of Arnoldo Alemán," *NACLA*, 30:2 (September/October 1996): 6–9.

33. On Nicaraguan Protestantism and its potential political influence, see Roberto Zub, *Protestanismo y elecciones en Nicaragua* (Managua: Ediciones Nicarao, 1993).

34. *El Nuevo Diario*, 24 October 1996, p. 16.

35. To get a sense of Ortega's thinking on political transition and the reform of the military, see Humberto Ortega Saavedra, *Nicaragua: Revolución y democracia* (Mexico City: Organización Editorial Mexicana, n.d.), esp. pp. 157–190.

36. These issues are reviewed in Roberto Cajina, *Transición política y reconversión militar en Nicaragua, 1990–1995* (Managua: CRIES, 1997), pp. 268–292.

37. Most of these groups receive further attention in Chapter 5. This section just introduces the players, sets them in the context of an operating political system, and briefly assesses their political weight within that system.

38. Richard Stahler-Sholk has done the best academic work on unions in contemporary Nicaragua. See, in particular, "Breaking the Mold: Economic Orthodoxy and the Politics of Resistance in Nicaragua," paper presented to the LASA congress, Washington, DC, 1995.

39. Trevor Evans, coord., *La transformación neoliberal del sector público* (Managua: Latino Editores, 1995), is the best source.

40. Similar if slightly less forceful policies aimed at limiting the power of unions could even come from parties of the left, as happened in Australia, New Zealand, and Spain.

41. Rose Spalding, *Capitalists and Revolution in Nicaragua* (Chapel Hill: University of North Carolina Press, 1995), pp. 156–188. Though mainly about the Sandinista regime, Spalding has a very useful chapter on business-government relations under Chamorro.

42. Karen Kampwirth, "The Mother of the Nicaraguans," *Latin American Perspectives* 23:1 (1996): 67–86.

43. Ibid., p. 73.

44. Florence Babb, "After the Revolution: Neoliberal Policy and Gender in Nicaragua," *Latin American Perspectives* 23:1 (1996): 27–48; cf. Anna M. Fernández Poncela, "The Disrputions of Adjustment," *Latin American Perspectives* 23:1 (1996): 49–66.

45. Karen Kampwirth, "Confronting Adversity with Experience: The Emergence of Feminism in Nicaragua," *Social Politics* 3:3 (1996): 136.

46. Kampwirth, "The Mother," pp. 76–77, offers an example of such cooperation; consider also the assembly's election of a new vice president for Nicaragua in 1995, described in the next chapter.

47. Chapter 6 treats foreign aid and Nicaragua's foreign debt.

48. John Aldrich, *Why Parties? The Origin and Transformation of Political Parties in America* (Chicago: University of Chicago Press, 1995).

49. The Costa Rican Social Christian Unity Party (PUSC), by far the best organized and most efficient party of the right in Central America, offered to help the UNO set up and run its campaign but was rebuffed. A PUSC official, Cristobal Zawadzki, later minister of housing, was at a loss to explain the Nicaraguans' behavior (interview, San José, Costa Rica, 17 January 1990).

50. This phenomenon, called "co-government," is examined in the next chapter.

51. On the FSLN in the 1990s, see Gary Prevost, "The FSLN," in *Nicaragua Without Illusions,* ed. Thomas Walker (Wilmington, DE: Scholarly Resources, 1997), pp. 149–164.

52. Examples of this pattern can be found in many developed constitutional democracies, for example, Canada (Progressives, Social Credit, and Cooperative Commonwealth Federation [CCF]), France (the Poujadistes and Front National), and Italy (Lombard League). Entering ordinary parliamentary politics reduces the extent and intensity of rank-and-file participation, producing discontent. An excellent study of this phenomenon is Leo Zakuta, *The CCF: A Social Movement Becalmed* (Toronto: University of Toronto Press, 1964).

53. *CAR,* 29 June 1990, pp. 87–88.

54. Richard Stahler-Sholk, "El ajuste neoliberal y sus alternativas: La repuesta del movimiento sindical en Nicaragua," *Revista Mexicana de Sociologia* 56:3 (1994): 3–21, and "The Dog That Didn't Bark: Labor Autonomy and Economic Adjustment in Nicaragua Under the Sandinista and UNO Governments," *Comparative Politics* 28:1 (1995): 77–101. Labor's role in the politics of the Chamorro administration receives more coverage in Chapters 4 and 5 herein.

55. *CAR,* 28 February 1992, p. 44. The Sandinistas proved again the old adage of the French left that there is more political difference between two Communists, one of whom is a deputy, than between two deputies, one of whom is a Communist.

56. *CAR*, 28 June 1991, p. 191, and 9 August 1991, pp. 233–235.

57. *CAR*, 14 January 1994, p. 3; 4 February 1994, p. 3; 11 February 1994, pp. 3–4; and 4 March 1994, pp. 3–4.

58. *CAR,* 30 September 1994, p. 7; 4 November 1994, p. 3; 20 January 1995, pp. 2–3; and Steven Kent Smith, "Renovation and Orthodoxy: Debate and Transition Within the Sandinista National Liberation Front," *Latin American Perspectives* 24:2 (March 1997): 102–116.

59. José Rizo, interview, Managua, 5 October 1995.

60. Eusebio Núñez, interview, 20 October 1995, Managua, Nicaragua.

61. These two governments are the Northern Atlantic Autonomous Region, of which Puerto Cabezas is the seat of government, and the Southern Atlantic Autonomous Region, headquartered in Bluefields.

62. Rizo and Núñez interviews.

4

How the System Worked

Individuals make politics work. They make the decisions and cause the conflicts. Institutions, processes, and structures channel individual actions in more or less predictable directions. But understanding the politics of a given place at a particular time demands knowing about more than individual actors and key institutions. Interaction among individuals and institutions produces unforeseeable results, and these results can become factors that throw the predictable workings of formal politics into disarray.

In President Chamorro's Nicaragua three originally unforeseen elements emerged to form part of the framework for her administration. One, high rates of political violence and elevated levels of protest that produced threats to Nicaragua's governability, was inherent in the political conditions the new government faced. The other two, debilitating conflict between the legislature and the executive and *co-gobierno,* cooperation between the FSLN and the president, were not. All, however, demanded able responses from the administration.

In considering how Doña Violeta's government met these challenges, there are several factors to bear in mind. First, this was the first fully functioning constitutional democracy in Nicaragua's history. The country had never before had limited government. Against this backdrop, Chamorro might look weak to the extent that she stayed within the confines of even the relatively permissive 1987 constitution. Further, President Chamorro was governing a war-torn country. Not only was there a tremendous job of rebuilding ahead, but reconstruction would necessarily be impeded by the deteriorated state of the nation's transportation and communications infrastructure. As a result, things would not be done in a timely fashion, people would become impatient, and the government would be blamed. Finally, Nicaragua is a poor country. All governments have to make choices about allocating public resources, but a poor country's resources do not run very

93

far. Even an administration of exemplary ability and efficiency will leave many things poorly done or simply undone.

Violence and Governability

Nicaragua has never been a peaceful country politically. Its history since independence is a saga of civil wars, occasionally interrupted by brief periods of peace. Though the Sandinistas may have felt that defeating the Somoza family dictatorship and beginning to build socialism would finally usher in an era of extended peace, in the end their regime, too, knew violence and disruption. President Chamorro was elected on a platform of national reconciliation and the promise of peaceful reconstruction. But like all her predecessors, Chamorro could not tame the violent land.

Much of the violence was simply criminal, an adjunct of social decay. For example, in 1985, the police investigated 15,189 crimes, which produced a crime rate of 49 per 10,000 people, rising to 30,896 (84 per 10,000) in 1991.[1] By 1995, the rate had risen to 118 per 10,000, or a total of 48,737 crimes. Crimes against persons rose from 9392 in 1991 to 17,934 in 1995. The most striking increase in this latter category was in rapes: 427 were reported in 1991, 1,037 in 1995.

More important politically for the Chamorro administration was the frequency of armed conflicts between the national security forces (mainly the army, but also the police) and rearmed groups. The United Nations Development Program (UNDP) in Nicaragua reported the following figures:[2]

Number of confrontations

1991	238
1992	378
1993	554
1994	390

Number of victims

1991	216
1992	281
1993	422
1994	329

As long as civil violence remained high, the stability of the new administration would be in question.

Rearmed Groups: The Rearmados

In reality, the prospects for violence were quite high when Doña Violeta was inaugurated in April 1990. Throughout the decade of Sandinista government, the country was racked by insurgent warfare. That the insurgents were financed, trained, and supplied by the United States was important to the conduct of the war, but it did not effect the building of the peace.[3] For the end of formal armed conflict between the Sandinista state and the counterrevolutionary rebels left Nicaragua with a scourge known to every postwar environment: unemployed, demobilized soldiers.

If anything, Chamorro's problem was more serious than most of this sort. First, she had to find a way to accommodate the two warring sides within the bosom of a single state. *Compas,* or government troops, and contras had been at each other's throats for ten years, each painting the other as evil incarnate. It was not clear that old hatreds could be forgotten and life taken up anew by the old enemies. Second, economic stringency would hamper her in two ways. The more obvious of these was that the new administration would not have funds available to dedicate to retraining, rehabilitation, and creating government jobs to occupy the young men whose only skill was mayhem. But budgetary pressures would also demand that the president quickly shrink the army, swelling the ranks of the demobilized and leaving her with fewer troops to contain any outbreaks of violence that might occur.

A further complication was that the contras felt that the UNO government owed them quite a bit. Indeed, they asserted that they had actually prevailed militarily over the EPS. Though this was inaccurate, it was true that years of conflict had worn down the Nicaraguan people and made them ready to vote for the peace party. So the contras had a legitimate claim to some kind of material recognition from the new government. Thus one of the new president's first priorities was to find a way to compensate the contras, a task that included disarming them and reintegrating them into civilian society.

Though talks between the Resistencia Nicaragüense (RN), or the Resistance, the newly fashionable name for the anti-Sandinista fighters, and the FSLN began before the election,[4] Mrs. Chamorro's landslide victory stiffened their resolve to press for the full demobilization of the EPS. This, of course, was rejected by President Ortega, and elements of the RN resumed operations in the country's north soon after 25 February.

On 23 March 1990, however, the first of what would be a long series of deals with all or part of the demobilized forces was concluded in Honduras. The Toncontín Agreement, named after the Tegucigalpa airport where the deals were signed, called for voluntary demobilization, setting 20 April, four weeks hence, as the effective date. Though the agreement promised logistical support to move the RN back from Honduras, it did not apply to guerrillas in Nicaragua itself. Neither did it provide for the disarmament of the irregulars.[5] There was still much work to be done.

It was late May 1990 when the first serious, concrete proposal for dealing with demobilized contras came forth. The Managua Protocol called for assigning 25,000 hectares of land, including much of Nicaragua's southern frontier, as a resettlement zone. Within this zone the new administration established eleven development poles and agreed to finance schools, hospitals, and other parts of the necessary infrastructure. Moreover, Chamorro's government promised immediate benefits to the contra widows and orphans.[6]

The most striking thing about the early days of this process of demobilizing troops and providing for their reintegration into civilian life is that it was largely ad hoc. Though Doña Violeta's campaign had stressed reconciliation, just how this would be secured was unclear. Certainly she said nothing about how men who knew only combat would be transformed into useful civilians. Even more, the first round of contra resettlement presaged future problems, because it paid no heed to the EPS troops who would soon be discharged or to the peasants who had been caught between the contending forces.

If the government was unprepared, so, too, were the guerrillas. Other than demanding the impossible—namely, that the EPS be dissolved or that key figures in the administration be sacked—contra leaders lacked an agenda. For example, they did not seek guarantees of funding for any of the programs promised in the Managua Protocol.[7] This may stem from the singular nature of the insurgency the contras waged.[8] Unlike most insurgents, the contras had neither a well-developed political outlook nor close relations with the residents of the areas where they operated. Depending on U.S. logistical and intelligence support, they had no need for local support bases and the good relations required to sustain them. Thus the contras relied far more on stark violence and gave less attention to political skills than had the Sandinistas when they were guerrillas.

Whether it was the contras' innocence of politics or the administration's failure to appreciate how complicated demobilization would be, many ex-combatants turned to arms again with a year. The first *Rearmados* were "recontras," who appeared early in 1991. Their return sparked the rearming of demobilized Sandinista troops, who became the "recompas."[9] Eventually, recompas and recontras joined forces in some places and became the *revueltos,* or "scrambled" bands.

Land shortages and poverty were the immediate causes of renewed violence. According to a report by the Instituto Nacional de la Reforma

Agraria (INRA), the agrarian reform institute, even after a year just over half of the roughly 22,500 ex-contras had received land and some 25,000 ex-EPS and noncombatant peasants were also seeking land.[10] This helps explain why the earliest actions by the *Rearmados* were land seizures.[11] But by early 1992, rearmed forces were moving against towns.

In January 1992, the government reached a deal on disarmament with a majority of both recontras and recompas. Within three days, however, Yatama, the Miskito front, returned to armed struggle. The Miskitos, indigenous inhabitants of Nicaragua's Atlantic coastal region, had neither received the allowances that nonnative groups in the country's west got nor had they been permitted to form their own police force. On 17 February 1992, Yatama forces seized the town of Waspam, killing two soldiers. At the same time, Yatama supporters occupied government buildings in Puerto Cabezas, the administrative center of the northern Atlantic coast. Then, on 6 March, violence escalated in the west, as Ocotal was attacked by *Rearmados*.[12]

Violence peaked between March and August 1993, bringing conflict between recontras and recompas. The first ominous signs appeared early in March as recompas began mobilizing after a period of inactivity.[13] Recontras then seized the Nicaraguan embassy in San José, Costa Rica, holding the building for thirteen days and negotiating a ransom with the Chamorro government.[14] July 21 saw an estimated 120–200 armed members of the Revolutionary Campesino Worker Front (FROC) occupy the northern city of Estelí. These recompas held the historic Sandinista stronghold for three days before being ousted by the army. Officially, forty-five died (forty-one recompas, two civilians, and two soldiers), and ninety-eight were wounded.[15] Incredibly, worse was to come.

On 19 August, Northern Front 3-80, a recontra group that would stay in business for the duration of the Chamorro years and even into the Alemán administration, took forty-one people hostage in Quilalí, in northern Nicaragua. Among the forty-one were FSLN deputies Doris Tijerino and Carlos Gallo. They were in the region with other members of the National Assembly's Human Rights Commission, the head of the Special Disarmament Brigades, and other officials involved in the reinsertion of ex-combatants in civilian life. The leader of 3-80, José Angel Talavera ("El Chacal"), sought a mediation team made up of Cardinal Obando y Bravo; Pablo Antonio Cuadra, Nicaragua's leading conservative intellectual; and Francisco Mayorga, onetime Central Bank president. El Chacal also demanded the immediate dismissal of Humberto Ortega and Antonio Lacayo, standard fare among the country's right.

What he got was a retaliatory kidnapping of the Political Council of the UNO the very next night. The Dignity and Independence Commando, a recompa group, held Vice President Virgilio Godoy; two ex-presidents of the National Assembly, Alfredo César and Miriam Argüello; former Assembly vice president Luis Sánchez; and fourteen others. Daniel Ortega and Vilma Nuñez, head of a left-wing human rights group, began negotiations the next day and won the release of all but a handful of the hostages, the men in their underwear people around the world saw on CNN.

The standoff was soon resolved peacefully, and the level of tension fell. Though rearmed groups maintained their operations (more banditry than politics) throughout the administration's remaining years, the country did not return to the brink of chaos. However, this owed as much to popular exhaustion as to new governmental initiatives.

During its six and a half years in office, President Chamorro's government undertook several measures to secure the peace promised in her campaign. Besides the resettlement grants mentioned above, the Nicaraguan government offered ad hoc material deals (e.g., with El Chacal in early 1994)[16] and amnesties. As to the latter, the government always claimed that those not accepting its offer would be treated as common criminals, that the need to deal with a succession of newly formed (reformed?) recontras and recompas amounted to a rolling amnesty, and that it may be that rearmed leaders counted on catching the next round. The army's Special Disarmament Units were the main enforcement arm in this process.[17] Operating between 1992 and 1995, these units collected:

- 53,475 firearms of all types: rifles, machine guns, grenade launchers, even light artillery;
- 23,473 grenades of various types;
- 7,072 mines—antipersonnel and antitank;
- 105,405 kilograms of explosives;
- and 10,000,000 rounds of ammunition for various arms.

But the army estimated in late 1996 that there were still between 10,000 and 15,000 military weapons (i.e., discounting hunting rifles and shotguns or small-caliber handguns) in civilian hands.

Why was the Chamorro government so unsuccessful in implementing what should have been the linchpin of all its policies? Two factors stand out, each indicating a lack of strategic thinking on the part of both the state and the ex-combatants.[18] First, each appeared to be playing for short-term advantages chosen without much thought to what was really needed to successfully reintegrate thousands of ex-soldiers into a crippled civilian economy. Second, too many people received too few material benefits: the demobbed EPS soldiers, the Miskitos, and peasants who had been displaced by the war. There was always someone ready to turn to arms to get the same treatment as their old adversaries.

Violent Political Protest

In addition to confronting less-than-demobilized ex-guerrillas and former soldiers, Chamorro's government faced more conventional forms of political violence emerging from strikes and protests. This combined with rising crime rates to make Nicaragua seem, if not ungovernable, at least under-governed.

Labor unrest. During the Sandinista years civil political protest was mainly, though not exclusively, the property of the political right. Organized labor seldom went on strike or otherwise protested its declining economic fortunes, because the main union confederation, the CST, was intimately linked to the FSLN. Once the elections brought President Chamorro's conservatives to power, however, organized labor began to shift for itself. Without friends in government, Nicaragua's workers rediscovered direct action after only three weeks under the new administration.

There were two immediate precipitants. One was a 200 percent devaluation of the cordoba, the national currency. This meant that imported goods became three times dearer and produced a general inflationary spiral. More important, the new government suspended the Civil Service and Administrative Careers Law, threatening the job security of all public-sector workers.[19]

For a week, 10–16 May 1990, 70,000 workers from the Unión Nacional de Empleados, the public service union, and the CST were on strike. They paralyzed the country by halting transportation, closing the airport, and occupying public buildings. Talks between the labor minister and union leaders finally settled on a 100 percent pay raise and the establishment of a committee to propose reforms to the law. Both sides claimed victory in the wake of this first installment of austerity-generated political conflict.[20]

Less than two months later, the newly formed National Workers' Front called its 41,000 members out on strike, this time adding concerns about privatization to its economic claims. President Chamorro again took a hard line toward the strikers, dismissing them as tools of a Sandinista conspiracy to destabilize her government and refusing to negotiate. The result was a massive strike, involving an estimated 130,000 people, that shut down the capital. Street fighting followed, leaving six dead and over a hundred injured. Negotiations were resumed and the crisis resolved by promising to slow the pace of privatization and give labor a formal role in wage policy.[21]

At this point, it looked as though direct action by organized labor had won concessions. By March 1991, however, the government had devalued the cordoba by 500 percent but only raised wages by between 35 and 200 percent. As it had in 1990, the FNT again called a general strike of the public service.[22] This deflationary shock, like the one a year before, was designed to stabilize the economy by reeling in massive (13,000 percent) inflation. Though this time the therapy did work against inflation, it did so at great social cost. By early 1992, unemployment was estimated at 60 percent, a figure reaching 89 percent in some rural areas.[23] Obviously, protest politics were not turning government priorities toward alleviating poverty.

The confrontations did not stop. Labor unrest peaked in September 1993 with a huge transport workers' strike occasioned by gasoline price rises and new taxes on vehicle ownership. The protest quickly turned violent, killing two and leaving many injured. As in 1990, the government backed away from its proposals.[24] But this time few could believe that a significant change had occurred, and it was no surprise to find transport workers striking again in May 1995.[25]

Direct action of a different sort seemed to bring better results in the realm of privatization. Workers in the state-owned enterprises resisted attempts to convey full control to new owners, holding out for a stake in the firms. A deal reached in the August 1991 *concertación* guaranteed labor 25 percent control of the privatized firms. However, by February 1992, the FNT was pressuring a reluctant government to enforce the accord in the privatization of Aeronica, the national airline.[26]

As with wage and employment issues, privatization remained contested territory, with two issues dominating debate. One was the level of worker participation in management, which took the form of conflicts over the proportion of shares in the enterprise to be reserved for its employees. The other was the privatization of basic public services, centered on TELCOR, the telecommunications company, and INE, the electricity firm. Both questions remained unresolved when Alemán received the presidential sash in January 1997.

A few examples will illustrate the nature of these conflicts. A sugar workers' strike in February 1993 was called because the National Sugar Workers' Federation, a Sandinista-affiliated union, claimed that the National Public Sector Corporations (CORNAP) was trying to reduce the shares available to workers.[27] TELCOR's privatization first generated protests in mid-1994, as FNT workers protested plans to sell off 40 percent of the firm. Proposing a similar fate for INE brought objections from its workers as well. In both cases, potential job losses and loss of national control over the monopolies, which would almost certainly be sold to foreign-controlled, multinational firms,[28] sparked confrontation.

Though the policies toward labor that the Chamorro administration followed were fundamentally those that Margaret Thatcher employed in the UK, that Ronald Reagan used in the United States, and that a host of other democratically elected right-of-center governments around the world enacted in the eighties and nineties, they produced a singular result in Nicaragua.

In Britain or America, Canada or Costa Rica, these pro–big business conservative policies all undid years of work by unions and parties of the center and left to assure working people better lives and a stronger political
voice. They did not, however, roll back rights that had been won through
revolutionary struggle. In the world's established constitutional democracies throughout the twentieth century, ordinary political action (votes,
strikes, lobbying, party work) could secure marginalized groups democratic
rights; but in Nicaragua it took protracted political violence to achieve that
same end. So even if the concrete results of President Chamorro's policies
for labor were no different from what conservative presidents and prime
ministers were doing everywhere, their symbolic weight must have been
greater.

Student protest.   University students were an important part of the
Sandinistas' original base and were reliable supporters of the FSLN during
its years in power. To repay them and protect them from possible reprisals
by future governments, the lame-duck Sandinista government passed a law
fixing university funding at 6 percent of the national budget. It is now a
constitutional requirement (Article 125), having been among the amendments ratified in 1995.

However, the 6 percent provision first generated conflict in 1992 when
the legislature considered the university grants set out in the national budget.[29] The administration allotted the country's public postsecondary institutions 6 percent of the revenues generated by tax collections. Though
seeming to meet the letter of the law, this sum was significantly smaller
than the government's total revenues, which included foreign aid and loans.
The government would not move toward a higher grant, because it believed
that its focus should be on primary education. As a result, university grants
fell from U.S.$30 million in 1990 to U.S.$25 million in 1994, even though
enrollment increased from 32,000 to 36,000 students.

Whether due to shrinking transfers or putting the 6 percent minimum
in the constitution, student agitation for a larger slice of the budget was
stronger than ever in 1995. On 12 December, three days before the National
Assembly had to pass the next year's budget, 1,000 students staged a four-
hour blockade of Managua's international airport to reinforce their
demands. Though they left voluntarily, the next day 3,000 students mounted a mass march down the Avenida Bolívar, the city's main thoroughfare. It
was a peaceful demonstration, but the police met it with tear gas and bullets. One demonstrator died and forty-nine were wounded.

After New Year's the demonstrations began again. A 10,000-strong
march to protest both violence and budget cuts went off smoothly. Then, at
the end of January, 200 student leaders occupied the Foreign Ministry; they
were evicted the next day and 107 were charged. Although there was no

further violence, the matter was not resolved and returned to haunt Mr. Alemán after he succeeded Mrs. Chamorro.[30]

Beyond the obviously political forms of violence, Nicaragua also witnessed a curious wave of bombings, directed against Catholic churches. From May 1995 to February 1996, some twenty churches were bombed.[31] Though no one was injured, the symbolic weight of these attacks was great, especially since Pope John Paul II was coming to visit Nicaragua in February 1996. When police in León charged fifteen known Sandinistas with the crimes, many remembered the pontiff severely chastising the revolutionaries in 1983. The FSLN quickly distanced itself from the attacks and denounced the bombers. Although the party was doubtlessly not behind the outrages (the party would not risk this kind of extraparliamentary action), that some of its followers would find violence an appropriate political tool says a lot about conditions in the country toward the end of President Chamorro's term.

The Military

In 1990, most conservatives would not have bet on the Nicaraguan armed forces becoming a nonpartisan, professional force. The Sandinista Popular Army was the direct descendant of the guerrilla force that overthrew the Somoza dictatorship and had been cultivated to become the military arm of the revolution. Though it had not directly intervened in politics (i.e., to seize power and govern), it was a highly politicized military, intimately related to the FSLN. So close were the ties that the anti-Sandinista opposition in the 1980s regularly denounced the EPS as a partisan army. Is was, then, no surprise that the military became one of the right's targets once the Sandinistas had lost power. The most radical factions wanted the military's abolition but had to be content with significant budget cuts and the force reductions they demanded.[32]

Yet even had the FSLN kept hold of the government, Nicaragua's military would have been reduced. At its peak strength in 1986, the EPS counted over 120,000 soldiers, some 75,000 of whom were enlistees or draftees on active duty.[33] In January 1990, the global figure (including reservists) had already dropped to 86,000. Discontinuing the draft, dissolving the reserves, and beginning to lay off soldiers on active duty brought troop strength to 27,864 by November 1990. By 1996, the Nicaraguan military, now rechristened the Nicaraguan Army, had but 14,000 soldiers, the smallest of any military establishment in Central America. These cuts allowed the government to reduce defense spending from U.S.$182 million in 1989 to U.S.$31 million in 1995.

During the Chamorro administration the military also came under civilian control for the first time in its history, with President Chamorro serving as her own secretary of defense. Moreover, in 1994, Nicaragua's defense forces began operating under a new military code that redefined their functions and operations in ways that conformed more closely to the canons of military professionalism.[34] During the Chamorro years, therefore, the country's military got smaller and cheaper to run, had its first experience with a civilian boss, and began to be professionalized.

But these changes may have come at a very high cost. Robert Cajina asks if 14,000 soldiers can adequately maintain public security in Nicaragua.[35] Though protecting citizens from ordinary criminals is the job of the police, which was also significantly reformed and dramatically downsized after 1990, controlling politically motivated insurgents and large rural bandit gangs falls to the military in most of Latin America. If there are not enough soldiers to suppress large armed bands, Nicaraguans will never be truly secure. And a citizenry that fears for its life and property is not the best material for constructing democracy.

Though the president set out to give Nicaragua the rule of law (*el estado de derecho*), in the end she was scarcely delivering law and order. Carlos Carranza and Jose Chinchilla suspect that prolonged economic austerity limits a state's ability to conciliate conflicting interests.[36] Such conditions could make recourse to self-help attractive. However, this situation should be only temporary, lasting until government revenues are sufficient to permit effective management. Things look worse if important segments of society decide that they cannot count on the state to provide equal justice, for then the struggle of each versus all becomes the rule.

It was still too early to make a definitive judgment in this matter when Doña Violeta left office, but there was no doubt that the country's first exercise in constitutional democracy had not made the political use of violence unthinkable. Perhaps the high levels of violence Nicaragua experienced between 1990 and 1996 were the normal aftermath of a civil war. Remembering that American politicians could "wave the bloody shirt" to get elected for a generation after the U.S. Civil War says something about how deep hatred can run. And because Nicaragua's civil war involved irregulars, there were large caches of arms around for use in settling scores or just making an easy living. Maybe, then, time will make violence a less attractive way to settle disputes and ease Nicaragua's way to constitutional democracy.

Executive-Legislative Conflict

Perhaps the only trait shared by the Somocista and Sandinista regimes was that neither saw significant conflict between the president and congress. True, the FSLN did see conservatives walk out of the Council of State and it withdrew or amended bills after confronting serious criticism throughout its time in office, but it never lost control of Nicaragua's representative assembly. Mrs. Chamorro, thus, had the misfortune of being the first president in over fifty years to face a rebellious and recalcitrant legislature. What made her situation even more novel was that her principal opponents came from within her own party.

Having already examined how the UNO split (Chapter 3), that theme needs only a brief review here. Most of the UNO members of the legislature wanted rapid reforms to roll back a decade's revolution and were far more willing than the president to confront the Sandinistas to get what they wanted. Because the 1987 constitution granted the National Assembly important powers, the more radical UNO politicians were able to use the legislature to advance their agenda. Adding to them the Sandinista caucus, the "official" opposition controlling 43 percent of the seats, produced a fractious house that could turn on the administration from both the right and the left. Though this gave Nicaragua a representative assembly with political weight for the first time in the twentieth century, it also contributed to the destabilization of national politics.[37]

Conflicts between the two branches of government arose over several issues. The two most significant, property, due to its persistence, and the constitution, for its virulence, receive only passing reference here, because they are the subject of Chapter 6. This section focuses on economic controversies—notably, the budget—but it also examines the Assembly's role in naming a new vice president in 1995 and the lame-duck legislators' creation of a final constitutional crisis in late 1996.

The budget.   Article 138.6 in both the 1987 and 1995 constitutions empowers the National Assembly to debate and approve the national budget; the amended 1995 clause also lets the Assembly track the executive's implementation of both the revenue and the expenditure sides of that law.[38] Though budgetary debates began under the Sandinista administration, it was only during President Chamorro's term that these became meaningful. Once the UNO caucus realized that the power to review and pass the budget gave it the chance to derail parts of the executive's program, the budget became a battleground.

The main point of contention in the 1991 budget, debated by the new legislature in late 1990, was the defense allocation. One of Chamorro's key policies was shrinking the military, and she accomplished this rapidly. In the seven months between her inauguration and the budget conflict, the president reduced the military from some 80,000 troops to 28,400 and cut its budget from U.S.$166 million to U.S.$78 million.[39] This, however, was not enough for the UNO caucus. They wanted to punish their old nemesis, General Humberto Ortega, without whose compliance the cuts would have certainly been harder to make, and get more money for populist programs. To this end, they sliced a further U.S.$20 million from the defense estimates, a reduction that would have meant laying off an additional 10,000 soldiers. The president vetoed the budget passed by the National Assembly, and after a week's intense lobbying by the executive (and a promise to chop defense spending by a further U.S.$8 million), the legislature sustained her veto, in a 69-to-21 vote.

A year later the same scene was played out again. Chamorro sent the legislature a budget asking for about U.S.$42 million to maintain a military establishment with 21,000 troops. The UNO caucus, however, wanted deeper cuts, complaining that the army had done badly controlling riots that had broken out the week before.[40] Thus, they deleted U.S.$4.3 million from the president's proposal. Again Chamorro vetoed the budget, and again her veto was sustained, but this time by two votes, 47 to 45, as eight UNO dissidents voted with the thirty-nine Sandinistas.

There were no further executive-legislature showdowns over economics, save for the related but independent property issue, for the rest of Doña Violeta's term. This was partly due to increased backing from the FSLN on certain key issues, but even more crucial was the executive's power to keep much of the economic portfolio exclusively in its hands. However important the budget was, the key to Nicaragua's economy in the early 1990s was what sort of deal the country could strike with multilateral international lenders, like the International Monetary Fund. As the National Assembly had no power to review the state's international financial engagements, a source of grave conflict between the two branches of government was absent until the constitution was amended in mid-1995. Further, the unamended 1987 constitution also let the executive tax by decree, taking another thorny issue from the Assembly's purview.

Choosing a new vice president.   Because the revised constitution demands that a sitting vice president who wants to run for the presidency must resign that post twelve months before the next election (Article 147.4.b), Virgilio Godoy stepped down in October 1995. It was the National Assembly's responsibility (Article 138.22) to fill the newly vacant position. No one suspected that fulfilling this duty would bring the Assembly into conflict with President Chamorro once again.

On 22 October, the Assembly met in special session.[41] For about a week previously, the Managua media had been floating the names of possible replacements and evaluating their chances. Four men, all Conservatives of some stripe, dominated the discussions: Nicolas Bolaños, a wealthy businessman and brother of Enrique, who became Arnoldo Alemán's vice president; Eduardo Paladino, a lawyer and member of a Conservative faction that was out of favor with the administration; Fernando Zelaya, an old-line *zancudo*.[42] Conservative whose roots went back to the days when his part of the party collaborated with the Somozas; and Hernaldo Zuñiga, a former Supreme Court justice who left the bench in the mid-1980s to protest the Sandinista government's interference with the judiciary. The clear favorite was Zelaya, who Chamorro had indicated was her preferred choice. At the end of the day, however, it was none of the four Conservative men who became vice president of Nicaragua, but a Liberal woman, Julia Mena.

Mena's candidacy was introduced by a member of her own party, the Independent Liberal Party, which was also the party of the departed vice president. As a result, few paid much attention to her. It was only politics to have a candidate from the same party as Godoy, and Mena was a member of the National Assembly's executive committee, the Junta Directiva (ID), so she had some name recognition. Yet this alone would not have secured her victory. What made Julia Mena Nicaragua's vice president was the work of Dora María Téllez.

Téllez first came to public attention in 1978 as part of the Sandinista squad that seized the Congress and held the congressmen, including Fernando Zelaya, hostage. She was "Comandante Dos," less famous than Eden Pastora, "Comandante Cero," who took off his mask at this operation so the world could put a face on the guerrillas, but Téllez was steadier. She carved out a political career for herself within the FSLN but eventually broke with it to join Sergio Ramírez and his MRS in 1994. Because Ramírez did not have his own seat in the Assembly (having been Daniel Ortega's alternate), Téllez became the MRS's house leader. Further, like any good congressional politician, she made alliances across party lines, especially with the other women deputies to build an informal women's caucus.

When Téllez began moving from desk to desk among deputies on both sides of the floor, the backers of the four Conservative nominees began to sense that something was afoot. As there was a potential majority of Mena supporters coming from the various Sandinistas, the PLI, the Christian Democrats (who appreciated her work as an executive of the assembly), and some others, the Conservatives withdrew their candidacies and left the floor.[43] The idea was to have so many deputies leave that the house would be counted out for want of a quorum and the session adjourned. This would have given the Conservatives time to regroup behind Zelaya and return better prepared to win.[44] However, fifty-three members remained after the walkout and the Assembly's quorum was forty-six, so the vote went ahead and Julia Mena became the first woman to serve as Nicaragua's vice president.

Though this is only indirectly an instance of conflict between the legislature and the administration, it still provides important insights into the dynamics of Nicaraguan politics. At least some members of the Assembly took the institution seriously enough to learn how to make it work. In this case, it was Dora María Téllez and her allies. Those more closely linked to the administration seemed to have assumed that President Chamorro's choice would be automatically confirmed. While this might have happened earlier in her term, some of the president's magic had worn off five years into it.

But there may have been another reason why a majority of deputies stayed to vote for Mena. The 24 October edition of *La Tribuna* reported that a plan had been concocted by Antonio Lacayo,[45] whose presidential aspirations, you will recall, had been dashed by a constitutional amendment that prohibited the sitting president from being succeeded by a close relative (Article 147.4.c). Apparently, Chamorro was to step down on Zelaya's selection as vice president, making him the country's chief executive and opening the way for Lacayo to make his own run for the top office. Though this seems convoluted, it is the sort of scheme that deputies suspicious of the administration could have found just plausible enough to make them look for an alternative to Zelaya.

The Christmas rush, 1996. The curious constitutional calendar in place in Nicaragua has created a situation where defeated deputies have to approve the budget for the government-elect, fill positions in the executive, and look after their own future economic interests.[46] None of this was new and should not have been unexpected. The infamous Sandinista *piñata* of 1990 was itself made possible by this calendar. Because the budget must be passed before the end of the calendar year—15 December is usually the last session, and a newly elected government only takes office on 10 January—not only are the lame ducks able to do mischief, but the new administration must work for a year with a budget not its own. Until some thoughtful reformers set this right, Nicaragua can look forward to a flurry of unedifying activity by some part of its government every five years.

In fact, there are a number of reasons why election years are bound to be problematic under this system. Deputies who want to campaign pay little heed to their duties in the National Assembly. As a result, work gets backed up. In 1996, there were forty-one bills—including the budget, amendments to the Central Bank Act, and a major privatization bill along with several minor ones—waiting for the deputies when they returned from the election recess. They had a little over four weeks to consider these measures. Further, some deputies linked to the president-elect, for example Jaime Bonilla and Adolfo Jarquín, both members of the chamber's executive committee, were not necessarily keen to see the lame-duck session act on too many of the proposals before it.

A further election year complication is that not all incumbents who run will win, but the losers will have a month or more during which to make policy. The elections of 1996 were particularly hard on those seeking reelection, as only eight incumbents were returned to the house, so more than eighty deputies would soon be out of work. Though a few had positions outside public life to sustain them, most did not. Searching for a sinecure became the order of the day.

However, pursuing a job with the state did not mean that an about-to-be-ex-deputy was just looking for a golden parachute. Unlike 1990, the 1996 Nicaraguan election was almost as much a matter of voting against a candidate or party as for one. Both Alemán and Ortega excited animus in the souls of their opponents, and this affected the political class as well as ordinary citizens. Indeed, it may have affected the former more, as there was a general understanding that the president-elect was going to reward his friends and punish enemies, including those who ran against him. Thus, filling key positions with Alemán opponents would stymie the new leader's plans.

The National Assembly reconvened in mid-November amid rumors that anti-Alemán interests would try to tie the new president's hands by usurping some of the executive's appointive power; that the president-elect's supporters would walk out, hoping to leave the legislature unable to act; that the parties and candidates who had to repay the money the state advanced them for their campaigns would legislate themselves immunity; and that the defeated deputies would fashion themselves a rich severance package. All of this actually happened.

On 25 November, with Liberal deputies unofficially boycotting and only forty-three members present (three short of the quorum), acting president Edmundo Castillo, a Conservative, adjourned the session. However, the FSLN, the MRS, and several other small parties staged a coup and convened another sitting, at which they elected a new executive from their number. At this point, President Chamorro, who had already declared herself opposed to the National Assembly's efforts at self-interested legislation, began talking about vetoes and court challenges. Others contented themselves by denouncing either Sandinista-inspired chaos or Liberal attempts to paralyze the proper workings of the state.

Eventually and inevitably, the matter made its way to the Supreme Court. On 20 December, the Court announced that all but two of the laws passed by the National Assembly in its preholiday lame-duck session were valid. Only the legislature's attempt to name the Central Bank president and the attorney general (*procurador general*) were ruled unconstitutional, because these appointments were presidential prerogatives. After Christmas, however, the Supreme Court reconsidered its position and, on 7 January 1997 rendered a decision declaring everything passed in the fevered session invalid. As Alemán would be inaugurated on 10 January, it was obvious that the incoming legislature would have to add this backlog of legislation to its labors. Whatever steps were taken by President Chamorro toward institution building and laying the foundations for a state wherein the rule of law prevailed seemed to vanish in the postelectoral political maelstrom that convulsed Nicaragua at the end of 1996.

Co-Gobierno

Presidents and prime ministers often have to reach accommodation with opposition parties in order to get parts of their programs adopted, at times even to assure that the machinery of state continues to function. The French, first in 1987 and then again in 1997, have seen Gaullists and Socialists "cohabiting," each secure with its own independent power base. Had the president, Socialist or Gaullist, not found a way to get along with the prime minister, his partisan opposite, France might have ground to a halt. Rather more frequent are the occasions when a U.S. president has to negotiate with his congressional opponents, some of them from his own party. These bipartisan deals weaken the president's agenda but avoid crisis and may even produce better laws.

But what has been acceptable, if not desirable, between Democrats and Republicans or Gaullists and Socialists proved much harder to tolerate in Nicaragua during President Chamorro's administration. Unable to rely on the support of her fellow UNO members in the legislature, Doña Violeta found Sandinista votes to carry through parts of her program. Both parties plainly had to compromise to permit this Nicaraguan cohabitation, something that might have been read as a welcome sign of pragmatism and political maturity. Instead, the bipartisan, interbranch alliance was reviled. Labeled co-gobierno (co-government) by its foes, the marriage of convenience was painted variously as a Sandinista takeover of the administration or a Sandinista sellout to the administration.

The first signs of cooperation between the FSLN and the executive appeared in the settlement of the public service strikes of 1990. Daniel Ortega began working with Antonio Lacayo to settle the conflicts and get people back to work. Apparently the two saw eye to eye, because over the next six years the Sandinistas often would support Lacayo's positions. Further, Ortega's willingness to cooperate on the strike question bespoke not just seizing an opportunity to get a better deal for his followers, but also a predisposition toward pragmatism. It was as if Ortega recognized that his and his party's fates over the next few years depended on his ability to maintain good working relations with the new president and her cabinet.

Thus, he and the FSLN drew on the ability to make deals that they had developed during their decade in power to maximize their influence while out of power.[47]

President Chamorro also benefited from Sandinista readiness to set rhetoric aside and search for workable, mutually profitable solutions. A very important instance of this attitude showed itself in the series of *concertaciones*—the familiar tripartite summits—the government convened on economic issues. The model for cooperation was established at the first such summit in the Chamorro years, where Daniel Ortega and the FSLN accepted significant elements of an austerity package against the wishes of the Sandinista unions. In return, the state agreed to respect the outlines of Sandinista land reform, driving COSEP, the organized voice of Nicaraguan big business, to oppose the administration.[48]

Thus, to get assurances on the property question, the FSLN moderated its criticism of the government's austerity policies. This was a sensible reading of the avenues open to it. Pressures from international lenders meant that no government could avoid budget cutting, so many Sandinista social programs were beyond salvation. Besides, the real heart of the Sandinista revolution was not schools or hospitals, something any development-minded government could provide, but rather the democratization of property, a genuinely socialist legacy. As long as the rural and urban poor had land and houses received from the Sandinista state, a return to the gross inequalities of the old days was impossible, the FSLN would have a ready pool of support, and the sacrifices exacted by the revolution would not have been in vain. To get to that bottom line, accepting unavoidable austerity was a small price to pay.

Simple cooperation between the president and Sandinistas in public forums is not, however, co-government. The term implies a symbiosis, a relationship that is both mutually beneficial and necessary for the survival of each party. This began when the administration started relying on the FSLN and the Center Bloc (originally, a small group of UNO backbenchers who sided with the president and not the caucus) after the December 1991 vote to sustain Chamorro's veto of the budget. Co-government really became evident where the property question and constitutional reform were involved. Though these issues are too complex for more than brief treatment here, some consideration must be given to why President Chamorro's opponents made them their centerpiece.

Perhaps because Nicaragua had never seen a sitting government lose power to another via elections before 1990, there was an aura of "winner take all" around the UNO camp. Controlling both the National Assembly and the presidency, the way was open to use the power of the state to pursue the victors' objectives. The opponents of the revolutionary regime had a long list of changes to make, but two were vital to their program: restoring property expropriated by the revolutionary state to its original owners, or providing satisfactory compensation where that was impossible, and rooting out all remnants of Sandinista influences from governmental institutions, including the constitution. This was nothing less than a project for reshaping state and society to reflect the winners' values. It was the core of the counterrevolution.

Unquestionably, the Sandinistas recognized this and went to great lengths to keep it from happening. If the urban poor lost the roofs over their heads and the rural poor were stripped of the parcels of land they worked, then the old relations of power and privilege would be restored, along with the practices of exploitation that went with them. It is, though, ironic that in defense of the poor the FSLN leadership also defended itself and its elite lifestyle. It is also ironic that in opposing constitutional reforms, when these finally came, the Sandinistas blocked not the far right but the democratic center of Nicaragua's political spectrum.[49]

The administration, for its part, appreciated that a property policy based on counterexpropriation or full restitution in cash was untenable. It also enjoyed the flexibility that the 1987 constitution afforded the president, allowing the legislature to be sidestepped when it got too boisterous. Thus, when the FSLN presented itself with a large legislative caucus and a reasonably responsive extraparliamentary following that could be applied to securing ends sought by the presidency, it was a natural match. President Chamorro would add Sandinista votes to those of her own party who still backed her, and the FSLN would preserve larger quotas of power and show its supporters that the party could still deliver for them.

But how much of the Sandinista-Chamorro entente deserves the name co-government? To what extent was it an alliance of near equals that significantly altered the president's agenda? For a while, particularly in 1992, the fates of the executive and the FSLN were clearly joined. But even then the Sandinistas were not brought into cabinet and were therefore excluded from the most critical aspects of policy formation. And the president's near-total dependence on the Sandinistas was not permanent, for once UNO legislative radicals began pressing their case through unconstitutional channels, the ranks of pro-Chamorro UNO deputies began to grow. Further, the president's decision to announce the termination of General Humberto Ortega's term as military chief of staff in September 1993 did not sit well with the Sandinistas, illustrating the limits of the supposed alliance. Finally, the FSLN's National Assembly caucus, while still led by Sergio Ramírez in 1993, was a key player promoting constitutional reforms that were vigorously opposed by the administration.

By 1994, however, Daniel Ortega had ousted Ramírez from his legislative post and driven the pro–constitutional amendment members of the legislative caucus from the party. At that point, the FSLN again began backing the president, because it, too, had decided to defend the 1987 constitution. Though Ramírez took the bulk of the legislative delegation into his new party, the Sandinista Reform Movement, even the reduced voting strength of the FSLN became a welcome asset in President Chamorro's struggle against the forces of constitutional change arrayed against her in the National Assembly. One must, though, wonder if the administration did not realize that it held the trump card, whether that was an approach to the property issue that stressed stability or a stand on constitutional reform emphasizing retaining a strong presidency. A moment's reflection suggests that throughout Doña Violeta's presidency, what was most often present was a mix of pragmatism, opportunism, perhaps even a bit of statesmanship, and the recognition of an interest the government shared with the FSLN in avoiding cataclysmic confrontations. This is bipartisanship, but it is a long way from coalition government.

That a president without an assured majority in her congress would patch together a relatively stable alliance is to be expected. Nor is it unusual that the main legislative partner in this sort of venture would slip into opposition and then return to support the administration. This sort of behavior seems perfectly consistent with an outlook that puts short- or medium-term advantage above abstract principle. In most places, at most times, most people would declare that this is just the way politics works. That some in Nicaragua between 1990 and 1996 took this as evidence of betrayal is powerful testimony to the absence of consensus that marked those years.

The strongest proof that the compact between the FSLN and the Chamorro administration was mainly utilitarian is that it collapsed as election year approached. The last stand the allies made was in defense of the presidential prerogatives sketched in the 1987 constitution, a fight that ended in June 1995. Standing then only sixteen months before Nicaraguans would decide the occupant of every national and local electoral office in the land,[50] the time had come for each party to stake out its own position. As well, by mid-1995, the administration was beginning to look weak. The economy was not responding as expected to austerity policies in place since 1990, the government's control over the rearmed groups was still questionable, and its advocacy of the highly presidentialist 1987 constitution seemed more self-serving than principled.[51] With Chamorro legally unable to succeed herself, one result of the 1995 amendments, there was little sense in staying aboard her ship of state.

Managing Instability in the Chamorro Years

Chamorro's government was not a strong one. To borrow a medieval description, its writ did not run far. A modern political scientist might say that it failed to integrate the political system. This showed itself most obviously in the state's inability to control violence. Though the violence was never so great as to threaten the state's survival, it was a big enough problem for anyone unlucky enough to be caught up in it. People suffered because the government lacked the power to assure its citizens peace, order, and good government.

The biggest reason why the Chamorro government was weak was that it was divided against itself. The president, her cabinet, and advisers had an agenda that differed radically from the plans of important parts of her legislative caucus. Thus, President Chamorro relied for a time on the votes of the opposition Sandinistas to carry her policies. Eventually, the FSLN split, too.

Behind the instability of Nicaraguan politics under the country's first liberal democratic, constitutional government lay two kinds of problems. We have encountered them before in this study and will do so again, but they still bear noting here. On the one hand was the shortage of resources. The uneven and ill-planned policy of reintegrating the compas and contras into civilian life was exacerbated by not having the money to tend to the legitimate needs of all of these men. It may seem trite to say so, but it really is harder to govern with little money. On the other hand was Nicaragua's political class, the men and women who ran or aspired to run the state, who simply did not share a governing philosophy: there was no common view of the ends toward which the authority of the state should be used. One faction wanted to erase all traces of the revolution; another wanted to take it apart carefully; and a third wanted to preserve it fundamentally intact. None was strong enough to impose its view, but each was sufficiently powerful to make its convictions felt and to impede its opponents.

Perhaps it is best to think of President Chamorro's years in office as an experiment in subsistence government. It was a government that was able to survive, indeed it had to overcome substantial obstacles in order to survive. It was always able to find enough allies to meet whatever grave challenge confronted it. Like a subsistence economy, it sustained life, but it was not able to set aside a surplus, a bank of investable capital on which to build the future.

In a curious way, subsistence government might have been the best thing for post-Sandinista Nicaragua. Not that the country needed instability, violence, and ceaseless political bickering. Rather, after ten years of war on top of intense social and political experimentation, Nicaragua could have profited from a government that could distinguish between the satisfactory and the optimal, and be happy to take the former. Unfortunately, tolerance and pragmatism came packaged too often with a certain confusion, as the government confronted opponents who were committed to getting what they wanted and willing to pay any price for it. To have maintained a low-profile administration in those conditions would have demanded a political genius. Violeta Chamorro may have been courageous, dedicated, and scrupulous, but she lacked the touch of greatness. Fortunately for her, so did her most obdurate foes.

Notes

1. All crime statistics that follow are from Ministerio de Gobernación, Policía Nacional, *Compendio estadístico, 1991–1995* (Managua: Policía Nacional, 1996), pp. 32–36.
2. UNDP, "Contributions to the Analysis of the Nicaraguan Transition," report presented to the Consultative Group on Nicaragua, 1995, p. 3.
3. David Close, "Counterinsurgency in Nicaragua," *New Political Science,* nos. 18–19 (1990): 5–19.
4. Angel Saldomando and Elvira Cuadra, *Los Problemas de la Pacificación en Nicaragua,* Documento de Trabajo No. 94/2 (Managua: CRIES, 1994), pp. 1–8.
5. *CAR,* 23 March 1990, p. 88, and 30 March 1990, pp. 93–94.
6. *CAR,* 10 June 1990, pp. 166–167.
7. David Dye et al., *Contesting Everything, Winning Nothing* (Cambridge, MA: Hemisphere Initiatives, 1995), pp. 32–42.
8. Close, "Counterinsurgency."
9. Included among the demobilized Sandinista forces were veterans of both the EPS and the Ministry of the Interior, which had its own troops.
10. *CAR,* 21 June 1991, pp. 181–182.
11. *CAR,* 19 October 1990, pp. 318–319.
12. *CAR,* 6 March 1992, pp. 58–59, and 15 May 1992, pp. 134–135.
13. *NNS,* 19 February–4 March 1993, pp. 4–5.
14. *CAR,* 25 March 1993, pp. 81–83.
15. *NNS,* 19–25 July 1992, pp. 1–3. The official figures for army casualties seem low, since it took house-by-house street fighting to push FROC out of Estelí.
16. Dye et al., *Contesting Everything,* p. 40.
17. These units are also referred to as the aforementioned Special Disarmament Brigades. Figures on their activities are drawn from an interview with Captain M. Sandoval, Ejercito de Nicaragua, Managua, 9 October 1996.
18. Dye, et al., *Contesting Everything,* pp. 40–41; Saldomando and Cuadra, *Los Problemas,* pp. 31–34.
19. Some saw this as heralding a purge of Sandinistas from public service, but radical cuts to public-sector employment are integral parts of contemporary austerity programs.
20. This material is drawn from *Mesoamerica,* June 1990, pp. 9–11; and *CAR,* 18 May 1990, pp. 138–140.
21. *CAR,* 6 July 1990, pp. 193–194; 13 July 1990, p. 203; and 20 July 1990, pp. 213–214.
22. *Mesoamerica,* March 1991, pp. 9–10, and April 1991, pp. 6–7.
23. *Mesoamerica,* April 1992, pp. 1–2; *CAR,* 8 May 1992, p. 123.
24. *CAR,* 24 September 1993, pp. 281–282, and 15 October 1995, pp. 305–306.
25. *CAR,* 26 May 1995, p. 7. The first five years of Mrs. Chamorro's tenure saw 330 national strikes; see Tim Johnson, "Nicaraguans Make Discontent a Way of Life," *Miami Herald,* 20 July 1995, p. A16.

26. *CAR,* 28 February 1992, p. 54. These issues are discussed by Richard Stahler-Sholk in his, "El ajuste neoliberal y sus opciones: La respuesta del movimiento sindical en Nicaragua," *Revista Mexicana de Sociologia* 56:3 (1994), and in his "Breaking the Mold: Economic Orthodoxy and the Politics of Resistance in Nicaragua," paper presented to the LASA congress, Washington, DC, 1995.

27. *CAR,* 12 March 1993, p. 67.

28. *CAR,* 17 June 1994, p. 7, and 9 June 1995, p. 8.

29. This section is based on "Nicaragua Needs a Miracle," *Envio* 15:175–176 (February/March 1996): 3–10.

30. *NNS,* 30 January 1997, pp. 1–2.

31. *CAR,* 25 August 1995, p. 4; 20 October 1995, p. 3; 26 January 1996, p. 4; and 6 February 1996, p. 2.

32. The conflict over the defense budget is discussed later in this chapter.

33. All figures relating to military strength and budgets in this section come from Roberto J. Cajina, *Transición política y reconversión militar en Nicaragua, 1990–1995* (Managua: CRIES, 1995), chap. 5.

34. Ibid., p. 363.

35. Ibid., pp. 317–368.

36. Carlos Carranza and Jose Chinchilla, "Ajuste estructural en Costa Rica, 1985–1993," in *Los Pequenos paises de América Latina en la hora neoliberal,* coord. Gerónimo de Sierra (Caracas, Venezuela: Editorial Nueva Sociedad, 1994), pp. 39–68.

37. Despite the conflictive relations between Nicaragua's executive and legislature, the data I have indicate that President Chamorro used her veto only ten times over the course of her term. Only three of these, however, were sustained, all of them in the administration's first two years. Moreover, after the National Assembly passed the constitutional amendment package of 1995, which is examined in Chapter 6, it became possible for the president of the assembly to order the publication of bills the president of the republic has refused to sign but has not vetoed (Article 142). This provision was used twice in President Chamorro's administration.

38. The Spanish text of the article is less specific. Article 138.6 states that the National Assembly shall *"conocer, discutir y aprobar el proyecto de Ley Anual de Presupuesto General de la República, y ser informada periodicamente de su ejercicio, conforme al procedimiento establecido en la Constitución y en la ley."*

39. David Close, "Nicaragua: The Legislature as Seedbed of Conflict," in *Legislatures and the New Democracies in Latin America,* ed. David Close (Boulder, CO: Lynne Rienner Publishers, 1995), pp. 59–61.

40. These riots broke out after a bomb damaged the tomb of Sandinista hero Carlos Fonseca. Rioters attacked Managua's city hall and an anti-Sandinista radio station; see Close, "Nicaragua," p. 63.

41. What follows is based on what I saw from the visitors' gallery, which stretches behind both sides of the aisle on the floor level of the Nicaraguan National Assembly building. Managua's four daily newspapers—*La Prensa, Barricada, El Nuevo Diario,* and *La Tribuna*—all carried extensive stories the next day, 23 October 1995.

42. *Zancudo* means "mosquito" and has long been applied to the Conservative wing that worked with the Somozas between 1936 and 1979.

43. Though Paladino withdrew with the rest, his party leader, Miriam Argüello, declared to a group of reporters that they were withdrawing for reasons specific to their party and not because they wanted to derail Téllez's movement.

44. This was confirmed to me that day by Alejandro Solórzano, a Socialist deputy who walked out.

45. *La Tribuna,* 24 October 1995, p. A3.

46. The material in this section comes from the following sources: *NNS,* between the weeks of 24 November 1996 and 5 January 1997; the electronic edition of *La Prensa,* at: http://www.tmx.com, from 16 November 1996 to 8 January 1997; and the electronic edition of *Notifax,* at: http://www.notifax.com, from 15 November 1996 to 8 January 1997.

47. I want to thank Michael Wallack for this suggestion. While in office the FSLN did make numerous accommodations, for example, on the 1987 constitution. On this, see David Close, *Nicaragua: Politics, Economics, and Society* (London: Pinter Publishers, 1988), pp. 138–144. What neither the former Sandinista government nor the new Chamorro administration did, however, was trade away key parts of their programs.

48. *CAR,* 2 November 1990, pp. 334–336.

49. Of course, Sandinista support of the existing constitution centered on executive power and securing Daniel Ortega's right to run again for the presidency.

50. This statement holds true for all offices except the regional councils of the two autonomous regions of the Atlantic coast that were elected in 1994.

51. Chapter 5 takes up the state of the economy and the administration's economic policy; Chapter 6 presents an extensive examination of the constitutional question.

5

Getting the Economy Right?

Trying to manage Nicaragua's economy would be a daunting task for any government. Never wealthy or developed by international standards, Nicaragua has made its way in the world by exporting a succession of agricultural staples, augmented by small quantities of minerals. In this it is like most of the countries of the Third World, with which it competes to sell its products to the industrialized countries. Short of finding an economic philosopher's stone, there is little a government can do to reorient the Nicaraguan economy in the short or medium term.

Despite this, governments past and present have tried to restructure Nicaragua's economy on many occasions. In the 1890s, the Liberal administration of José Santos Zelaya built a railroad, opened banks, and promoted the cultivation of coffee. He also sought unsuccessfully to have the country be the route for a trans-isthmian canal, and he eventually came to woe after seeking German and Japanese money to back a Nicaraguan canal to compete with the one the Americans were just finishing in Panama. After World War II, Somoza built roads and encouraged big landholders to grow cotton. The Sandinistas were perhaps the most enthusiastic state interventionists Nicaragua had seen since Spanish days, proposing that the state be responsible for economic accumulation. That President Chamorro's administration turned its hand to reshaping the nation's economy is thus hardly novel. What distinguishes Chamorro's efforts from those of her predecessors is that her government worked to get the state out of economic affairs.

The last two decades of the twentieth century will be marked by future economic historians as an era of increasing market deregulation. Where managed, Keynesian capitalism had been the economic faith of the post–World War II generation of finance ministers; the economic crisis of the 1970s brought free market polices back into fashion. Yet just as the first market economy, Britain in the early nineteenth century, needed state action to come into existence,[1] so, too, would this return to orthodoxy require the aid of a strong governmental hand. Laws had to be repealed or amended, and the entire array of economic interests that had come to count on government assistance had to be cut adrift. Because government acted to change the way the economy worked, it would be blamed every time one of its free market initiatives brought pain instead of gain.

A number of things combined to convince governments to risk unpopularity by taking the state out of ever larger parts of the economy. One was being confronted with an economic crisis that statist economic policies were unable to cure. Though the industrialized world knew its share of economic problems between 1975 and 1990, these were minor compared to what most of Latin America faced. Growth ground to a halt; unemployment and underemployment grew steadily; inflation took off as governments printed money, trying to get their economies fired up again; and foreign debts multiplied as the combination of shrinking export markets and rising interest rates on international loans contracted earlier produced a disastrous balance of payments. Grave problems generally lead to looking for novel ways to solve them. But why return to the free market?

What ensured that market economics became the policymaker's instrument of choice was the earlier conversion of aid donors and multilateral international lenders to the precepts of unalloyed capitalism. Where development agencies and IFIs (including USAID and the World Bank) once counseled having big public sectors, by the early 1980s, they had swung around to back a new version of the night-watchman state. Always important to the economic well-being of poor countries, donors and lenders assumed a special relevance in this latest crisis. To survive, if not overcome, the crunch, Latin American countries needed access to international loans, both to reactivate their faltering domestic economies and to pay the interest on outstanding loans. To get these loans, the debtors had to convince their creditors that they were worthy recipients, and for reasons to be discussed later on, this could be done only by adopting free market policies.

Besides the two reasons noted above, a third factor was at play in Nicaragua's economic changes. Sandinista economic policy was not just very dirigiste in nature, but it also aimed to be highly redistributive and eventually bring about the victory of socialism over capitalism. Were that not enough, the revolutionary state expropriated the properties of those who abandoned the country or who were implicated in counterrevolutionary activities. The result was an anti-Sandinista coalition made up overwhelmingly of ready supporters of noninterventionist, sound business government.

However, in 1990, there were also many supporters of the Sandinistas' economic philosophy. Not that Nicaraguans wanted the hard times to continue, but the FSLN's redistributive policies and its antibourgeois populism found ready audiences among large parts of the population. Organized labor, especially the part in Sandinista unions, rural workers, and many small farmers would certainly prefer the direction of old-time Sandinista thinking to what the new government was offering. So economic policy in the Chamorro era would be colored by class politics, with the powerful generally supporting the new order and the dispossessed opposing it. And since the Sandinistas still had the political resources to mount a strong opposition both in parliament and in the streets, economic policymaking from 1990 to1996 was bound to be highly conflictual.

The State of the Nicaraguan Economy in 1990

Nicaragua's economy has the characteristics associated with an underdeveloped or Third World country. It has a weak industrial sector, it is structured around the export of raw or semiprocessed raw materials (staples), and it is poor. Such an economy generally supports a society that is poorly educated, has limited access to health care, and has a highly skewed class structure with a tiny upper class, small middle and industrial working classes, and an extremely large lower class.[2] The economic objective of the Sandinista revolution was to make a transition from underdevelopment to socialism. This did not mean Stalinist heavy industry or Maoist collective farms and backyard blast furnaces or even a Cuban-style nationalization of petty commerce. It did, though, aim at building a mixed economy in which the state sector was dominant and would channel more of its energies toward meeting the needs of the majority.[3] The revolutionary state failed to achieve its economic objectives and inadvertently left the country worse off materially than before the FSLN took power.

Basic Characteristics and Macroeconomic Performance

Nicaragua's economy has always been built around the export of raw or semiprocessed staples, particularly agricultural products (see Table 5.1). For nearly fifty years the mix of agricultural exports has featured coffee, cotton, and livestock. These commodities are sold in the international market where Nicaraguan goods compete against identical or competing products from tropical countries around the world, including its Central American neighbors. As a result, Nicaragua finds itself selling in a highly competitive buyers' market where its well-being depends on factors beyond its control.

But relying on staple exports and facing fierce international competition do not automatically condemn a country to endless poverty. A number

Table 5.1   Exports by Sector, 1981–1994
(as percentage of total exports)

Sector	1981	1985	1991	1994
Agriculture	60.0	79.0	79.8	81.3
Mining[a]	5.1	—	24.5	6.1
Manufacturing	34.8	20.0	6.5	12.6

Sources: Adapted from Close, *Nicaragua,* p. 77; and IADB, "Basic Socio-Economic Data," in *Nicaragua: Statistics and Quantitative Data,* electronic ed. (18 September 1997), at: http://database.iadb.org/int/basicrep/banic/html.
    a. Mining sector for 1991 and 1994 includes agricultural raw materials.

of countries—the United States, Canada, and Australia chief among them—have built modern industrial economies on a foundation of primary products. They did so by taking advantage of three types of linkages: (1) backward, by building machines needed to produce the staple, for example, farm implements; (2) forward, by processing the staple, for example, steel from iron ore; and (3) final demand, by opening consumer goods firms to meet the demand flowing from the incomes earned in the primary products sector.[4] Nicaragua has not been able to follow this path partly because foreign control stifled development[5] but even more because the country's production was based on a system of servile labor that worked against creating and taking advantage of the sorts of linkages that the British settler colonies used to grow and diversify. This is typical of the sort of structural problems that developing economies face.

Although staples are Nicaragua's main export, the primary sector—agriculture, fishing, mining—is not the largest employer in the nation's economy. Table 5.2 reveals that more Nicaraguans work in service occupations than in either the primary or the manufacturing sector. Though this has an air of the "new, postindustrial economy" about it, in fact the service sector of most developing economies has little in common with information economies evolving in the world's wealthiest nations. Rather, the tertiary sector is often inflated by a large informal sector, an economy of last resort populated by those unable to find wage labor. Instead of being composed of lawyers or consultants, the Nicaraguan service sector is dominated by men and women who make brooms or tortillas and hawk them up and down the streets. Somewhat better off, but still parts of the informal economy, are the women who sell soda pop in plastic bags from their stands along busy streets. Though this kind of work can assure survival, it is not the basis for a flourishing economy.

One of the most interesting approaches to the question of development

Table 5.2   Gross Domestic Product by Sector, 1981–1994
(as percentage of total)

Sector	1981	1985	1993	1994
Primary	20.2	22.6	27.3	31.3
Secondary[a]	30.5	32.2	19.0	20.2
Tertiary	49.3	45.1	53.7	48.5

Sources: Adapted from Close, *Nicaragua*, p. 76; and IADB, "Basic Socio-Economic Data."
   a. The 1991 and 1994 data for the secondary sector includes, besides manufacturing, public utilities (electricity, gas, and water) and construction.

is the Human Development Index (HDI), published in the annual *Human Development Report* of the United Nations Development Program. The HDI was devised as an alternative to per capita income as a quick measure of material well-being. Though per capita income is a simple and useful indicator, it can be misleading. For instance, countries with substantially equal per capita incomes can show very different levels of literacy, good health, and income distribution. All things being equal, a country with healthier, better-educated people, more of whom have some income, is the better bet to diversify and modernize its economy, as well as being a better place for people to live. Thus the UNDP designed a measure of development that takes into account life expectancy—a surrogate for health care, literacy and mean years of schooling, and an income element. All countries for which data are available are ranked according to the sum of their scores, running from 0.0 to 1.0, on these measures. Table 5.3 presents the 1990 HDI for Central America, excluding Belize, and the top and bottom three countries from the entire global ranking. The data on which the 1990 HDI is based are from the mid- and late 1980s.

Nicaragua did well in terms of relative human development, achieving an HDI ranking seventeen places higher than its gross domestic product (GDP) per capita position. Among Central American countries, only Costa Rica performed better, finishing twenty-six places higher on the HDI list than in the GDP standings. The Sandinistas' attention to health, education, and redistributive policies to help the disadvantaged were paying some dividends. Even more important, however, Nicaragua's performance in such areas as literacy, life expectancy, and infant mortality improved dramatically during the decade of FSLN rule,[6] testimony to the efficacy of at least some Sandinista initiatives. The incoming administration, therefore, received a basis on which to further develop Nicaragua's human capital.

Unfortunately, the country's generally positive record in promoting

Table 5.3   Central American Human Development Index, 1990

Country	Global Ordinal Rank	HDI	Difference Between HDI and GDP Ranking
Japan	1	.996	4
Sweden	2	.987	4
Switzerland	3	.986	–2
Costa Rica	27	.916	26
Panama	37	.883	5
Nicaragua	59	.743	17
El Salvador	71	.651	3
Guatemala	75	.592	–8
Honduras	79	.563	–2
Burkina Faso	128	.150	–10
Mali	129	.143	–13
Niger	130	.116	–19

Source: Adapted from UNDP, *Human Development Report, 1990*, pp. 128–129.

human development did not carry over into its overall economic performance. Before looking at this in detail, several points need to be mentioned. First, for all of Latin America, the decade of the eighties was an economic disaster. A combination of low prices for many primary products, high interest rates, growing foreign debt loads, and soaring unemployment left most countries no better off in real terms than they had been ten years earlier. Any government coming to power in Latin America in 1990 was going to have to rebuild its nation's economy. In Nicaragua, however, a second element came into play: war. War always distorts an economy by its inflationary effects and by shifting people from their regular tasks to work in war-related activities. Further, the postwar period always brings the problem of reintegrating veterans into civilian jobs just as the economy is shifting back to peacetime production.

But more striking than these general effects are the real, concrete costs of war. Paul Oquist reports that, beyond the war's horrible toll in human life (over 30,000 deaths), roughly half of Nicaragua's economic output during the 1980s was lost because of the war.[7] He argues that in addition to the direct costs arising from war-related damage (almost U.S.\$2 billion), a true picture of the total economic price of the war should include losses associated with the embargo (U.S.\$1.1 billion), extraordinary defense expenditures (estimated at U.S.\$1.9 billion), and secondary effects on the gross national product (e.g., reduced consumption, estimated at nearly U.S.\$4.1 billion).[8] The resulting figure is a little over U.S.\$9 billion. When one recalls that Nicaragua's GDP for 1989 was around U.S.\$1.8 billion,[9] the material impact of the contra war can plausibly be set at the equivalent of five years of total output.

With this background, the data presented in Table 5.4 become more comprehensible. Every country in Central America, except Panama, saw its economy shrink between 1980 and 1989. And all of them experienced dramatic increases in their foreign debt. Yet Nicaragua stands out among this set of somber statistics by having the worst record among the isthmian neighbors. And even these do not tell the whole story, particularly in regard to inflation. In the period 1980–1987, the inflation rate in Nicaragua averaged 87 percent annually,[10] the worst in the region but not catastrophic. However, in 1988, inflation soared to 33,603 percent, dropping to 1,609 percent in 1989,[11] to produce a horrific annual inflation rate of over 600 percent, a septupling of prices every year for the decade.

Table 5.4   Relative Economic Performance of Central American Countries, 1980s

	Average Annual Growth (%)	Average Annual Inflation (%)	Debt, 1989–1980 (%)
Costa Rica	−0.5	25.6	203.2
El Salvador	−2.4	19.0	184.4
Guatemala	−3.6	13.9	259.4
Honduras	−2.0	7.8	244.5
Nicaragua	−4.7	618.8	533.8
Panama	0.3	1.8	n.a.

Sources: Adapted from World Bank, *World Development Report, 1991* (New York: Oxford University Press, 1991), pp. 170–171; and Cardoso and Helwege, *Latin America's Economy,* pp. 101–102, 512–513.

Sandinista Austerity, 1985–1989

That President Chamorro and her new administration inherited a weak economy is self-evident. What is not so clear from the foregoing data is that Sandinista policies enacted during the Ortega government contributed to debilitating the economy in an unexpected way. Beginning in 1985, just after receiving the country's mandate in 1984, the revolutionary state started down the road of fiscal austerity and eventually came to adopt, if not embrace, the logic of the free market. This sounds odd, as in three years' time Nicaragua would be swept up in perhaps the worst hyperinflation in the Western Hemisphere. However, to meet the exigencies of the war and a defense budget that would soon command 60 percent of the country's resources, the state began to cut jobs in the public sector, reduce funding for social programs, and let wages fall relative to prices, not just in the public sector but throughout the economy, as inflation rolled on unabated. The result was austerity without the compensation of price deflation, a hyperinflationary austerity, and misery for millions of Nicaraguans.

The last good economic year the Sandinistas had was 1983. Beginning in 1984, the contra war escalated, making ever-greater demands on the economy; the overvalued cordoba was contributing to inflation and depressing exports; inflation was accelerating but interest rates had stayed low, producing negative real rates; and the revolutionary government's attempts to play "catch-up socialism"[12] had clearly left it overcommitted. To begin to repair this damage, the newly elected government of Daniel Ortega unveiled a dramatic new policy in February 1985. It would have many of the painful characteristics of the austerity programs prescribed by the IMF and the World Bank, but it would not bring with it the benefits (e.g., access to cheap loans) that came with participation in the multilateral lenders' schemes.

Nicaragua's new economic policy was a complex, integrated package that was designed to stimulate production, adjust salaries, shift resources toward the military, and improve material conditions in rural areas.[13] The first step in this direction was cutting government spending by eliminating subsidies on food and reducing them on public transport. Along the same lines, a hiring freeze in public service was enacted and public-sector investment rationalized. Beyond this, the government revised its exchange rate policies by decreeing a devaluation and tightened its credit policies toward the agricultural sector. Phil Ryan argues that the government did not get its credit policies right and that borrowers were soon luxuriating in negative rates that practically guaranteed profits.[14] Though that certainly would have spelled trouble for the FSLN's adjustment plan, the U.S. embargo of May 1985 and continued funding of the contras by the Reagan administration assured its failure.

Thus, on 14 February 1988, the Sandinistas had to bring forth another austerity plan.[15] This one was a grand theatrical gesture, because it introduced an entirely new currency (the new cordoba) effectively overnight, having concocted the plan over several months in complete secrecy. Nicaraguans had three days to convert their old cordobas for new ones at the rate of 1,000:1, up to a limit of ten million old cordobas, with amounts beyond that being frozen in special accounts. As the new currency was pegged at ten cordobas to one U.S. dollar, a unified value to replace the plethora of rates that existed previously, this meant that savings of as much as U.S.$10,000 could be immediately and legally exchanged. More important for most Nicaraguans was the generalized rise in the prices of consumer goods that increased the cost of buying various baskets of goods by up to 273 percent. Finally, in another attempt to rein in costs, the public sector was to be reduced through a policy of *compactación* (compression) that would merge ministries and allow layoffs.

When this plan, too, had failed (in June 1988), the Ortega government moved to further liberalize Nicaragua's economy, raising prices and devaluing the tarnished new cordoba along the way. By then, however, even such a radical shift was insufficient. Inflation continued on toward its historic national high of over 33,000 percent (though it fell to 1,600 percent in 1989), work for wages became increasingly scarce and increasingly unremunerative as pay was always behind skyrocketing prices, and the economy continued to decay. By the end of 1989, after a decade of Sandinista rule, per capita income in Nicaragua stood at about half of what it had been in 1970, and what had cost 100 cordobas (C$) in 1980 fetched C$458 million, in constant values.[16]

Harry Vanden and Gary Prevost observe that "the socialist orientation of the mixed economy was significantly gutted by the economics [of] the last two years of Sandinista rule," adding that the "nature of the June 1988 reform was evidenced by the relatively warm reception it received from the anti-Sandinista business sector."[17] By adopting the polical economy of austerity, the FSLN was unwittingly falling into line with the behavior of other socialist governments. Labour Party governments in Australia and New Zealand and Socialist administrations in France and Spain also abandoned historic positions and adopted more business-friendly economic policies in the eighties. None of those four, however, had come to power through a revolution, none was really engaged in a project to build socialism,[18] and certainly none was fighting a costly counterinsurgent war. That the Sandinistas needed more revenues was evident. That they apparently thought they could collect the needed funds from their staunchest supporters was an act of supreme shortsightedness.

The Economic Policies of the Chamorro Administration

In one sense, the economic policy choices open to President Chamorro must have looked simple and straightforward: do the exact opposite of whatever the Sandinistas had tried to do. Thus, the new government would restore investor confidence by cutting back the role of the state and emphasizing the market. Moreover, it would put the country's fiscal house in order by adhering to the prescriptions of the IMF and the World Bank. And it would reopen trade and aid ties with the United States. In the end, though it did all of these things to at least some extent, the economic management record of Doña Violeta's administration is not impressive. She and her cabinet did find ways to bring Nicaragua's destructive hyperinflation to heel, but they did not find the means to reactivate the economy until the end of their time in office. So Nicaragua, because its economy had been disrupted by nearly constant turmoil since the late 1970s, would spend another stagnant six years.

The General Model: Structural Adjustment

Not just Nicaragua but nearly every poor country in the world has found itself a candidate for a structural adjustment program in the last fifth of the twentieth century. "Structural adjustment" has become shorthand for a series of policies prescribed by the IMF and the World Bank for countries facing chronic international debt problems. Though SAPs were first applied to a few African countries in the late 1970s, they become nearly universal in the 1980s and 1990s. The programs have a dual objective: to eliminate the current debt problem and then to so restructure a country's economy and economic policy that debt problems do not recur. Despite their admirable aims, SAPs have been vilified as often as they have been praised. As the economic policy of the Chamorro administration can be seen as a lengthy, though not totally successful, exercise in structural adjustment, it is useful to describe the logic and operating principles of SAPs.[19]

A bit of history is needed to understand why structural adjustment programs exist. This background will also make understanding their objectives easier. The 1950s and 1960s saw many low- and medium-income countries—the underdeveloped countries or the Third World—record healthy rates of economic growth. Most of these poor countries used the state as a very important tool in building their economies; and although there were skeptics like Peter T. Bauer,[20] most economists and development agencies in the industrialized world accepted this model. However, the oil shocks and generalized recession of the 1970s brought an end to those relatively good times and ushered in an era of crisis.

First, both the 1973 and 1979 oil shocks raised energy prices, significantly adding to production and transport costs, especially in countries that relied on exports. Second, these shocks also affected industrial countries, raising prices and inducing a recession that depressed demand for imports. Third and ultimately most important, the 1973 shock put enormous windfall profits into the hands of oil producers who deposited many of their "petrodollars" in European and North American banks. The banks, in turn, began looking desperately for ways to loan these new deposits out to cover the interest they had to pay. Eventually, this led to "loan pushing"—high-pressure sales tactics applied to international banking—targeting sovereign borrowers, mostly developing countries. The banks professed to believe that sovereigns could not go bankrupt, making them the safest havens for loans.

This might have held true had not interest rates begun rising after the 1979 shock. When the short-term loans financed by petrodollars came up for renegotiation in 1979 or the early 1980s, countries saw 6 percent rates turn into 20 or 25 percent rates overnight, easily tripling the payments needed even to cover interest costs. In August 1982, Mexico threatened to default on its $85 billion debt, and the era of generalized structural adjustment programs had arrived.

Fundamentally, SAPs set out conditions that debtor countries must meet to qualify for loans from multilateral lenders, often the only ones willing to make loans to seriously indebted states. The conditions usually take the form of policies and economic performance standards, though increasingly political conditions relating to "governance" are being set.[21] The conditions are obviously related to the lenders' analysis of the country's problems, thus they focus on how to reduce the economic role of the state. Securing the SAP's objectives occurs through two separate but closely related steps.

First comes stabilization, or getting the immediate fiscal and monetary crisis under control. Austerity is the usual prescription, and it involves cutting budget deficits, laying off public-sector workers, privatizing SOEs, reducing subsidies, and eliminating programs. Education, health, and social services generally are the prime targets, because they are large, not well defended by any particular constituency, and do not contribute to immediate economic recovery. Special attention goes to reducing the foreign debt, because debt service diverts money that could be used for other public purposes or be the basis of a tax cut.

Once stabilization is achieved (two to three years is the usual guideline) structural adjustment proper begins. This entails setting policies that preclude a recurrence of the crisis. Given SAPs' emphasis on eliminating budget deficits, it is not surprising that strengthened fiscal administration is one part of the adjustment. The other part consists in forming policies that open the country to foreign trade and orient its economy toward world markets. Here the advice is to capitalize on existing comparative advantages— that is, specializing in those areas where the country is already an efficient (low-cost relative to others) producer. This is not the "competitive advantage," building the special skills that let a country move beyond relying on raw materials and cheap labor, that the Harvard management theorist Michael Porter describes, but rather the exact opposite.

As structural adjustment calls for changing a vast range of existing policies, the program reallocates costs and benefits in society, thereby producing opposition. One of the questions that occupied the early studies was what let a state successfully carry through a SAP. It should not be a surprise that governments that concentrated decisional power in the hands of an executive that operated with a high degree of independence from the legislature were the most effective in implementing SAPs.[22] It seems, therefore, that applying a structural adjustment program might well conflict with the sorts of policies and practices that are needed to build constitutional democracies, particularly creating a strong and independent representative assembly that is able to hold the executive accountable for its actions.

Skeptics, especially in Latin America, argue that SAPs want to recreate the political economy of the region as it was before the Great Depression. Optimists point to strengthened administrative structures and a healthier fiscal balance as the foundation for a better economic future. Unfortunately for Nicaragua, the country's experience with structural adjustment as implemented during the Chamorro administration leaves the skeptics with the better part of the argument.

Stabilization

Stabilization in Nicaragua was first and foremost about taming inflation. Though inflation fell from over 33,000 percent in 1988 to just over 1,600 percent in 1989, in the new government's first year, 1990, it again spurted upward to more than 13,000 percent. Clearly the Chamorro administration's initial approach to securing price stability was flawed. It had been based on the plan of Francisco Mayorga,[23] a Yale economics Ph.D. who became Doña Violeta's first Central Bank president, and was built around the introduction of another new currency: the *córdoba oro* (gold cordoba), set equal to the U.S. dollar. As is usual in such cases, the new money was to be based on sounder policy and be tightly enough managed to drive inflation out of the nation's system. There were confident predictions that only 100 days would be needed to bring prices under control, and though things would be tough, the short, sharp shock would produce a rapid cure. According to Mayorga:

> What we want to do with the gold córdoba is to erase the memory of hyperinflation in the people's minds. No one will believe a promise to allow just a little inflation. If you want to convince people in a country like this, you have to have a firm commitment that inflation will disappear.[24]

Mayorga was wrong: the new currency (the bills featured pictures of Sandino and Pedro Joaquín Chamorro, among others) did not halt the hyperinflationary spiral. Part of the reason this happened was that the new currency was introduced gradually, according to plan. At first, the gold cordoba was used only to pay taxes and utility bills. However, people were still paid in the old "pigsty cordoba" (*córdoba chanchero*), whose popular name reflected the public's assessment of its value. As the *chanchero* was pegged to the *córdoba oro* just as the new money was pegged to the dollar, every dip in the national currency's value (and there were twenty-five devaluations in the administration's first few months) meant that ordinary people's everyday living costs soared ever further beyond their capacity to meet them. This confounded the government's expectations, as the slow replacement of the old currency by the new was supposed to protect people's purchasing power by retarding inflation. As a further complication, the dollar also served as a parallel currency, making "investing" in U.S. dollars a better and safer bet than investing in Nicaraguan businesses.

The failure of the plan led to Mayorga's dismissal in October 1990, just four days after the government concluded its first deal with organized labor over economic policy.[25] Perhaps had Nicaragua not been so conflict-prone or its working class so militant, people would have accepted the costs that came with Mayorga's shock treatment. It is certainly plausible that the plan was definitively undone by the two great strikes that took place in the new administration's first 100 days.[26] Nevertheless, it is surprising that the administration would commit itself to a policy that had so much potential to incite opposition. Either the new government overestimated its capacity to repress confrontational dissent or the apolitical technocrats who staffed the administration's upper reaches grossly misread the character and temperament of Nicaraguans.

Though Mayorga was a handy scapegoat, it is unfair to saddle him with the whole blame for the Chamorro administration's rocky start on the road to stabilization. Faced with the enormous problem of resettling returning contras and reorganizing government, the government's deficit for 1990 grew to 14.3 percent of GDP from the 5.1 percent it had been the year before.[27] And that, in turn, was in some part the product of the tardy arrival of promised economic assistance from Washington: of the $300 million promised President Chamorro after her election, less than half had arrived a year later.[28]

Despite these unpromising beginnings, prices began to come under control. By mid-1991, the monthly inflation rate had fallen to less than 1 percent; prices remained relatively low for the rest of Chamorro's term (see Table 5.5). What finally got the process started was an anti-inflation plan introduced in March 1991. The Lacayo Plan, named after Antonio, the minister of the presidency, who superintended it, the scheme brought a 400 percent devaluation of the currency (making each revalued córdoba worth about 40 billion pre-February 1988 cordobas).[29] Unlike the Mayorga Plan, however, the Lacayo Plan brought in social policies to help absorb part of the shock.[30] Whereas this gave the new approach a chance to work without having to be revised in the face of general strikes, there were other

Table 5.5   Nicaraguan Macroeconomic Performance, 1991–1994

	1991	1992	1993	1994
Inflation	2945%	23.7%	20.4%	7.8%
Debt/GDP	584.4%	606%	619%	632.8%
GDP per capita	U.S.$464	U.S.$450	U.S.$456	U.S.$460[a]
Growth	–0.2%	0.4	–0.4%	3.3%

Sources: Adapted from IADB, "Basic Socio-Economic Data"; and USAID, "Nicaragua."
   a. The World Bank, gives Nicaragua's per capita income as U.S.$340 (*World Development Report, 1996* [New York: Oxford University Press, 1996], p. 188).

elements at work. Popular exhaustion, resulting from a year's constant mobilization while trying to cope with personal economic distress, combined with paying off some $300 million in arrears on loans from the Somoza period[31] to make a great contribution to ending hyperinflation.

Restoring price stability was the great economic achievement of the Chamorro administration. However, mastering inflation was not enough to spur reactivation. Because the economy remained depressed through most of the term, revenues were low, deficits large, and the multilateral prophets of fiscal stabilization were left less than completely satisfied.

Structural Adjustment in Chamorro's Nicaragua

Table 5.5 paints a gloomy macroeconomic picture. Structural adjustment is supposed to avoid the macroeconomic dilemmas in which Nicaragua found itself at the end of President Chamorro's term. To understand why this happened we have to be able to assess how much of the problem should be attributed to poor execution by the government, how much to ill-conceived structural adjustment policies, and how much to the interaction of these two effects.

An overview.   Although the new administration began its term with a tough austerity policy, it did not have a structural adjustment agreement in place. In fact, the Chamorro government's first internationally supported steps toward economic reform were financed by USAID.[32] It was only in September 1991, after almost eighteen months in office, that its initial loan was arranged with the IMF. Soon deals were struck with the other major multilateral lenders: the World Bank and the Inter-American Development Bank (IADB). Eventually, the IADB would take a more flexible approach to Nicaraguan restructuring, but the others, especially the IMF, continuously hewed an orthodox line.

The adjustment program itself was conventional. It consisted of laying off government employees and decreasing other expenditures to move toward a balanced budget. There were also the usual calls to reduce tariffs and other barriers to international trade, and to privatize SOEs, both to generate revenue and to reduce the state's role in the economy. The money saved through cuts and raised through privatizations was targeted toward paying down the country's massive foreign debt (U.S.$11 billion, six times the annual GDP). From the perspective of abstract economic logic, the policy was unassailable. Austerity would restore price stability and lower wages, thereby opening the way to new investment and jobs. Free trade would bring consumers cheaper goods and push inefficient local firms to match their international competitors. Paying down foreign debt would bring lower debt service charges (interest payments), allowing the government more fiscal flexibility. The only flaw was that all these policies were likely to produce a strong economic contraction by taking money out of the economy; and in 1991, Nicaragua's economy had very little money to spare.[33]

Besides this inherent problem, individual programs did not work according to plan. Personnel reductions were to be achieved by offering people substantial incentives to leave the public service through a program called "occupational reconversion" that proved less attractive than anticipated. Though the proportion of the national budget allotted to health and education stayed steady during the administration's six years, the country faced enormous difficulties in responding to public health crises, especially an outbreak of hemorrhagic dengue in 1995, that were blamed on the government's austerity policy. And though there were tax reforms, for example, raising the sales tax from 10 to 15 percent and reducing top marginal income tax rates, monitoring agencies complained that some taxes were being applied unevenly, suggesting political favoritism. Tariff reductions, too, fell short of expectations, generating little foreign investment.[34]

Despite the difficulties associated with structural adjustment, had the government not accepted the stipulations of the multilateral lenders it would have had no access to low interest loans. By accepting terms that were doubtlessly congenial in principle, the Chamorro administration also became eligible to renegotiate its outstanding debts with the Paris Club, the name given to practices to deal with international debt payment problems developed since 1956 by the world's creditor countries.[35] Only debts arising from government loans or private loans backed with official guarantees qualify for Paris Club treatment. Negotiations can lead to rescheduling payments or forgiving up to one-third of loans taken at commercial rates. As about 20 percent of Nicaraguan foreign debt was held by Paris Club countries in the early 1990s, it was in Managua's interest to take advantage of the Club's offer. However, the Paris Club only deals with countries that have a program with the IMF; so negotiating with the Paris Club is conditional upon having accepted the restructuring conditions of the IMF.

From the outset, however, the Chamorro administration faced problems in meeting the stipulations set by its creditors. It was consistently tardy in reducing its deficit, unsuccessful in laying off the requisite numbers of state employees, could not meet guidelines for international reserves, and did not achieve on time all the privatization goals set for it. Beyond these chronic dilemmas, the Chamorro government was occasionally upbraided for not bringing the property question to a satisfactory conclusion and for the serious problems of governability the country occasionally displayed. In October 1996, all these problems came together as the IMF suspended disbursements under the Enhanced Structural Adjustment Facility (ESAF)—a special SAP available to low-income countries that offers assistance on concessional terms—it had concluded with Nicaragua in 1994. The IMF continued to monitor Nicaragua's performance, but it would not make payments until the country improved its economic performance.

Why did the Chamorro government have so much trouble meeting the conditions of its SAP? One thing to note is that Nicaragua was not the only country, even in Central America, to run into problems with the multilaterals. Neighboring Costa Rica saw payments suspended in 1995 due to its inability to meet budget deficit goals. This suggests that poor countries may have structural characteristics that make it hard for them to shape their economies to fit the IMF–World Bank template. But Nicaragua had unique problems stemming from its need to rebuild after years of war and due to the special burdens brought by its exceptionally confrontational, high-stakes politics. Together, these two factors make a persuasive case for exceptional treatment, but even that might not have brightened the country's economic prospects. Most of its neighbors and overseas competitors adopted the multilaterals' prescriptions well before Managua; to have delayed making fiscal adjustments could have set Nicaragua back even further.

Privatization. It was Prime Minister Margaret Thatcher of Britain who introduced the world to systematic policies of privatization, the process by which the state sells its assets to private owners. Harvey Feigelbaum and Jeffery Henig suggest that there are three distinct types of privatization: systemic, where it is part of a project to remake the state's economic role; pragmatic, the logic of which is saving money; and tactical, which implies it is used to secure short-term political advantage.[36] Nicaragua's privatization policy clearly falls into the systemic category, though it also had pragmatic, revenue-generating goals. It is best to view the policy as having two parts, one concerned with SOEs that were either nationalized by the Sandinistas or created by them, the other with conventional public utilities.

The Corporaciones Nacionales del Sector Público, or the National Public Sector Corporations, was created in May 1990 to bring 351 SOEs under one roof and facilitate their eventual disposition.[37] This number excluded public utilities like the electric company (INE), the phone company (TELCOR), and the waterworks (INAA), though all three would eventually be targeted for privatization as part of the ESAF. However, among the 351 firms within CORNAP's purview were the national airline (Aeronica); corporations responsible for the production and marketing of bananas (BANANIC), coffee (CAFENIC), sugar (CONAZUCAR), and tobacco (TABANIC); the biggest brewery (Victoria); the Pepsi-Cola bottler (ENSA); as well as car rental agencies, construction firms, and the agency that regulated the marketing of basic grains like beans, corn, and rice (ENABAS). Structurally, CORNAP was an independent agency, reporting directly to the president of the republic. Indeed, it was so independent that even the country's controller general (Nicaragua's functional equivalent of the U.S. General Accounting Office or Canada's auditor general) had no knowledge of its financial operations.[38]

CORNAP disposed of the 351 SOEs under its control through 1,532 separate actions, because in most cases an SOE is not sold whole. For example, CONICSA, a construction firm, sold most of its buildings and equipment to private owners, but some of the machinery was given to the workers, and one building was rented out to private interests.[39] In some instances, the state retained control of an SOE, as was the case with the bulk of the enterprises making up COFARMA, a pharmaceutical firm, most of whose constituent enterprises were transferred to the Ministry of Health.[40] However, the majority of privatized firms, or their holdings, went to private purchasers (see Table 5.6).[41]

Far more interesting and important than the institution set up to privatize the FSLN's patrimony, however, was the politics surrounding that process. The tripartite *concertación* of September 1990 provided that workers in public-sector firms slated to be privatized could acquire shares in the enterprises.[42] These firms, some urban, some rural, would form the Area of Workers' Property (APT). Rural properties could be wholly owned by the workers, but urban workers could control only 25 percent of their workplaces.[43] Besides the APT, some rural properties also went to ex-RN fighters and former Sandinista soldiers.

Privatizing the Nicaraguan state sector was a task calling for great political subtlety and sophistication. Inevitably, there were conflicts, generally involving attempts by owners to strip the workers and soldiers of their rights. Two cases are illustrative: Prego Soap and La Fosforera.[44] The soap company, located in Granada, was claimed by workers but returned to its

Table 5.6   Disposition of Properties by CORNAP, 1991–1994

Recipient or Buyer	Number of Transactions	Percentage of Transactions	Value of Transactions (C$)	Value of Transactions (%)
Government (transfers)	39	2.55	n.a.	n.a.
Private business	790	51.57	666,360,469	59
Ex-combatants, both EPS and contras	241	15.73	15,383,857	1.36
Workers	358	23.36	333,905,257	29.57
Others (includes liquidations)	104	6.79	113,750,214	10.07
Totals	1,532	100	1,129,339,798	100

Source: Adopted from CORNAP, *Avance del proceso de privatización,* p. 48.

owners, the Pregos. Though the union staged a long occupation of the factory, its members netted six trucks. La Fosforera is the national match company, located in Managua. Of its total stock, 50 percent went to its employees and 50 percent to its former owner, Pedro Ortega Macho. Ortega Macho, however, attempted to sack the worker-owners and decapitalize the plant. A court decided for the employees and put out a warrant for Ortega Macho's arrest.

Even after disposing of the 351 firms under CORNAP's jurisdiction, Nicaragua was not finished with privatization. The World Bank and the IMF wanted to see TELCOR, INE, and INAA sold. Selling public utilities to the private sector is a common SAP strategy, promoted because the sale brings in a onetime injection of money and because the state no longer has on its books an enterprise that may cause a drain on the treasury. Due to the deterioration of the country's municipal water systems, INAA was a bad bet for privatization. The electrical monopoly, now named ENEL, and the phone company, rebaptized ENITEL, should have been more attractive. Nevertheless, protests by unionized workers in both firms significantly retarded privatization; in fact, both were still unsold late in 1997. That may be just as well, because when public utilities are privatized there has to be a solid regulatory regime in place. Unfortunately, neither the Chamorro cabinet nor the National Assembly gave serious thought to this matter.[45]

A final problem besetting the administration's privatization policy was the taint of corruption. Though there has been no systematic evidence of illegal procedures reported—indeed, there has been no serious investigation of the matter undertaken by a competent authority—it was common to hear Nicaraguans, both ordinary citizens and political insiders, talk about the "Chamorro *piñata*," equating this government's disposal of state holdings to the Sandinistas' dispersal of public assets after they lost power in 1990.[46] Complaints involving sweetheart deals for friends and relatives of top officials figured most prominently. Large-scale privatizations in poor countries often generate charges of corruption, especially where the need to shed state resources rapidly produces what look like fire-sale prices.[47]

What was most interesting about the Chamorro *piñata,* however, was that it received little coverage in the opposition press. Neither the Sandinistas' own *Barricada,* including its international edition, *Barricada International,* nor the left-leaning *El Nuevo Diario* pursued the stories with great vigor.[48] Articles in the media about privatization usually focused far more on the layoffs that would result than on possible sweetheart deals or kickbacks. Job losses, and even more the loss of the "sweat equity" workers had invested in nationalized companies during the 1980s, were probably what these papers' readers were most concerned about. Still, scandal sells newspapers and gives the opposition a club to use against the government, so the low profile given to possible shady dealings is surprising.

Foreign aid. It is estimated that between 1990 and 1995, Nicaragua received U.S.$3.2 billion in foreign economic assistance.[49] Though as much as 80 percent of this went toward debt service,[50] the country never-theless came to depend on these financial infusions. The Institute of Latin American Studies of the University of Stockholm reported in 1994 that "Nicaragua is a country completely dependent on foreign aid, not only to cover its budget deficit, but to finance domestic investment."[51] Another measure of its reliance on foreign aid comes from the World Bank, which estimated that 46.1 percent of Nicaragua's GDP, not just its budget but its total income, derived from aid.[52] To put this into perspective, no other Central American country got even 10 percent of its income from outside assistance, and to get proportions higher than Nicaragua's, one has to look at Rwanda or Mozambique. But it was neither the amount of aid received nor the conditions attached to the aid—nor even the government's depen-dence on donors' generosity—that aroused the most interest. That distinc-tion went to the politicization of American aid by conservative members of the U.S. Congress, most notably Senator Jesse Helms.

In considering this matter, we need to keep three things in mind. One is the symbolic importance of U.S. aid to the Chamorro government. President Bush had been one of Mrs. Chamorro's greatest supporters, and the restoration of American assistance had been one of the trump cards held by Chamorro in the campaign of 1990. The second is the actual dollar value of the aid and how its suspension affected the fragile Nicaraguan economy. Lastly, there is the role that Nicaraguan conservatives, members of President Chamorro's party, even of her administration, played in encour-aging the U.S. Congress to impede the flow of money to their own country.

Though some members of the Chamorro campaign team talked about getting $1 billion from Washington to jump-start Nicaragua's economy, in the new administration's first year, the United States actually approved $300 million in aid. The defeat of the Sandinistas and the progress made in peace talks in El Salvador, which would produce an accord by the start of 1991, moved Central America back toward its usual, less-significant place on the U.S. foreign policy agenda. Not all U.S. politicians lost interest, however. Thus, when two years had passed without the full de-Sandinization of the Nicaraguan state, Senator Helms convinced his fellow senators to freeze aid to President Chamorro's government.[53]

It was an official Senate report, authored by the senator's aide, Deborah DeMoss, and released 31 August 1992, that brought matters to a head. The document charged that Nicaragua was run by "Communists, terrorists, thugs, and assassins," implying, of course, that the Sandinistas still held effective power. Remedying this condition demanded, inter alia, replacing all former FSLN security forces with ex-contras; returning all properties confiscated from U.S. citizens—meaning everyone who was a U.S. citizen on the date the report was issued, not necessarily when the property was expropriated; and replacing all judges as part of a total overhaul of the judiciary. The Chamorro administration dismissed the charges as ludicrous, but it did move quickly to oust police chief René Vivas, a longtime Sandinista.[54] Though the accusations were ill-founded and the recommendations politically impossible for the Nicaraguan government to implement, they had their desired result as the undistributed portion ($104 million) of Washington's 1992 aid was withheld. Worse, from Managua's standpoint, this event established a precedent for setting political conditions on the release of U.S. assistance to Nicaragua, and the drama was played out again in 1994.[55]

Not only was this a psychological blow, but it was also economically important. Every dollar of foreign aid that Managua did not get it had to squeeze out of Nicaragua. In 1992, for instance, $104 million would have been just under one-fifth of the nation's expenditure budget. To put that into perspective, a proportional drop in revenues in the United States in 1992 would have been over $250 billion. Nicaragua would have to choose between paying down its debts more slowly, cutting more expenditures, dipping into its foreign reserves, or some mix of these to find the money. Whatever course it chose would harm the economy and cause more problems with the multilateral bankers who supervised the country's progress.

The most galling part of the whole affair for President Chamorro and her cabinet must have been the support radical UNO politicians gave the Helms initiative. Alfredo César, once a Chamorro loyalist, was the leading figure, joined by fellow deputy Humberto Castillo and Vice President Godoy.[56] Still, Mrs. Chamorro should not have been surprised. Ever since the United States became the final arbiter in Nicaraguan affairs after 1909, both governments and opposition factions in Managua have made their way to the U.S. embassy and even to Washington searching for support. As long as the U.S. government has not so much the power to influence events in Nicaragua, something it will possess for a very long time, but more so the seeming inclination to employ that power, it will remain the object of entreaties from the Nicaraguan political class.

The Bottom Line:
Nicaragua's Economy at the End of the Chamorro Years

Understanding the economic state of Nicaragua in the mid-1990s requires examining evidence from two sources. The first is composed of macroeconomic indicators that allow the comparison of Nicaragua and its Central American neighbors (see Table 5.7). Figures on growth, debt, trade balances, and income are straightforward enough to impart a sense of the country's relative economic condition. Equally unambiguous, even if not always measured as precisely as GDP, are the data on social conditions that form the second body of evidence.

Table 5.7 Comparative Macroeconomic Performance: Central America, 1990 and 1994

Country	Trade Balance (in millions U.S.$)		Debt (% GDP)		Growth (%)		GDP/Capita (U.S.$)	
	1990	1994	1990	1994	1990	1994	1990	1994
Costa Rica	−443	−606	65	55	0.9	2.1	1,924	114
El Salvador	−152	−18	40	27	2.8	3.6	1,034	1,202
Guatemala	−213	−638	34	24	0.2	1.1	857	892
Honduras	−93	−311	118	127	−2.9	−4.3	633	644
Nicaragua	−306	−524	508	632	−3.0	3.3	480	460
Panama	207	−519	107	71	6.0	1.1	2,216	2,620

Sources: Adapted from IABD, "Basic Socio-Economic Data"; and USAID, "Nicaragua."

Though no Central American country took off economically in the first half of the 1990s, Table 5.7 shows Nicaragua having the largest relative debt load and being the region's laggard in income per capita. For all its travails, however, the government in Managua did post economic performance numbers not appreciably worse than those of Honduras. Still, Nicaragua's income slide has not be halted, and it would have made no headway in reducing its debt had not substantial portions of it been written off by creditors; for instance, Russia forgave 80 percent of the loans extended by the Soviet Union.[57]

Yet these numbers do not tell the whole story. During the 1980s, while the United States financed a war against Nicaragua and imposed an embargo on the country after 1985, aid flowed freely to the other states of the region. Admittedly, El Salvador could not take full advantage of the assistance as it, too, was caught up in civil war, but Costa Rica and Honduras, and to a lesser degree Guatemala, benefited by receiving U.S. official development funds. They did not slide as far back as did Nicaragua, and even similarly war-ravaged El Salvador fared better. Though there is little question that President Chamorro's policies did not restore Nicaragua to full economic health, when her record is considered in the light of economic performance of the entire region, there appear reasons to temper one's criticism.

Turning from the more purely economic data to look at the country's social indicators, however, brings back the gloom. We can start by examining the Human Development Index numbers reported in the 1996 *Human Development Report* (Table 5.8).[58] Every Central American country except Honduras saw its HDI fall between 1990 and 1996, but in Nicaragua's case the decline was disastrous. Only Iraq experienced a similar fall,[59] and it had suffered a military defeat and was bound by UN trade sanctions. In Nicaragua the culprits were unemployment and underemployment and the generalized poverty they spawned.

With "poverty" defined as having to spend all one's resources to get the minimum daily caloric requirement (2,226 calories per adult), and "extreme poverty" defined as being unable to meet that daily requirement even by committing all one's resources to getting food, a joint UNDP–United Nations Children's Fund study carried out in 1993 made some startling discoveries.[60] Of 4,458 homes included in the survey, only 25.2 percent were classified as "not poor"; 31.2 percent were "poor"; and 43.6 percent lived in extreme poverty. Conditions were worst in rural areas, with the 41 percent of the country classified as rural providing 63 percent of the poor and 78 percent of the extreme poor. Some rural areas were particularly afflicted: 23 percent of Nicaraguans live in the Northern (Jinotega and Matagalpa) and Segovias (Esteli, Madriz, and Nueva Segovia) regions, but these zones produced 46 percent of the extreme poor.

Table 5.9 puts Nicaragua's plight in perspective, comparing its poverty data with those of the other countries of Central America. Though the numbers are slightly different from those in the UN survey cited above, the

Table 5.8   Central American Human Development Index, 1996

Country[a]	Global Ordinal Rank[b]	HDI[b]	Difference Between HDI and GDP Rankings
Canada	1	.951	6
United States	2	.940	0
Japan	3	.938	6
Costa Rica	31 (27)	.884 (.916)	23
Panama	43 (37)	.859 (.883)	0
Guatemala	112 (79)	.580 (.592)	−26
Honduras	114 (75)	.580 (.563)	7
El Salvador	115 (70)	.576 (.651)	−5
Nicaragua	117 (59)	.568 (.743)	−4
Somalia	172	.221	−10
Sierra Leone	173	.219	−20
Niger	174	.204	−17

Source: Adapted from UNDP, *Human Development Report, 1996*, pp. 135–137.
a. As with Table 5.3, Central American data exclude Belize, and the top and bottom three countries from the entire global ranking are included here for comparative purposes.
b. Numbers in parenthesis following the 1996 data represent points below 1990 rank.

Table 5.9   Poverty in Central America, 1993

Countries	Poverty(%)	Unemployment: Open + Underemployed (%)	Illiteracy (%)	Infant Mortality (per 1,000)
Costa Rica	17	21 (4 + 17)	7	13
El Salvador	50	55 (10 + 45)	28	51
Guatemala	76	39 (6 + 33)	49	54
Honduras	65	40 (9 + 31)	32	53
Nicaragua	70	62 (24 + 38)	28	60
Panama	50	58 (13 + 45)	10	21

Source: Adapted from *CAR,* 31 March 1995, p. 8.

picture is the same. Nicaragua has the worst unemployment and infant mortality figures in the region and the second worst poverty results. Whatever can be said about President Chamorro's economic policy, it is impossible to claim that it produced better numbers than those recorded by

Nicaragua's neighbors or that the policy substantially benefited the average citizen.

The World Bank's analysis of these data led it to criticize the government for not having a strategy to attack poverty. It also singled out the insecurity of land tenure, though it did not indicate whether it referred to individuals who had received land from the Sandinista agrarian reform or to those whose lands were redistributed in that reform. Finally, the Bank noted the problems of small and medium producers in getting credit and in dealing with the woefully deteriorated infrastructure of rural Nicaragua. It did not, however, suggest that its policy prescriptions could have contributed to the malaise.

Consistent with these poverty figures are estimates of combined unemployment and underemployment upward of 65 percent.[61] Regarding unemployment alone, a 1995 survey carried out by the Central American University in Managua reported 32 percent of Nicaraguans unemployed.[62] Contributing to the high levels of un- and underemployment was the closure of many small businesses. Antonio Chavez, president of Nicaragua's small business federation (CONAPI), argued in 1994 that of the 40,000 small businesses that existed ten years previously, only 6,000 were still operating.[63] The Chamorro years were at best years of recession that bordered on being years of depression for many Nicaraguans.

But why did the administration not do better as an economic manager? One would think that the technocratic Young Turks who filled the administration's upper ranks would have been Nicaragua's best and brightest, the very ones to chart a course to prosperity. Reflecting on their six years in power, we find that there was no single problem that defeated the policymakers, but rather a series of difficulties that came together to make sound economic management beyond the reach of President Chamorro's team. Part of the explanation that is easy to miss is that the heightened political conflict of 1990–1996 took so much of the government's energy that it was unable to look after the economy properly. This is doubtless true, but it nevertheless begs the question of why there was so much political conflict; it also ignores the point that economic distress likely fed at least some of the political turmoil. Oscar Neira identifies a second contributor: the SAP's fixation on reducing the external debt.[64] Overemphasizing this aspect of recovery drained so much liquidity from Nicaragua's economy that reactivation was impossible. And this leads to a final question: Why did the Chamorro government not work harder to alter the structural adjustment policies? A two-part answer is needed here. On the one hand, the economy the new administration inherited was so straitened that it had little bargaining room and effectively had to take what was offered. On the other hand, the absence of trained economists with prior government experience from

the upper levels of the administration might have played a role by effectively assuring that the government would not generate well-founded alternatives to the views of the multilaterals.

Conclusion: A Counterrevolutionary Political Economy?

Unquestionably, the economic policies of the Chamorro administration
were inspired by a desire to radically change Nicaragua's economy.
Carrying out the desired reforms meant nothing less than undoing most of
the economic work of the Sandinista revolution, though not quite all of it.
Though this course of action might not have been what many of those who
voted for the president in 1990 expected, it was the most logical path for
her to pursue. Besides reflecting the background and general ideological
disposition of the president and her advisers, Chamorro's economic policy
gave the world undisputable evidence that Nicaragua had reentered the
ranks of capitalist respectability.

What we forget in focusing on what Doña Violeta did is that Daniel
Ortega would doubtless have done many of the same things had he been
reelected. His government had mounted its own harsh austerity program,
albeit one even less successful than Chamorro's. And Daniel would have
faced an even more hostile group of international lenders. Though it is possible that an FSLN returned to power could have found ways around the
shoals that wrecked the Chamorro administration, a more likely scenario
would have been a choice between Cuban-style autarky and abandonment
of most of the economic ground the revolution originally gained. Though
the Sandinistas would certainly have labored diligently to save jobs and
find a property settlement that left the poor with secure titles, the political
economy of counterrevolution might have been Nicaragua's destiny regardless of who governed.

That being the case, it is pointless to criticize the Chamorro administration for following an austerity policy. A more legitimate target for comment and complaint is the content of the program and its application. In
particular, it is fair to target Nicaragua's dependence on foreign assistance.
Though this began under the Sandinistas, President Chamorro and her
chief minister, Antonio Lacayo, neither broke the pattern nor used the aid
they got particularly effectively. True, the conditions of its structural
adjustment agreements committed the government to paying down its
accumulated foreign debt. Yet there was very little evidence of planning
for a "postdebt" future by the administration. Had more thought been
given to what Nicaragua had to do to prosper in an international economy
far different from what it had been when the FSLN took power at the end

of the 1970s, the country might have had more to show for its years of suffering than low inflation, high debt, feeble growth, and generalized poverty.

Notes

1. Karl Polanyi, *The Great Transformation* (Boston: Beacon Press, 1944); cf. Andrew Gamble, *The Free Economy and the Strong State* (London: Macmillan, 1987).

2. For exceptions to this pattern, see any of the annual *Human Development Reports* published by the UNDP. The 1990 edition clearly sets out the notion of "human development" used in these publications; see UNDP, *Human Development Report, 1990* (New York: Oxford University Press, 1990).

3. For details about the economic system of Sandinista Nicaragua, see David Close, *Nicaragua: Politics, Economics, and Society* (London: Pinter Publishers, 1988), pp. 73–106. Much of the material in the present section comes from this book.

4. Melville Watkins, "A Theory of Staples-led Growth," in *Approaches to Canadian Economic History,* ed. W. T. Easterbrook and M. H. Watkins (Toronto: McClelland & Stewart, 1967), pp. 49–73.

5. John M. Talbot, "The Struggle for Control of a Commodity Chain: Instant Coffee from Latin America," *Latin American Research Review* 32:2 (1997): 117–135, provides some insight into this process.

6. ECLAC, *Statistical Yearbook for Latin America and the Caribbean, 1994* (New York: United Nations, 1995), pp. 58, 15, 53.

7. Paul Oquist, "The Sociopolitical Dynamics of the 1990 Nicaraguan Elections," in *The 1990 Elections in Nicaragua and Their Aftermath,* ed. Vanessa Castro and Gary Prevost (Lanham, MD: Rowman & Littlefield, 1992), pp. 7–10.

8. Ibid., pp. 7–8.

9. IADB, "Basic Socio-Economic Data."

10. UNDP, *Human Development Report, 1990,* p. 171.

11. Eliana Cardoso and Ann Helwege, *Latin America's Economy* (Cambridge, MA: MIT Press, 1992), p. 214.

12. The phrase is from Phil Ryan, *The Fall and Rise of the Market in Sandinista Nicaragua* (Montreal: McGill-Queen's University Press, 1995).

13. Alejandro Martínez Cuenca, *Nicaragua: Una década de retos* (Managua: Editorial Nueva Nicaragua, 1990), pp. 119–126, 229–230.

14. Ryan, *The Fall and Rise,* p. 166.

15. Martínez Cuenca, *Nicaragua,* pp. 129–144, 250–252; and Ryan, *The Fall and Rise,* pp. 206–215.

16. World Bank, *Social Indicators of Development, 1996* (Baltimore: Johns Hopkins University Press, 1996), p. 252; ECLAC, *Statistical Yearbook, 1994,* pp. 434–435.

17. Harry E. Vanden and Gary Prevost, *Democracy and Socialism in Sandinista Nicaragua* (Boulder, CO: Lynne Rienner Publishers, 1993), p. 99.

18. However, President François Mitterrand certainly came to power in 1981 with plans to radically reshape French capitalism.

19. Rather than attempt to review the extensive literature on structural adjustment, I shall simply list a short selection of works that can serve as a starting point

for further reading. Cardoso and Helwege's text, *Latin America's Economy,* introduces the elements of structural adjustment in chapters 5–7. Victor Bulmer-Thomas, *The Economic History of Latin America Since Independence* (Cambridge: Cambridge University Press, 1994), treats the theme in chapter 11. More specialized works include: Stephen Haggard and Robert Kaufman, eds., *The Politics of Economic Adjustment* (Princeton, NJ: Princeton University Press, 1992); Tony Killick, *A Reaction Too Far: Economic Theory and the Role of the State in Developing Countries* (London: Overseas Development Unit, 1989); Joan Nelson, ed., *Economic Crisis and Policy Choice* (Princeton, NJ: Princeton University Press, 1990); Adam Przeworski, ed., *Sustainable Democracy* (Cambridge: Cambridge University Press, 1995); and Gavin Williams, "Why Structural Adjustment Is Necessary and Why It Doesn't Work," *Review of African Political Economy* 60 (1994): 214–225.

20. Peter T. Bauer, *Dissent or Development* (London: Weidenfeld & Nicolson, 1972), and *Reality and Rhetoric: Studies in the Economics of Development* (London: Weidenfeld & Nicolson, 1984). Also, any World Bank *World Development Report* from the mid-1980s will present a similar view.

21. Adrian Leftwich, "Governance, Democracy, and Development in the Third World," *Third World Quarterly* 14 (1993): 605. See also the special issue of *IDS Bulletin* 26 (April 1995) dealing with the question of governance.

22. Nelson, *Economic Crisis and Policy Choice,* pp. 3–32, 321–361.

23. The Mayorga Plan is discussed in Oscar Catalan Aravena, "The Logic Behind the Stabilization Politics of the Chamorro Government in Nicaragua," in *Economic Maladjustment in Central America,* ed. Wim Pelupessy and John Weeks (London: Macmillan, 1993), pp. 41–52.

24. Quoted in Mark A. Uhlig, "Nicaragua Using a New Currency Pegged to Value of Dollar," *New York Times,* 16 September 1990, p. 8.

25. Richard Boudreaux, "Nicaragua Fires Author of Its Economic Plan from Central Bank," *Los Angeles Times,* 1 November 1990, p. A18. The settlement reached in the first tripartite economic negotiation included preferential water and electricity rates for low wage earners and a minimum wage sufficient to cover the cost of a basket of basic goods and services (*canasta básica*), all items that would slow anti-inflationary measures; see *CAR* , 2 November 1990, pp. 334–335.

26. This is implicit in Richard Stahler-Sholk, "Structural Adjustment and Resistance: The Political Economy of Nicaragua Under Chamorro," in *The Undermining of the Sandinista Revolution,* ed. Gary Prevost and Harry E. Vanden (New York: St. Martin's Press, 1997). The strikes themselves are described in Chapter 4 of this book.

27. Data for GDP and government deficit from USAID, "Nicaragua: Selected Economic Data," *USAID 1996: Latin American and the Caribbean Selected Economic and Social Data: Country Economic Data,* electronic ed. (8 August 1997), at: http://www.lanic.utexas.edu/la/region/aid/aid96/Country_Economic/niccen.html.

28. *CAR,* 5 April 1991, pp. 94–95.

29. This is the official rate just before the February 1988 devaluation. John Weeks, "The Nicaraguan Stabilization Program of 1989," in *Economic Maladjustment in Central America,* ed. Wim Pelupessy and John Weeks (London: Macmillan, 1993), p. 39n.

30. Stahler-Sholk, "Structural Adjustment and Resistance," pp. 87–88.

31. *CAR,* 27 September 1991, p. 287. The money was borrowed between 1960 and 1980. When the World Bank ceased making loans to Nicaragua in the early 1980s due to U.S. pressure, the Sandinistas stopped paying interest on the earlier

loans. It is worth noting that the Sandinistas started their time in office as heirs to a U.S.$2.1 billion foreign debt and empty coffers. Mrs. Chamorro's government certainly began no better off.

32. Trevor Evans, "Ajuste estructural y sector público en Nicaragua," in *La Transformación neoliberal del sector público,* coord. Trevor Evans (Managua: Latino Editores, 1995), pp. 191–193; cf. Angel Saldomando, *El retorno de la AID* (Managua: CRIES, 1992).

33. The recessionary tendencies built into Nicaragua's SAP are considered and criticized in the following: Adolfo Jose Acevedo Vogl, *Nicaragua y el FMI: El pozo sin fondo del ajuste* (Managua: Latino Editores, 1993); and Oscar Neira Cuadra, coord., *ESAF: condicionalidad y deuda* (Managua: CRIES, 1996).

34. Stahler-Sholk, "Structural Adjustment and Resistance," pp. 92–94.

35. Surprisingly little is written about the Paris Club. Relatively easily available sources are: Alexis Rieff, "The Role of the Paris Club in Managing Debt Problem," *Studies in International Finance, No. 161* (Princeton, NJ: International Finance Section Department, Princeton University, 1985); David Sevigny, *The Paris Club: An Inside View* (Ottawa: North-South Institute, 1990); and R. P. C. Brown, "IMF and Paris Club Debt Rescheduling," *Journal of International Development* 4 (1992): 291–313.

36. Harvey B. Feigelbaum and Jeffery R. Henig, "The Political Underpinnings of Privatization: A Typology," *World Politics* 46:2 (January 1994): 185–208.

37. The descriptive, technical material in this section comes from CORNAP, *Avance del proceso de privatización al 31 de diciembre de 1994* (Managua: CORNAP, 1995).

38. *NNS,* 12–18 March 1995, p. 3.

39. CORNAP, *Avance del proceso de privatización,* p. 54.

40. Ibid., p. 57.

41. Unfortunately, the data presented in the CORNAP report do not allow us to determine easily and with assurance which properties were restored to original owners.

42. This question is best covered by Evans, "Ajuste estructural y el sector público," pp. 241–258.

43. The 25 percent rule came out of the 1990 *concertación,* but it was not inviolable. Evans (ibid., p. 254) presents a table showing thirty-nine firms given over entirely to workers. But employees and their unions also had to fight to keep CORNAP and the government from reneging on promises to reserve portions of enterprises for the workers; see *CAR,* 20 November 1992, p. 352.

44. Information on La Fosforera is from *NNS,* 11–17 December 1994, p. 1; 12–19 December 1994, p. 3; and 25 June–1 July 1995, p. 3. That on Prego Soap is from *CAR,* 7 March 1992, pp. 81–82, and 17 July 1992, pp. 201–202. Specific data on the division of goods is from CORNAP, *Avance del proceso de privatización,* p. 58.

45. Trevor Evans, interview, Managua, 20 November 1995. This was confirmed by David Dye, Managua correspondent for the *Christian Science Monitor,* interview, Managua, 22 November 1995.

46. One Sandinista member of the National Assembly even spoke of a Somocista *piñata,* a Sandinista *piñata,* and a Chamorrista *piñata;* Julio Marenco, interview, Managua, 30 November 1995. *Envio,* the monthly publication of the Central American Historical Institute, noted the matter several times in 1995; for example, 14:167 (June 1995): 3–13, and 14:169 (August 1995): 3–9.

47. The problem is well treated by Daniel Kaufmann and Paul Siegelbaum,

"Privatization and Corruption in Transition Economies," *Journal of International Affairs* 50:2 (winter 1997): 419–458.

48. This is based on my personal observation of, first, the daily press, radio, and televison coverage during trips to the country in 1991, 1994, 1995, and 1996; and, second, what I saw reported in the biweekly *Barricada International,* the weekly *Nicaragua News Service,* and the monthly *Envio.* This is not to say that questions of malfeasance regarding the privatization of state properties were not raised, only that they occasioned less comment than I expected.

49. *NNS,* 4–11 June 1995, p. 3.

50. *NNS,* 16–22 January 1994, p. 3.

51. Quoted in *CAR,* 7 October 1994, p. 8.

52. World Bank, *World Development Report, 1997* (New York: Oxford University Press, 1997), pp. 214–215.

53. This section draws on *CAR,* 12 June 1992, p. 162; 3 July 1992, p. 189; 16 September 1992, pp. 273–274; 2 April 1993, pp. 92–93; 23 April 1993, p. 107; 6 August 1993, p. 227; 17 August 1994, p. 94; and *NNS,* 9–15 August 1993, p. 8; 13–19 September 1993, p. 4; 28 November–4 December 1993, p. 5; 20–26 February 1994, p. 4. See also *New York Times,* 4 June 1992, p. A9; 3 September 1992, p. A3; 12 April 1993, p. A16; 13 February 1994, p. I3; and 25 July 1995, p. A7. Longer analyses are found in *Envio* 11:133 (August 1992): 3–10; 11:134 (September 1992): 3–8; and 12:143 (June 1993): 4–10.

54. Vivas was replaced by Fernando Caldera, another Sandinista from within the ranks of the police, but one who did not prompt such a strong reaction.

55. Senator Helms assumed a slightly different role in Nicaraguan politics in 1994 by taking up the claims of U.S. citizens seeking compensation for property expropriated by the revolutionary government. This is treated in Chapter 6 in the context of the property question.

56. Godoy had been isolated from the beginning by the administration and became a leading spokesperson for the anti-Sandinista hard-liners. César had led an unsuccessful attempt in 1991 to force the president's hand on the property issue and would in late 1992 attempt a coup from within the legislature.

57. Germany and Venezuela each forgave 90 percent of Nicaragua's debt, and the United States wrote off about $900 million in arrears; *CAR,* 27 September 1991, p. 287, and 5 March 1993, pp. 60–61.

58. UNDP, *Human Development Report, 1996* (New York: Oxford University Press, 1996).

59. Ibid., p. 136; cf. UNDP, *Human Development Report, 1990,* p. 129.

60. Data on poverty are drawn from World Bank, "Nicaragua: Poverty Assessment Summary," *Summary of Poverty Assessments Completed in Fiscal 1995,* electronic ed. (7 August 1997), at: http://www.worldbank.org/html/hcovp/povertyfy95pa.html; and "La pobreza en Nicaragua," *El Observador Económico* 43 (July 1995): 24–28.

61. World Health Organization and Pan-American Health Organization, "Datos basicos socioeconomicos: Nicaragua, 1996," *Datos Basicos Nicaragua,* electronic ed. (7 August 1997), at: http://www.ops.org.ni.

62. *Mesoamerica* 14:10 (October 1995): 9–10.

63. *NNS,* 16–22 January 1994, pp. 4–5.

64. Oscar Neira Cuadra, "El ESAF y la transición política en Nicaragua," in *ESAF: Condicionalidad y deuda,* coord. Neira Cuadra.

6

The Big Issues:
The Constitution
and Property

Two political questions above all others preoccupied President Chamorro's administration. One, reforming the constitution, nearly paralyzed the Nicaraguan state during much of 1995. The other, the handling of claims for property expropriated by the Sandinista, not only vexed the government throughout its time in office, but also provoked an attempted coup in the National Assembly. Neither of these issues is truly representative of the problems the Chamorro administration faced, thus they give a somewhat distorted picture of the government at work. Their importance lies in the fact that the acute conflict that arose over the constitution and the more protracted dispute over property policy each held the potential to destroy Nicaragua's tentative progress toward democratic consolidation. And even though the crises associated with these conflicts did not put an end to democracy, they certainly affected its development.

The Constitution and the Constitutional Crisis

We have already observed that President Chamorro began governing under the 1987 constitution that was wrought by the Sandinistas. That instrument gave exceptional powers to the executive and conferred on the state a central role in economic management, while still managing to keep much of the form and substance of liberal democracy. It was sufficiently flexible to permit the Chamorro administration to function adequately for three years. But when the government showed signs of losing its grip over the country in 1993, there were calls from across the political spectrum to restructure the state.

What Constitutions Are and What They Do

It is conventional to think of constitutions as doing three things.[1] First, they provide a statement of the principles on which the state is founded or which it seeks to secure. For example, the U.S. Constitution was instituted to "establish justice, ensure domestic tranquility, provide for the common defense, promote the general welfare, and secure the blessings of liberty." The objective of Canada's constitution is to provide "peace, order, and good government." These principles, usually contained in a preamble, are the goals of the elites who draft the constitution. And it is an elite that composes a constitution, even when the resulting package must be approved by the whole citizenry. Constitutions are complicated legal instruments that treat matters of limited interest to most people.

A second feature common to all constitutions is that they establish a basic legal framework for the state. They set out the respective rights and duties of governors and those governed, often in the form of a charter of individual rights and liberties. These documents also define the scope of the state's authority by indicating those areas in which government is authorized to act. This will also include specifying who is authorized to act and under what conditions, thus identifying the principal officers of the state. Constitutions further define the territorial structure of a state: whether it is federal or unitary, as well as simply identifying the geographic zones into which the nation is divided for administrative ends.

Closely related to providing a basic legal framework for the exercise of public power is a third function of constitutions: they serve as a power map. Constitutions routinely describe not just who holds what authority, but also the processes that must be followed in exercising that authority. They may indicate what a president must do to declare a state of emergency, how a parliament passes a law, or the proper procedures for holding elections. All constitutions of course provide for their revision, often setting out in some detail an amending formula. In all instances it will be harder to change a country's constitution than its ordinary legislation, because a written constitution is the organic law of a state, the very foundation of its legal existence.

Putting these three general attributes of constitutions together produces the picture that most people have of constitutional government: a government of laws, not of men. There are known procedures for making laws, established means for applying them, and recognized mechanisms for contesting a law or its application. Citizens of the world's historic constitutional democracies all share this perspective. But not all countries belong to this class. Many, Nicaragua unfortunately among them, have histories in which constitutions were either nonexistent, unobserved, or revised constantly to provide a patina of legitimacy to whatever the ruler of the day had decided to do.

It is, I believe, important to bear in mind when examining the battle that arose over efforts to amend Nicaragua's 1987 charter that the country does not draw on a long tradition of constitutionalism. It is equally important to recall that the constitution being reformed was the Sandinistas' handiwork, designed to institutionalize their revolution. Thus this was not a constitutional document revered as is the U.S. Constitution or even respected and accepted as is its counterparts in Canada, Costa Rica, or India. At best, it would be judged according to its utility, its efficacy as a problem solver. At worst, it would be thought a partisan document that had to be removed and replaced by one of equal partiality, although benefiting a different party.

Beyond this, there is the complication that President Chamorro's accession to power marked the beginning of a new regime. Regime transition received extended treatment in Chapter 2, so it is only necessary to present a simplified sketch of the concept here. Essentially, a new regime brings a new basis of political legitimacy (e.g., by election); imposes a different system of accountability (i.e., the manner by which and to whom government answers for its acts); changes the pattern of influence over and access to governors; and revises the relationship among the state, citizens, and civil society. It changes the basic rules of the political game, sometimes so much so that someone accustomed to the old rules will be unable to play by the new ones.

A government representing a new regime will want to change the old constitution for a variety of valid reasons. It will, first, want to mark the demise of the old system with a clear, legal monument. Beyond that, the new regime will have its own priorities that differ from those of its predecessor and will want its standards to have full constitutional status. The simplest, yet often most pressing, reason is that the old regime's constitution may not let the new government do the things that it feels are necessary. In the case of President Chamorro's government, the 1987 constitution was usable, and indeed the administration would defend some of its provisions fiercely, but significant elements of the Nicaraguan political elite saw it as an impediment to creating their preferred political system. As was too often the case in Nicaragua between 1990 and 1996, however, different parts of that elite put forward conflicting and irreconcilable visions of what that preferred system should be.

The Context of Crisis and the Prelude to Reform

Some of the factors that combined to cause the crisis that precipitated a push for far-reaching constitutional amendments were born with the new government. An obvious contributor was the absence of elite consensus that underlay the failure of the political class to conclude a viable foundational pact. Absent an accord concerning the character and purpose of Nicaragua's new political order among those who would direct the state, any serious problem the government encountered would be the pretext to call for its resignation and the imposition of new rules, instead of banding together to preserve peace or even trying to fix whatever had gone wrong. To this we must add the ambiguous mandate of the UNO and the divisions within the alliance that arose over how to interpret 1990's victory. Earlier chapters have examined some of the consequences of these obstacles to unity (Chamorro's early conflicts with the UNO caucus in the National Assembly over the budget, for example). Three years into her term, the president had not found a recipe for reconciling the dissidents in either her party or society as a whole.

Exacerbating these partisan and ideological antagonisms were the results of the government's frequently ineffective administration. Although inflation had been subdued by 1993, economic recession still gripped the country. Strikes and labor problems went on unabated. Violence, crime, and the challenges to governability that came with them continued ravaging the land. As the constitution did not provide for midterm elections, there was no immediate, legally sanctioned way to bring new forces and fresh ideas into the political fray. Therefore, when Nicaragua witnessed an unparalleled eruption of savagery (reciprocal hostage takings) and chaos (a debilitating and bloody transport strike) in mid-1993, it was evident that the existing governing formula was exhausted. Unless another was found quickly, increasing ungovernability loomed large.

The initial response came after the September 1993 strikes ended. As was becoming customary, the first attempted step was to call for a national dialogue among all the main political players. Like the *concertaciones* on economic issues held under both the Ortega and Chamorro governments, national dialogues brought government together with nongovernmental actors in the search for solutions to pressing problems. Political summitry of this sort can be useful. When all works right, a national consensus can emerge that focuses enormous energy toward addressing critical issues. Even when dialogues collapse or do not achieve their potential, government can gain some credit for seeking solutions and it will be able to blame its opponents for any failures. However, continued resort to extraordinary congresses suggests that the state lacks ordinary institutions able to manage society's problems. And institutionalizing *concertaciones* and dialogues, making them part of the normal pattern of governing, carries its own complications, because these top-level consultations are by their nature opaque in operation, leaving those involved in them free from the ordinary constraints of accountability.

Against this background there began to form a group of like-minded politicians in the legislature, led by the small Christian Democratic Union

(UDC) of Luís Humberto Guzmán. Guzmán, a German-trained political scientist, first came to public attention in the 1980s as a member of the Popular Social Christian Party, a radical offshoot of the older Social Christian Party. The PPSC and some of the PSC joined the UNO, and Guzmán was elected to the National Assembly in 1990. What distinguished him from most of his fellow Unistas was that he came to appreciate the institutional debilities that held the potential to undermine Nicaragua's progress toward constitutional democracy. As 1993 drew to a close, other deputies joined the drive to amend the constitution.

Though Guzmán and increasing numbers of legislators were to form the vanguard of effective constitutional reform, they were not the first to make a political issue of the constitution. The conservative elements of the UNO, joined by Cardinal Miguel Obando y Bravo and some individuals from big business, had called for a constitutional convention even before the 1993 crisis.[2] By the time the legislature decided to take up amending the constitution, however, the right had seen much of its political base disappear. Moreover, the presence of a Democrat in the White House meant that Washington would not be sympathetic to proposals with the potential to destabilize Managua's fragile experiment in liberal democracy. Thus, constitutional reform in Nicaragua would be carried out by and in the National Assembly, much as the original 1987 document had been drafted.[3]

The assembly was the constitutionally prescribed (Articles 191–192, 194–195) venue for amending, though not rewriting, Nicaragua's constitution. Still, the fact that the changes wrought in 1995 amounted to a substantial revision of the constitution that benefited the legislature may seem suspicious. There were doubtless conflicts of institutional interest, but these probably would have arisen even if a special assembly had been convened to draft a new constitution. Moreover, it is not certain that a drafting convention would have reflected the array of national interests any more accurately than the National Assembly did. Add to that the extra costs that the country would have had to bear to elect the delegates, plus whatever expenses maintaining a constituent assembly would have brought, and the practicality of using the legislature is manifest. Finally, since neither the president nor the vast majority of the legislature wanted a constitutional convention, constitutional change would come from the National Assembly of Nicaragua or it would not come at all.

The actual process of revision began late in 1993.[4] Reacting to the political crisis that had been growing in the country since July of that year, the UNO and the FSLN agreed to discuss a national dialogue that would involve the constitution. When these discussions broke down in mid-November, the UDC was ready to present its package of constitutional amendments. The timing was propitious for the forces of change. The FSLN was altering its policy of supporting the administration, because the president had forced Humberto Ortega's resignation as military chief of staff. Moreover, the UNO's leadership, especially its Political Council, had alienated many of its Assembly members by, first, banishing from its ranks any party supporting the UDC initiative, including the UDC proper, and then demanding that the legislature's executive committee order all the parties that had broken with its line in the past to return to the fold. As a result, the reformers faced little opposition in the chamber.

The First Steps

Before the 1993 session of the legislature ended in mid-December, the National Assembly had begun setting out a complex package of over 100 amendments. These can be grouped into five classes:[5]

1. *property rights,* including compensation for expropriated property;
2. *national defense,* covering abolishing the draft and renaming the military;
3. *political rights,* mainly focused on guaranteeing that soldiers could vote;
4. *economic matters,* stipulating that privatizations and international economic undertakings would henceforth have to be passed by the National Assembly;
5. *state reforms,* the longest and most important section, proposing increasing the legislature's role in key appointments, forbidding the reelection of the president, and excluding close relatives of the incumbent president from succeeding to that office.

More important in the short term, the chamber passed an amendment to Articles 192 and 195 to permit in the future the amendment of the nation's constitution by a 60 percent majority in a single session. The existing wording of those articles called for amendments to be passed by a 60 percent supermajority in two consecutive sessions of the Assembly, for example, in 1993 and then again in 1994. Returning to work after Christmas, the National Assembly revised the amending formula, but fortunately, President Chamorro refused to sign the measure. Had she done so, constitutional amendment would have become ridiculously easy and the constitution reduced to something hardly better than an ordinary piece of legislation.

By April 1994, what would become a long battle between the executive and legislative branches of Nicaragua's government was joined. The Assembly approved a bill exempting school supplies and medicines from the regular 15 percent sales tax. The executive's reaction went beyond the expected criticism of the legislature's openhandedness with government revenues to stake a remarkable claim. Article 150.4 of the 1987 constitution conferred on the president the highly unusual authority to issue fiscal decrees. The standard in constitutional democracies, of course, is that all fiscal matters (taxing, spending, or setting tariffs) fall solely within the purview of the legislature, and the executive cannot undertake financial actions not previously approved by the legislature. Chamorro and her advisers, however, asserted that only the president was constitutionally empowered to deal with fiscal issues. Thus they argued that the Assembly was trenching on executive jurisdiction in adopting a tax measure. Curiously and disturbingly, there was little response from the press, certainly nothing like the beating a U.S. president would get for proposing even a timid foray into the fiscal powers of Congress.

What drew both more attention from the media and more fire from the executive were the amendments that defined the conditions of presidential succession. Nicaragua, like too many of the world's poor countries, has seen presidents amend the constitution to permit their perpetuation in office. If a chief executive found that course unpalatable, putting up a close relative to watch things for a term was a common alternative. As a result, many Latin American constitutions forbid at least the immediate reelection of a president; some limit her or him to one term with no reelection; and some exclude close family members from succeeding one another in the chief executive's office.[6] The National Assembly's amendment package made immediate reelection impossible and also excluded close relatives from following immediately in the footsteps of their kin.[7] The memory of the Somoza dynasty obviously was part of the inspiration for this restriction, but the possible succession of one Ortega brother by another and of Mrs. Chamorro by her son-in-law, Antonio Lacayo, doubtless also figured in some deputies' calculations.

In the end, it was only Lacayo who was directly affected by the prohibition. He would fight the ban fiercely, but would lose when the Supreme Electoral Council decided on the merits of his case in 1996. Since the polls showed Lacayo with the support of less than 5 percent of the electorate, his case raised a significant political question: Did Nicaragua need this sort of familial exclusion? Arguing in its favor is the interrelatedness of the Nicaraguan elite, described by Carlos Vilas,[8] and the country's experience with the Somozas. Against this one can assert that in a democracy it should not matter if a president is succeeded by his or her sister and that a constitutional inhibition will not dissuade a dictator from doing what he or she wishes. At the heart of the issue is whether a country like Nicaragua can become a stable, habitual democracy without a rule to guard against one family dominating politics.[9]

The key issue in this batch of amendments, then, was the relative powers of the executive and the assembly. David Dye, a reporter with long experience in Nicaragua, wrote that this was an attempt to reduce the powers of the country's president to the Latin American norm.[10] Even Daniel Ortega, who would come to oppose the reforms within a year, lauded them on their introduction. He declared them "a leap forward in the country's democratization because a balance between the branches of government will be attained and greater stability and joint administration through consensus will be possible."[11]

The executive saw things differently. Tomás Delaney, the president's chief adviser on legal matters, objected to losing financial powers, as it would limit the administration's capacity to make economic policy.[12] The World Bank and the International Monetary Fund also opposed strengthening the legislature's economic jurisdiction, as both preferred to deal with governments whose executive held the decisional authority necessary to enact tough austerity policies quickly. And though President Chamorro made a point of not criticizing the consanguinity prohibitions, Lacayo and his wife once mooted the possibility of divorce to let him run for the nation's highest office.

In September 1994, the National Assembly set to work to pass the reforms. This was the first significant constitutional reform initiative ever to have come from a Nicaraguan legislature, and the chamber set about to assure that everything was done well. First, it struck a special committee of eleven members, including some originally opposed to the project. To assure the widest consultation possible, the committee held hearings in all of the country's sixteen departments during October 1994, taking evidence from forty-five different organizations.[13] It reported to the house on 15 November 1994, and the plenary accepted the report in principle two days later. On 24 November, Assembly president (speaker) Guzmán announced that the house would not adjourn until the amendment package was passed. At 1:30 A.M. the next morning, the National Assembly adopted by a vote of 70 to 0, with two recorded abstentions, the last of sixty-five amendments to twenty-one articles, about half what had been in the original proposal a year before. The legislature then turned to consider the budget and other ordinary business until the 1994 session ended in December.

Returning in January 1995 to start a new session, the National Assembly reelected Guzmán as its presiding officer. On 3 February, the legislature passed the bill amending the constitution in the second consecutive annual session and with the required 60 percent majority (64-0-0, twenty-eight deputies were not present).[14] But the new law would take effect only when it was published, and President Chamorro had indicated no disposition to do so. Before examining the details of the crisis that convulsed the country from February to June 1995, we should look more closely at the constitutional reforms that caused all the trouble.

How the Assembly's Amendments
Changed Nicaragua's Constitution

What emerged from the National Assembly's year of work was a constitution that fit post-Sandinista Nicaragua better. Numerous elements of the 1987 document had become functionally dead letters, because they were obvious and intimate parts of the apparatus of a revolutionary state. Changing these to give the constitution greater real applicability was important and uncontroversial. More contentious were the changes that would affect parts of the constitution that, though very much part of a revolutionary regime's political logic, were used daily by the conservative Chamorro government. And the bitterest disputes involved attempts to include the executive branch in a system of real checks and balances. Although it is possible to criticize the content of individual amendments, even claim that the whole enterprise was mean-spirited and motivated by personal ambition, a dispassionate reading of the central reforms leads one to conclude that the revised constitution is a far better instrument for securing the rule of law, *el estado de derecho,* that Violeta Chamorro promised Nicaraguans.

Rather than analyze all sixty-five amendments, some of which received only cosmetic changes, I shall examine only those reforms that transformed the constitution in a fundamental way. These critical changes are grouped to reflect their effects on the three functions of a constitution that were noted earlier: stating principles; establishing legal bases, and mapping power.

Basic principles. The principles in question are those of the Sandinista revolution. Though the preamble remains unchanged, still recognizing the works of Sandino, Carlos Fonseca, and the "Heroes and Martyrs of the Revolution," the section defining the state's fundamental principles was revised. The changes mainly "derevolutionize" the document's language, but they also add a specific recognition of the rights of indigenous communities "to maintain and develop their identity and culture, have their own forms of social organization, . . . and maintain their communal forms of property" (Article 4). And while Article 68 still recognizes a social role for the mass media, the amended version explicitly denies the state the right of prior censorship, a trait shared by both the Sandinista and Somocista systems.

Some of the other changes that reflect the new philosophical foundations of the Nicaraguan state are subtle. For instance, Article 56 still deals with veterans' affairs, but where once the focus was EPS veterans and their families, the state is now obliged to offer assistance to all "victims of war." Similarly, the constitution retains six articles on agrarian reform, but two

(106 and 107) have been changed to no longer speak of "revolutionary transformation" and to ensure that due process is followed in expropriating "idle lands" for redistribution. Along the same lines, Article 104 no longer demands that "the economic plans of enterprises be prepared with the participation of workers."

Perhaps the most noticeable amendments were those concerning national defense (Articles 92–97), one consequence of which was changing the military's name from the Sandinista Popular Army to the Nicaraguan Army. This is now defined as a professional army, just as the National Police (formerly the Sandinista Police) is now a professional police force, instead of a revolutionary one. Especially striking is the change in Article 96. In the 1987 constitution, this article defined a citizen's duty to bear arms; but since 1995, it outlaws conscription and forced recruitment. Despite the depth of the changes, there was little opposition to these reforms. The FSLN objected only to revisions that it saw imperiling the democratization of property it brought about during its decade in office.

Legal bases.   The legal effect of the amendments falls into three different categories: legal and civil rights, property rights, and qualifications for candidates for public office. Under the first rubric, one finds a fuller elaboration of the conditions that must be met to justify a search without a warrant (Article 26); a reduction in the time a suspect can be held without being charged from seventy-two to forty-eight hours (Article 33.2.2); and a clearer double-jeopardy provision (Article 34.10). Article 71, which deals mainly with the right to form and maintain families, was amended to include a definition of children's rights.

The new Article 44 guarantees the right of "private" property, where its predecessor spoke of "personal" property. The distinction between the two forms of property is that the former includes "moveable goods and real estate, and the instruments and means of production"; the original referred to "essential and necessary goods for the integral development of the person." Moreover, the reformed article prohibits the confiscation of property but also speaks of the possibility of expropriating, with due compensation (*justa indemización*), real property when the public good requires it. Though not entirely a matter of property rights, the revised constitution does indicate that the state and its employees can be held responsible for damages attributable to them (Article 131), something not contemplated in the Sandinista constitution.

Finally, the 1995 amendments define a new set of qualifications for officeholders. Articles 134 and 147.4 set residency requirements for deputies and the president and vice president, respectively; Articles 134.4.1 and 147.4.f[15] demand that those holding executive office at any level resign that post before running for national office. More far reaching is the series of disqualifications contained in Article 147.4.a–g. Some, like the exclusion of ordained ministers or those who renounced Nicaraguan citizenship, were uncontroversial. However, Articles 147.4.a and 147.4.c created a great stir, because of their obvious political implications. The first prohibits the immediate reelection of a president and limits an individual to two terms as chief executive. The second article lays out the consanguinity exclusions: no one related to the incumbent president by blood within the fourth degree (second cousin) or by marriage within the second degree (immediate in-laws) may even stand for election. Article 130 pursues a similar purpose by prohibiting the appointment of close relatives by any official in any branch of government, though here the aim is more to curb nepotism than to prevent the monopolization of executive power.

Power map.   Potentially more consequential than any of the above were the amendments recasting the balance of power between the legislative and executive branches of Nicaraguan government. The National Assembly granted itself the right to sufficient funding from the national budget (Article 132). It also granted itself the power to approve treaties and international economic agreements, for example, with the World Bank (Article 138.12). Though it had previously been able to call members of the executive to appear before it, the Assembly now has the legal power to compel them to come (Article 138.4). As well, it increased its control over the appointment of Supreme Court justices, magistrates of the Supreme Electoral Council, and the controller general (Articles 138.7–138.9). Regarding appointments, both the legislature and the president are to submit lists of names from which the legislature is to choose. If, however, the president does not submit a list, the Assembly's suffices.

Interestingly, the National Assembly did not seek to remove the president's line-item veto. It did, though, curb the president's de facto and unlimited pocket veto. Previously, the president had been allowed to neither sign nor veto a bill, but rather do nothing in the hope that the Assembly would make the changes she wanted. Article 142 now gives the speaker of the National Assembly authority to deem a bill passed and order it published if the president has not acted on the measure after fifteen days.

The executive's losses were as impressive as the legislature's gains. Article 150.4 was amended to remove the president's right to tax and spend by decree. In fact, before 1995 the Nicaraguan president's decree powers were virtually limitless, because she could issue decrees on any topic, at any time, even with the legislature in session less than a block away from her office.[16] Nor was the decree power confined to details, for the Central Bank Act was the product of a decree (Decree 46-92), as was the law establishing enterprise zones (Decree 46-91) and that establishing the Nicaraguan Women's Institute (Decree 36-93). Further, where previously the president assumed full legislative powers whenever the National Assembly was not in session, now the president has only the right to ask the speaker to recall parliament (Article 150.7). The president also lost the authority to reorganize the state (e.g., creating or dissolving agencies or ministries) by decree; Article 151 stipulates that this be done by legislation. And the president also lost the right to approve the national budget herself, should she have declared a state of emergency (Article 185). Even the transitory measures (Article 21 of the bill) hobbled the executive: the amendments would take effect when published in any print media, not just *La Gaceta: Diario Oficial* (the Nicaraguan Official Gazette). This last point would precipitate Nicaragua's constitutional crisis of 1995.

Institutional Deadlock

Given the restrictions the National Assembly's amendment package placed on the executive as an institution and on President Chamorro and Antonio Lacayo as individuals, the president's reluctance to sign and publish the measure is understandable. Nevertheless, after passing its amendments on 3 February 1995, the Assembly made it clear that it expected to see these changes published within fifteen days. Chamorro took the position that the reforms approved by the legislature went beyond the simple amendment of the constitution; therefore she would not order them published. Rather, she would hold out for a national dialogue, perhaps as a surrogate constitutional convention, where the executive would have more friends and be able to undo some of the chamber's work.

Under normal circumstances the president and the Assembly would have tested their claims before the courts. However, a significant obstacle precluded choosing this course in February 1995. The amended constitution reorganized the country's Supreme Court, increasing its membership from seven to twelve and setting up four *salas,* or divisions, one of which specialized in constitutional matters. As the president did not recognize the Assembly's amendments, and as the Assembly held that its version of the constitution was now the law of the land, each branch effectively acknowledged a different Supreme Court. Even had the two sides agreed to accept the jurisdiction of the unreformed Court, nothing would have happened, because it did not have enough members for a quorum. And each branch had its own version of the proper procedure for naming Supreme Court justices. That is how Guzmán came to publish the amendments on 24 February 1995 in two newspapers: the independent, left-leaning *El Nuevo Diario* and the Chamorro family's *La Prensa.*

Nicaragua now had two constitutions. The executive stood by the 1987 document, saying that any amendments had to be negotiated before the president would accept them. The Assembly, holding fast to its version, claimed that only implementing legislation, perhaps deferring the entry into effect of the consanguinity provisions until after the 1996 elections, could be discussed. Legally, the National Assembly was right, because it had followed the rules laid down in 1987 for amending the constitution. Politically, the executive had the upper hand, because a constitution rejected by one-half of a country's government was not going to solve anybody's problems.

To attempt to break the impasse, five countries offered their good offices. This "Group of Friends" (Grupo de Apoyo) was made up of Canada, Mexico, the Netherlands, Spain, and Sweden. Besides the five official members, the U.S. ambassador maintained a discreet but important presence.[17] Though Washington could not take an active role without eliciting cries of intervention, all parties knew that U.S. approval would be needed for any deal to have a chance of success.

The first meeting arranged by the Group of Friends on 24 March 1995 brought agreement that President Chamorro would finish her full term, foreclosing any possibility of early elections. Otherwise, little progress was made. In fact, things took a turn for the worse in early April as the assembly acted unilaterally to fill the vacancies on the Supreme Court with its appointees. A month later the executive's case got a welcome boost when the Court, still without a quorum, ruled to sustain a motion filed in February in a district court and invalidated the amendments. In its decision the Court ordered the president to publish the reforms to make them valid, but it set no date by which this was to be done. For its part, the legislature ignored the whole affair, claiming the Court was powerless to act without a quorum. So the stalemate dragged on further into May, raising concerns that Nicaragua would be unprepared to meet with its principal donors on 19 June to discuss the renegotiation of its debt.

A last-ditch effort to come to an accord started in late May. Sponsored by the Group of Friends, with Cardinal Obando serving as moderator, and with the donors' meeting looming, these talks finally brought an end to the country's constitutional schizophrenia. On 15 June, an agreement was reached that would see the amendments published in *La Gaceta,* in return for which the Assembly would pass a Framework Law to spell out how and when the amendments would take effect.

The Framework Law was, in itself, an interesting bit of political engineering.[18] Among its thirty-two articles were provisions to defer the application of nepotism rules until January 1997 and, rather more significant, undertakings by the legislature to cooperate with the executive on certain issues. For example, the National Assembly agreed not to raise spending above the limit set in the executive's budget. It also committed itself to draft certain key bills with the executive to assure their broad acceptability and to work with the executive to establish a joint list of nominees for the Supreme Court, the CSE, and the controller general.

Outcome: A Step Toward a Governing Consensus?

Nicaragua now has a constitution that holds more promise for the construction of a constitutional democracy. A less powerful executive, a representative assembly with more usable authority, and citizens' rights defined in ways that are more plausibly enforceable all are desirable attributes of a liberal democratic state. But Nicaragua cannot yet confidently be counted a constitutional democracy. In constitutional democracies all—ordinary citizens, senior civil servants, elected politicians—expect the rule of law to prevail. At bottom that means that policymakers, elected and appointed, work on the assumption that it is easier, not just morally better, to operate within the framework of the constitution than to do what "must be done" and legalize the details after. This in no way implies being bound by every word in a constitution as if it were sacred: ways must often be found around cumbersome provisions in order to secure the commonweal. Rather, it connotes an acceptance that public policy must be made transparently and according to commonly known rules.

Arriving at that point can take a long time.[19] Part of the reason for this is that constitutional norms have to develop. Norms are not the same as laws. They are expectations that people will behave in certain ways and that institutions will operate in certain ways. Such expectations are not enforceable by law, but they do have the weight of political sanction behind them.

The agreements struck in the Framework Law could have laid the foundation for a series of such norms in Nicaragua. They identified questions about which the two policy-initiating branches of government had to seek consensus. Further, the very fact of agreeing to compromise on matters of deeply held principle—here the proper balance of power between the executive and the legislature—constituted a turning away from the winner-take-all politics that had marked the country's past. To appreciate the significance of this development, one only has to recall the chaos that gripped Nicaragua during the months when the legislature and the president were at loggerheads. Had either side stuck to its guns and refused to negotiate, Nicaragua's progress toward constitutional democracy could have been stalled, even reversed.[20]

Perhaps if serious electoral campaigning had not started almost immediately upon adoption of the Framework Law, the nation's politicians could have begun establishing patterns for relations between the executive and legislature that would have been oppositional but not disruptive. This would have put political flesh on the bones of the constitution and given it greater meaning. Constitutionalism might have come to denote particular paths to follow when grave conflicts beset the country. Time, however, did not permit this, and the constitution was still a political instrument, though an important one, at the administration's close.

Yet the constitutional reforms initiated by the National Assembly do mark a step toward forming a governing consensus. A "National Front to Defend the Amendments," organized in February 1995, included Cardinal Obando y Bravo, former Sandinista cabinet minister Carlos Tunnerman, ex–Vice President Virgilio Godoy, and conservative political commentator Emilio Alvarez Montalván. This is a broader cross section of the country's political class than that which supported the 1990 Transition Accords.[21] Equally, the opponents of the package—the administration and the FSLN— did sufficiently suspend their reservations to accept the revised document. Unfortunately, even had the constitutional amendments been fully and enthusiastically received by all parts of the Nicaraguan community, the property question was still there to divide the country.

The Property Issue

With the fall of communism in the former Soviet bloc, the question of the disposal of state property loomed large on the agendas of post-Marxist governments. In the main, the central issue has been how to privatize the all-encompassing holdings of the state. The problems that have arisen include corruption, inability to sell some of the worst firms, and coping with administrative problems, such as those accompanying the distribution of shares to all citizens. These are certainly real and vexatious problems, but they are very different from those that came with the property question in Nicaragua.

What President Chamorro had to confront that her Central and Eastern European peers generally avoided was expropriated owners returning to claim their patrimony. In Europe time disposed of most of these claims. During more than forty years of Communist government, properties were repeatedly subdivided and transformed, and many of the original owners had died. The time period in Nicaragua, however, was ten and one-half years at most, and in the majority of cases less than that. People still remembered their old homes or businesses and had not so remade their lives in their places of exile that they harbored no desire to return to Nicaragua to take up the threads of the past.

But properties in Nicaragua, too, had been broken up and redistributed. Large ranches and plantations came to be owned by cooperatives or numerous small farmers. Land in a city that an investor had held for future development was home to hundreds of poor families. And though a commercial firm might still be in existence, its workers might deem themselves the real owners thanks to the sweat equity they had accumulated over a decade. In short, there were others besides the original owners with claims to the expropriated properties. The government could not simply return all expropriated holdings to those from whom they had been taken without regard to the estimated 170,000 families who now occupied those properties.

Making the task of the government and the lives of those occupying property awarded them by the revolutionary government more difficult was the Sandinistas' disregard for property law. Ernesto Castillo argues that this was not an oversight on the part of the FSLN, but rather a reflection of its disdain for the bourgeois institution of landed property: the Sandinista state was managing a transition to socialism that would make property rights (e.g., to use the property as collateral for a loan or to sell it) obsolete.[22] By refusing to imagine that they might fall from power, during their lame-duck period (26 February to 24 April 1990) the Sandinistas had to patch together legislation (Laws 85, 86, and 88)[23] ceding title to those who had received land or houses from the revolution—what became known as the *piñata*.[24] But this did not register the titles or quiet the claims of original owners, leaving the latter a legal basis for their claims.

Moreover, the property redistributed by the Sandinista state had come into its hands by a variety of mechanisms. Decree 3 (20 July 1979) seized all the goods of the Somoza family, soldiers, and officials of the old regime who fled the country. Nineteen days later, Decree 38 (8 August 1979) extended the confiscations to include "persons linked to somocismo," a broader and less-well-defined category. Then 1981 brought Decrees 760 (the Abandonment Law) and 782 (the Agrarian Reform Law), which allowed the expropriation of abandoned and idle or underutilized farm properties.[25] Urban properties came into the possession of the revolutionary state in 1979 through Decree 97 (Law of Illegal Land Divisions) and in 1991 via Decrees 895 (Law Expropriating Unused Urban Lands) and 903 (Law Expropriating Vacant Lots in the Center of the City of Managua). Beyond these measures there were also purchases (later claimed by the sellers to have been made under duress) and de facto recognitions of occupations of property.[26] Though Decree 3 was widely accepted as just, later land reform statues found notably less general approval.

In all, 5,968 rural properties, covering 2.8 million *manzanas* (4.9 million acres), were obtained; and there were 11,244 occupants of urban houses and 90,260 occupants of urban lots.[27] While President Chamorro's counterparts in Central and Eastern Europe were dealing with more property, the Nicaraguan administration still faced an enormous task. Even if all with claims to the property involved, present occupants and original owners alike, acted with restraint and in good faith, sorting out those claims was sure to tax, if not overload, the administrative capacities of a poor country emerging from a prolonged internal war. But since many of the claimants, especially though not only the former owners, were not disposed to be patient, no easy solution was in sight.

President Chamorro's Initial Approach

On 11 May 1990, President Chamorro issued two decrees that were the basis for her first property policy. Decree 10-90 provided for the privatiza- tion of all land and industries owned by the state or by cooperatives. These properties, which had formed the Area of Peoples' Property, had produced roughly 40 percent of Nicaragua's national income in 1989. As the sale of state-owned enterprises had become common in all capitalist societies, this action was expected and had little immediate bearing on the claims of expropriated property holders.

More pertinent to the property question was Decree 11-90, the Decree- Law for the Review of Confiscations. This transferred jurisdiction over the return of or compensation for properties from the courts to the attorney general.[28] Beyond that, it set up the National Commission to Review Confiscations (CNRC). This commission, composed of the attorney general and four other presidential appointees, was charged with "proceeding with the review of all the confiscations carried out by the past government . . . that in one form or another deprived natural or juridical persons of their goods, rights and shareholdings, respecting the rights of peasants, coopera- tives that fulfill their social and economic function, and of the underprivi- leged."[29]

Despite the CNRC's assurances that it would respect the rights of cur- rent occupants and its promise to abide by Decrees 3 and 38, there was con- siderable mistrust of the commission. Peasants saw it as an instrument for orchestrating a full-scale rollback of the agrarian reform. Their suspicions were fueled by the rash of attempts by former owners to evict peasants with agrarian reform titles and by UNO-backed invasions of Sandinista coopera- tives.[30] Police figures for 1991 show that 71 of 220 land seizures involved cooperatives; in 1992, the proportion fell to 18 of 162.[31] And the behavior of the CNRC in its first two years of operation unfortunately confirmed these forebodings, since the commission "ordered the return of 2,200 prop- erties, frequently without determining the circumstances of any existing occupation of the land."[32]

Not all land invasions were organized by the former owners. A good many were carried out by ex-contras, impatient for the land the Chamorro government had promised them and not hesitant to try taking it from their old Sandinista enemies.[33] Of course, the Sandinistas resisted, and blood began to be shed. The most troubling aspect of the violent conflict over land tenancy concerned the use of public security forces to dislodge peasants from land to which the latter claimed to hold titles confirmed by Law 88 of 1990.[34] This was an unwelcome reminder of the Somoza years when the National Guard was regularly used against the population.

Given the problems attending the president's first choice of instruments to address the property issue, she may not have been entirely displeased when the Nicaraguan Supreme Court struck down parts of Decree Law 11-90 in May 1991. The Court held that the transference of judicial responsibilities to the executive (i.e., letting the CNRC order the return of lands to their original owners) trenched on the judiciary's authority. In commenting on the decision, Chamorro reaffirmed her government's position that peasants who received land from the Sandinistas would get their titles and that "those who lost property unjustly would not be left without an answer."[35]

To provide that answer, the president issued Decree 35-91 on 19 August 1991. This set up the Office of Territorial Reordering (OOT). The OOT's job was to review all titling done under Laws 85 (urban houses) and 86 (urban lots) and to be part of an interinstitutional commission to review titles granted under Law 88 (rural lands). If the OOT found that an occupant's title was valid (that the person had only one property and had occupied it before 25 February 1990), it issued a *solvencia*.

A *solvencia* is not a title but a legal instrument that could be used to register a property and get a title. To get a *solvencia,* however, the occupant had to go to the OOT and make a case to receive that document. Failure to do so would leave the way open for prosecution and possible eviction. The process, though logical and reasonable to anyone familiar with legal proceedings, may have put the poor recipients of land and dwellings from the revolution at a disadvantage.[36] The Chamorro administration developed other administrative mechanisms to address the problems arising from conflicting claims to property, but before any of these devices really got a chance to work the National Assembly issued its own, more dramatic, solution.

Alfredo César's Legislative Coup

The National Conservative Party (PNC), one of several Conservative splinters in the UNO, introduced a bill in May 1991 to repeal Laws 85 and 86. This was indeed a drastic initiative, because it threatened all those occupying more than 100,000 pieces of property covered by the two laws. To express their discontent, the FSLN caucus walked out of the National Assembly in June. Other Sandinistas took more vigorous action to show their displeasure, bombing the office of Vice President Godoy and seizing the building housing Radio Corporación, Nicaragua's premier right-wing radio station.[37]

Attempting to preserve order, the president referred the issue to a *concertación* that brought together the government and representatives of both the political right (COSEP, representing big business, and the Congreso Permanente de Trabajo [CPT], a group of conservative unions) and the left (the FNT, the militant labor front, and UNAG, a Sandinista-affiliated farmers' group) to discuss the property issue. On 15 August, all but COSEP agreed to leave all properties expropriated before the 1990 election with their current occupants but to review those distributed during the two months between the election and President Chamorro's inauguration. With the property it had distributed secure, the FSLN returned to the legislature on 20 August. However, on 23 August, the party again walked out when the assembly, led by its president, Alfredo César, passed Law 133, which repealed all three Sandinista property laws.[38]

In their place, the UNO majority in the legislature proposed a complex scheme distinguishing between small and large holdings that provided a partial model for future legislation. More specifically, the law provided that urban properties valued at under the equivalent of U.S.$11,600 would be titled to their current occupants. Property worth more than that would have to be bought at its full market price or returned to the original owner; an estimated 5,000 units, about 5 percent of all properties covered by Laws 85 and 86, were affected. Rural properties under 45 *manzanas* (roughly 75 acres) would not be touched, but larger farms would be confiscated and returned to their former owners. Owners who did not get their property back would be paid by the state.

Law 133 would have been difficult to administer. Assessing the values of the urban properties would be difficult because there was not yet a well-established real estate market in the country. It is curious, therefore, that the Assembly ignored the proposal of the 1991 *concertación* to use house size to establish a cutoff point. Classifying rural property would not be much easier, because the lands assigned in the agrarian reform had never been properly surveyed. That about one-fourth of the land registers in the northern and central parts of Nicaragua had been destroyed during the war only added to the problem.

In the end, the president used her veto, claiming that the legislature was invading her jurisdiction. But just three weeks later, she withdrew her veto in return for an undertaking on César's part to negotiate a compromise. The speaker complied, sensing that he did not have the votes to override. Less than a year later, however, the same bill was back.

What was perhaps the strangest and most perilous occurrence of President Chamorro's term, even surpassing the "two constitutions" episode of 1995, began as a squabble in mid-1992 between the Sandinista and UNO legislative caucuses over the filling of two posts on the assembly's executive committee, the Junta Directiva.[39] César, still the chamber's presiding officer,[40] delayed holding elections for replacements because it was likely that his supporters would not win. To protest the speaker's dilatory tactics, the thirty-nine Sandinistas and eight Centrists (deputies who had defected from the UNO to support Doña Violeta, although it meant voting with the FSLN) walked out. The forty-seven boycotters made up over half the assembly's members, leaving the legislature unable to muster its constitutionally mandated (Article 141) quorum (46/92). The FSLN and Centrists returned to the house after a tidal wave devastated Nicaragua's Pacific coast on 1 September; however, they withdrew the following day when they saw that César was still maneuvering to gain the JD seats for his faction. This time, though, the speaker would not be denied and convened his own rump parliament with the forty-five remaining UNO members.

The FSLN and Centrists brought suit against the illegal Assembly and won a court order, but the UNO appealed it. While the matter was before the courts, César manufactured a quorum by the unconstitutional mechanism of calling the alternates of the boycotting Centrist deputies.[41] This let the UNO pass once more the property law vetoed by Chamorro a year earlier, this time assured it could override her veto. On 30 September, the day after the legislature passed a decree giving the JD the authority to name substitutes (not necessarily the elected alternates) for absent legislators, President Chamorro declared she would not recognize the legality of any National Assembly proceedings since 2 September. A Supreme Court decision in November found all the rump parliament's actions null and void, for want of a legal quorum. The president then likely exceeded her constitutional authority by dismissing the JD that had led the legislative coup, but its members were ill-placed to argue points of constitutional law. No more unilateral attempts to settle the property problem came forth from the National Assembly.

Property Issues in the Second
Half of President Chamorro's Term

In the wake of the chaos that accompanied attempts to solve the property puzzle through 1992, Doña Violeta's administration began relying on slower but surer methods built around the OOT. In 1992, the government reactivated the CNRC to determine whether compensation should be given to the original owners and added an Office for the Quantification of Indemnizations to set levels of compensation. These revised structures did regularize property proceedings and reduce the tensions that originally surrounded the issue. By 30 September 1996, 92.61 percent of the 12,415 cases associated with Law 85 had been treated; 81.11 percent of the 106,128 cases arising from Law 86; 90.83 percent of the 10,011 cases based on Law 88; and 72.02 percent of cases involving compensation or return of properties to the original owners.[42] However, titling lagged far behind, meaning that there was still potential for conflict. The administrative record, moreover, obscured the political battles fought along the way.

The crux of the property problem was always that there were expropriated owners who either would settle for nothing less than the return of their property or else wanted a generous cash settlement for losing their houses and lands. Though some properties were illegally occupied, even according to the 1990 Sandinista laws, thus making possible the eviction of the tenants, most were not. Any sensible government would blanch at the prospect of dislodging more than 100,000 families from their dwellings, even in a political climate less polarized than Nicaragua's. Yet any but a very rich government would be equally nonplussed by the challenge of finding the cash to compensate the old owners.

In Nicaragua the cost of such a buyout is usually estimated at U.S.$500–600 million, about one-third of the nation's annual GDP. Thus, the government had no realistic alternative to issuing bonds. It hoped that the *confiscados,* the ex-owners, would accept the bonds because they could either be held, cashed, or used to buy other state properties being privatized. But what sort of bonds could an impoverished state issue that would retain their value well enough to satisfy expropriated property holders? Unless this problem was resolved, no lasting settlement of the property dispute would be possible.[43]

An additional complication arose in 1994 when the U.S. Congress adopted the Helms-Gonzales amendment to the Foreign Assistance Act.[44] As discussed previously, Senator Helms, a Republican from North Carolina, adopted the cause of the anti-Sandinista Nicaraguan right as his own when it became evident that President Chamorro was not going to purge the revolutionaries from Nicaragua's public life; so he was a natural choice to defend the interests of Americans who had lost property to the Sandinista government. The bill he co-sponsored with Representative Henry Gonzales, a Texas Democrat, requires Washington to both suspend aid and vote against loans by IFIs to a country that has seized the property of U.S. citizens, unless the U.S. president certifies that the country has adopted policies to return or pay adequate compensation for that property.

The amendment is unusual in that it applies to people who were not U.S. citizens at the time their property was expropriated. International law generally limits a state to pressing claims for those who were its citizens when they lost their holdings. Yet most (69 percent) of the claims by U.S. citizens were filed by Nicaraguans who became naturalized Americans after fleeing to the United States. Because these claimants have the backing of the U.S. government, they not only stand to get preferential treatment, but also hold out for the terms they want, making the Nicaraguan government's job tougher.

The National Assembly acted in 1994 to make the bonds the government was offering more attractive by raising the interest they paid, but this was not enough. In an attempt to negotiate a way to a lasting property settlement, former U.S. President Jimmy Carter co-chaired the Property Issues Conference with former Prime Minister George Price of Belize in July 1995.[45] The conference brought together the main players in the property conflict: the government, the National Assembly, groups of *confiscados* and those who now held property, the Supreme Court, and political parties with an especially strong interest in the matter.[46] Although there was some disagreement, a general consensus emerged that those with small houses or plots of land should be protected. There was broad agreement that those who received larger properties should pay the full value of their holdings if they wished to retain them. The key accomplishment of the conference was reaching agreement on compensation for those who could not regain their properties. Money raised from the privatization of TELCOR, the telecommunications monopoly, would go to buy U.S. Treasury bills, to be placed in trust to back the compensation bonds. This, it was hoped, would make the bonds more desirable and lead more ex-owners to take them, drop their claims, and let life move toward normality.

President Chamorro had indicated several times during her tenure that she did not want to pass the property conundrum on to her successor. So she must have been pleased when, building on the foundation laid at the Property Issues Conference, the National Assembly passed Law 209 in November 1995. The Property Stability Law recognized *constancias* (documents acknowledging legal occupancy of property that were granted before a title is issued) and agrarian reform titles as provisional titles, thereby giving those who held them greater legal security. It also assured that those holding small properties (e.g., houses with a floor space of less than 100 square meters) would not have to make extra payments to receive their titles, though those with larger properties would. Finally, the law stipulated that those who could not recover properties expropriated by the revolutionary government would receive bonds.

Important though the details of the bill are, it is the fact of its passage that is most significant. That the assembly approved Law 209 shows how far the country had gone on the road to constitutional democracy since 1990. Earlier attempts to settle the property question were unilateral impositions. These episodes of in-your-face politics succeeded only in stiffening the resolve of the Sandinista opposition to make no concessions. By 1995, however, the prevailing view of what constituted good, workable politics had changed, and a property bill was passed that satisfied all of Nicaragua's key political players.

Law 209 was supposed to be the *punto final,* the last word, on the property controversy. It was not, for the debate started anew in President Alemán's term. Why and how this happened, and how the renewed dispute was yet again settled, will be considered in more detail in the concluding chapter. I raise the fact that the apparently sensible Law 209 did not provide a lasting solution to the property issue because it underscores the centrality of this question in Nicaraguan political life. Until some form of closure of the property debate is secured, Nicaragua will not be able to move on to other pressing concerns.

Final Thoughts

Either of the two political issues reviewed in this chapter could have brought the Chamorro administration down. Equally, either could have prompted Doña Violeta's government to abandon peaceable, legal paths in favor of authoritarian practices that would have halted the slide into disorder. That the president served her full six-and-one-half-year term and did so without recourse to states of emergency must be scored a significant accomplishment. What is more, it is an accomplishment as much for ordinary Nicaraguan citizens as for the president.

The Chamorro government really offered ordinary people very little in a material sense. It did, though, hold out the promise of the eventual establishment of predictable, peaceful rule. President Chamorro, with the very notable exception of the constitutional imbroglio, was usually on the side promoting peace and reconciliation. Even if her policies produced hardship and conflict, she was the one Nicaraguan public figure who generally steered clear of inflammatory discourse.

Whether most Nicaraguans recognized this and consciously decided to stick with the president or whether they simply could not or would not muster the energy for another political crusade makes little difference. When elites with projects opposed to the president's could not mount substantial popular support, they had few options. In other countries or in Nicaragua at other times, they might have turned to the security forces to strengthen their hand. But despite strongly partisan tinges, both the army and the police remained fundamentally politically neutral and worked to make themselves into professional services.

By avoiding breakdown, the Chamorro administration left the country a better constitution (though entirely against the government's wishes) and an emerging common ground on what to do about expropriated property.

These results were not obtained by brilliant statesmanship: there was a lot of luck and a lot of muddling through involved. One must, however, recognize that President Chamorro did learn from early reverses and did accept defeats with as much grace as a politician can command. A president more determined to be a "leader" might have pushed confrontation too far and led the country only into greater disaster. One might wonder if a male president would not have been more prone to histrionics, grand gestures, and drawing lines in the sand, thus to conclude that the fact that President Chamorro was a woman was critically important. It would not, however, take long to arrive at the cases of Prime Minister Thatcher and Prime Minister Ghandi and realize that presidential character and judgment are not related to gender.

Notes

1. In this section I am referring to written constitutions, that is, single documents that serve as the legal foundation for a state. Among modern constitutional democracies only Israel and the United Kingdom do not have such a foundational charter.

2. For one of several incidents where Chamorro's conservative opponents called for her removal and a new constitution, see *Mesoamerica* 11:9 (September 1992): 8.

3. There was one significant difference between the two constitutional processes. In assembling the package formally adopted in 1987, the FSLN used an extensive series of public consultations to test public reaction to and generate public support for its provisions. The National Assembly did not adopt this method in the period from October 1993 to February 1995, when it was considering its amendments. Rather, it struck a special committee. Though there was consultation, it was done more fully within the institutional context of the legislature.

4. The descriptive material bearing on constitutional reform is drawn from issues of *CAR, Mesoamerica, Envio,* and *NNS,* between October 1993 and July 1995, unless otherwise indicated.

5. *Barricada,* 29 November 1993, pp. 1, 12.

6. The constitutions of Argentina, Brazil, and Peru, for instance, have been amended since 1990 to permit presidential reelection. In Argentina, and even more so in Peru, these changes were the work of powerful presidents with strong personal followings.

7. The exclusions were to the fourth degree of relation by blood and the second degree of relation by marriage.

8. Carlos Vilas, "Family Affairs: Class, Lineage, and Politics in Contemporary Nicaragua," *Journal of Latin American Studies* 24:2 (1992): 309–344.

9. Small political classes make familial exclusions potentially problematic. Two of Costa Rica's last three presidents have been the sons of earlier presidents, though neither succeeded his father directly. Carrying a famous family name may have assisted Rafael Angel Calderón and Jose María Figures in their political endeavors, but it does not seem to have unduly influenced the Costa Rican electorate; indeed, they defeated Calderón twice before electing him in 1990.

10. David Dye, "Nicaragua Opens Era of Reform," *Christian Science Monitor,* 14 December 1993, p. 6.

11. Quoted in *Barricada,* 30 November 1993, p. 12.

12. Dye, "Nicaragua," p. 6.

13. Asamblea Nacional de Nicaragua, *Memorial legislativa, 1994* (Managua: Editorial el Parlamento, 1994), pp. 4–5, 16, 62. As the executive opposed the whole reform process, it would have been difficult to hold more extensive consultations. Further, the National Assembly was starting to use itinerant committees for important measures in 1994, so the Comisión Especial Dictaminadora del Proyecto de Reforma Parcial de la Constitución Política de la Republica, the committee's official name, was an integral part of the legislature's institutional development.

14. The earlier proposal to permit the amendment of the constitution with a 60 percent supermajority in only one session, which President Chamorro had indicated she would veto, was not carried over into the 1994 package.

15. The inconsistent numbering, that is, having both a 147.4.g and a 134.4.1, is in the original.

16. Luís Humberto Guzmán, the National Assembly's president from 1994 to 1996, indicated to me that the executive consciously and consistently refused to grant the legislature exclusive jurisdiction in any field (interview, Managua, January 1998). Though this may have been a holdover from the days of the Council of State, which recognized the executive as a fully qualified co-legislator, it also sounds remarkably like the royal prerogative, that is, the rights the crown exercises on its inherent authority until parliament acts to curtail them.

17. A Latin American diplomat told me in October 1995 that Canadian ambassador Paul Durant, actually stationed in San José, Costa Rica, was instrumental in the negotiations. The diplomat also added that John Maisto, the U.S. ambassador, played a crucial role in persuading the Chamorro administration to accept provisions of the new constitution it found unpalatable.

18. There is a good treatment of the Framework Law in *Envio* 14:169 (August 1995): 3–9.

19. And simply getting there is no assurance that later governments will not relapse into unconstitutional ways. Citizens of Canada and the United States, both consolidated constitutional democracies by any standard, can count too many instances of illegal governmental actions, running the gamut from improperly let contracts to state-sanctioned spying on citizens engaged in perfectly constitutional political activities.

20. I want to thank Michael Wallack for this observation.

21. The Transition Accords are treated in Chapter 2.

22. Ernesto Castillo, "The Problem of Property and Property Owners," *Envio* 16:196 (November 1997): 38–39.

23. Law 85 gave property rights to those occupying houses belonging to the state. Law 86 applied to those occupying urban land. In both cases no individual or family could occupy more than one house or lot, and the occupants had to hold their house or lot as of 25 February 1995. Law 88 converted agrarian reform titles, which were usufructuary and not possessory, to definitive titles conveying full property rights.

24. The *piñata* is discussed in Chapter 2.

25. "Idle" was defined as uncultivated for at least two years; "underutilized" applied to farms where less than 75 percent of their suitable land was in production or was not being grazed intensively enough. Details may be found in David Close,

Nicaragua: Politics, Economics, and Society (London: Pinter Publishers, 1988), pp. 90–99.

26. Excellent summaries of the property question are found in J. David Stanfield, "An Analysis of the Current Situation Regarding Land Tenure in Nicaragua," report prepared for the Swedish International Development Authority, November 1994; Latin American and Caribbean Program, Carter Center, "Nicaraguan Property Disputes," report prepared for the UNDP, April 1995; Ricardo Guevara Carrión y Javier Matus L., "Analysis de la situación actual de la tenencia de la tierra en Nicaragua," unpublished manuscript, April 1996. I wish to thank Dr. Alvaro Herdocia of the UNDP in Nicaragua for making these materials available to me.

27. Stanfield, "An Analysis," p. 2; Latin America and Caribbean Program, "Nicaraguan Property Disputes," p. 14.

28. It is interesting to note that Chamorro relied on Article 150.4 of the 1987 constitution, which gave the president decree power in "fiscal and other matters," for her authority to issue Decree 11-90. The rationale for shifting jurisdiction over the property process to the executive was that the courts, especially the Supreme Court, were filled with Sandinista appointees.

29. Republica de Nicaragua, *Decreto-Ley No. 11-90,* 11 May 1990, Article 1.

30. *CAR,* 7 September 1990, p. 267.

31. Nicaragua, Government of, Ministerio de Gobernación, Policía Nacional, *Comendio estadístico: 1991–1995* (Managua: Policía Nacional, 1996), p. 126.

32. Latin American and Caribbean Program, "Nicaraguan Property Disputes," p. 14.

33. For more details, see Chapter 4.

34. *CAR,* 31 July 1992, p. 219; the article reports on several expulsions.

35. *CAR,* 31 May 1991, p. 156.

36. The OOT and its performance receive consideration in Stanfield, "An Analysis," pp. 8–12, and in Latin American and Caribbean Program, "Nicaraguan Property Disputes," pp. 17–21.

37. *CAR,* 12 July 1991, pp. 201–202. It should be noted that the two sites attacked are relatively close together, both located in the Ciudad Jardín neighborhood of Managua. Though this is a long way from the government's administrative complex, Godoy kept his office here, in the building belonging to his Independent Liberal Party, because President Chamorro never assigned him space in any of the executive's offices.

38. Material on the 1991 property crisis comes from *CAR,* 30 August 1991, p. 254; *Mesoamerica* 10:9 (September 1991): 6–7, and 10:10 (October 1991): 10; and *Envio* 10:124 (November 1991): 17–18.

39. The section on the "legislative coup" follows David Close, "Nicaragua: The Legislature as Seedbed of Conflict," in *Legislatures and the New Democracies in Latin America,* ed. David Close (Boulder, CO: Lynne Rienner Publishers, 1995), pp. 62–64.

40. In 1991, the assembly changed its internal regulations to give all JD posts a two-year term. In 1993, these were changed back to one-year posts.

41. Every Nicaraguan deputy is elected with an alternate, whose name also appears on the ballot, who will replace the deputy should he or she resign, become incapacitated, or die before the next election. In fact, Nicaraguan practice, established in the case of Daniel Ortega, recognizes that a deputy who just wants to do something besides sit in the house can hand the seat over to his or her alternate and then reclaim it when he or she so wishes.

42. Ricardo Guevara Carrión y Javier Matus L., "Avances en la solución al problema de la propiedad: Situación al 30 de septiembre de 1996," draft document for the UNDP in Nicaragua, 1996, p. 3.

43. Ricardo Guevara Carrión y Javier Matus L., "El sistema de bonos en Nicaragua," report prepared for the Swedish International Development Authority, 1994, is a thorough treatment of the bonds question by an economist.

44. Carter Center, Latin American and Caribbean Program, "Nicaraugan Property Disputes," p. 10.

45. This section draws on the Carter Center, *Report on a Property Issues Conference,* 1995.

46. These political parties were the FSLN of Daniel Ortega, the MRS of Sergio Ramírez, the Liberal Constitutional Party of Arnoldo Alemán, and the National Conservative Party, which first introduced the repeal of the Sandinista property laws.

7

Ending the Chamorro Years: The 1996 Elections

On Sunday, 20 October 1996, Nicaragua held extremely problematic and controverted elections.[1] There were allegations of fraud, grave and obvious administrative flaws, and charges that the Roman Catholic hierarchy was guilty of overt partisanship. Yet there were no casualties, other than badly bruised reputations. In other settings that might have been enough to qualify the elections as a successful step toward democracy. Nicaraguans, however, had seen better. They knew that what they had been part of was not democracy working as it should.

Eventually, Arnoldo Alemán was elected president, taking a majority of the votes cast. His coattails, however, were not long enough to give his party, the newly formed Liberal Alliance (AL), which brought most of Nicaragua's Liberals on to one ticket, a majority in the National Assembly. The AL still emerged the largest party in the house, and more significantly, the FSLN took less than 40 percent of the seats, meaning that it could not block constitutional amendments by itself. Local elections, featuring directly elected mayors for the first time, were made more interesting by the presence of candidates running for local parties, not affiliated with any of the national organizations. Only one of these won, though, because in most municipalities fewer voters than expected strayed from their national preferences. Despite twenty-four parties or electoral alliances running for national offices, twenty-three of which contested the presidency, the 1996 Nicaraguan election was really a head-to-head, two-party fight between the AL and the FSLN (see Table 7.1).

Post-Transition Elections

Nicaraguans had good reason to be disappointed by the 1996 elections, even if their favorite party and candidates won. Under the Sandinistas, the

Table 7.1   Nicaraguan General Election Results, 1996

Registered voters	2,421,067
Ballots cast	1,865,833
Turnout	77.07%
Spoiled ballots	4.95%

Presidency: Parties with more than 1 percent of the vote	Number of Votes	Percentage of Votes
AL/Arnoldo Alemán	904,908	51.03
FSLN/Daniel Ortega	669,443	37.75
CCN/Guillermo Osorno	72,621	4.10
PNC/Noel Vidaurre	40,096	2.26

National Assembly of Nicaragua: Parties winning seats	Number of Seats	Percentage of Votes
AL	42	46
FSLN[a]	37	36.5
CCN[a]	4	3.7
PNC[a]	3	2.1
Proyecto Nacional (Pronal)	2	2.4
MRS	1	1.3
Nicaraguan Resistance Party (PRN)	1	1.2
Unity Alliance (Unidad)	1	0.8
PLI	1	0.7
UNO 96	1	0.6
National Conservative Action (ANC)	1	0.6

Central American Parliament: Parties electing deputies	Number of Seats
AL	9
FSLN	8
CCN	1
PCN	1
Pronal	1

Parties electing mayors	Number of Mayors
AL	91
FSLN	52
MRS	1
Local Parties	1

Sources: Council of Freely Elected Heads of Government, *The Observation of the 1996 Nicaraguan Elections* (Atlanta, GA: Carter Center, Emory University, 1997), pp. 60–63; and Telematix, Web site, at: http://www.tmx.com.ni/elecciones.
    a. Assembly delegation includes defeated presidential candidate.

country had organized two honest, open, and efficiently run contests. The first of these, in 1984, was not fully competitive, because several parties boycotted; but it was free, fair, and well administered.[2] In the 1990 elections, all parts of the system worked well and no one questioned the vote's honesty, since the incumbents lost.[3] The electoral authority, the Supreme Electoral Council, was competent, experienced, and professional. Whatever one's partisan views, there were grounds for believing that the one part of Nicaragua's governmental machinery that would be a strong, fully consolidated democratic instrument after the elections was the CSE.

Political science has said surprisingly little about "post-transition" elections, those held subsequent to the vote that ushers in the first avowedly constitutional democratic government. And what does exist projects from initial elections as much as it analyzes subsequent votes. However, the treatments that are available focus on two themes. The first concerns the administration of elections.[4] The second is the evolution of the party system, particularly what happens to the profusion of parties that contest the transition election.[5]

Electoral machinery and administration have to be part of this analysis. When the initial election returning constitutional democrats conforms to procedural standards acceptable in consolidated representative democracies, there is naturally a tendency to expect later elections to follow suit. Yet this confidence may be misplaced. A government could have organized "showcase" elections to prove to the world that it could hold honest elections. Or, more positively, it may simply have made an exceptional effort to mount meaningful elections. For example, in her study of Panama, Margaret Scranton reports that former Panamanian Vice President Ricardo Arias Calderón "joyfully exclaimed, 'We held a Costa Rican election!'"[6] She then notes that "subsequent tests will be required before the strength of the new institutions and procedures can be adequately assessed, much less taken for granted."[7]

How might this logic be applied to Nicaragua? In the case of the two Sandinista elections, it appears on reflection that the state put significant resources at the disposal of the electoral authorities and allowed them to carry out their professional mandate freely. It was essential that the revolutionary government do all that it could to guarantee clean elections, because so many, above all those in Washington, were so skeptical. But Chamorro's victory in 1990 changed all that.

With the exception of her most conservative compatriots and their U.S. allies, no one questioned the new president's democratic bona fides. So there was less reason to pay such strict attention to the CSE, the Electoral Law, and the other elements of electoral administration. When we examine in detail the causes of misfeasance in the 1996 elections later in this chapter, we shall indeed see that a combination of more partisan structures, a tight time frame, and scarce resources contributed greatly to the problems. This sort of "slippage" happens in other countries, too, as campaign finance scandals in the United States and Great Britain in 1997 make manifest. Obviously, democrats should not take fair and good electoral machinery for granted, even from one election to the next.[8]

Political parties constitute the other element to receive attention. Elections in a democracy are not just about machinery or campaign monitoring. People have to vote for or against something, and that something is almost always a party. It makes good sense that transitional elections see numerous parties in the fight, for there will not be established lines of partisan division or deeply seated patterns of partisan choice. Moreover, the promised emergence of a new regime will tempt many "political entrepreneurs" to try to make their names through parties of their own creation. The situation's fluidity results in an openness that does not exist at other times.

Arthur Turner's work on this question indicates that an explosion of parties is normal in "postauthoritarian" or transitional elections. For example, in 1974, Greek voters chose among 46 parties and 1,425 candidates. Spanish voters in 1977 found 161 parties. And there were 363 parties in Japan in 1946, 184 with only one member. In his analysis Turner discovered that parties did disappear in later elections and that the ones most likely to fail were those taking only a small proportion of the vote in the first place.[9]

Post-transition attrition among political parties, then, is a natural enough phenomenon. The weakest, who win nothing, will confront large debts, empty bank accounts, and the painful realization that the public did not care much for them. Those somewhat better off, by virtue of having a seat or two in the legislature, may find that advancing their program, which may be equivalent to their leaders' careers, demands merging with a larger party or several other small ones. This process will be accelerated where the electoral system works against fractionalization, for example, by setting a threshold vote that must be passed to gain representation, or where legislative rules decree that caucuses of less than a specified size cannot receive funds or other perquisites.

Assuming that there are enough parties seriously contesting elections to give voters sufficient choice,[10] thinning the ranks of parties should be accounted a good omen for consolidating democracies. On a crass material level, fewer parties will generally mean that the state will have to spend less money to mount elections. Ballots will be simpler, TV and radio time easier to allocate, and less public money will have to go toward financing campaigns. Where there is not state financing of election campaigns, these considerations do not apply, but most new democracies do support political parties with public money.

Having fewer parties to choose among can also help voters. A profusion of vanity parties (vehicles to promote an individual's career by making him or her a party leader) raises the possibility that voters will find the election too confusing or annoying and abstain. Proliferating parties can also make it harder for voters to focus on the issues that really concern them. A dozen or more parties, all receiving free media time and state funds to mount campaigns, make lots of noise and certainly remind voters that an election is under way; but their contribution to democratic government is questionable.

Finally, though this admittedly shades into the realm of pious hopes, reducing the number of parties might benefit those that remain. As the microparties take minuscule proportions of the vote, the elimination of competition should not be of much concern to democrats. Whatever costs this might bring by limiting the range of choices open to electors can be compensated for if the remaining parties decide to set themselves up on a permanent basis, establishing a framework that gives them a presence between elections. Further, where vanity parties are not useful mechanisms for political advancement for any but their founders, ambitious politicians will have incentives to join larger parties and make their careers within stronger, more stable organizations. Building robust, institutionalized parties can occur only where microparties do not flourish.

Accepting that Nicaragua had its transitional election in 1990, 1996 should have seen a significant reduction in the number of parties in the race. It did not. Though there were indications in late 1993 that the moderate legislative elements of the UNO and the FSLN were evolving toward becoming a new center party, as the elections drew nearer these all went their respective ways. Much of this fractionalization was an artifact of the electoral system that gives a seat to a losing presidential candidate who can garner 1.1 percent of the national vote. This can appear a more plausible task than getting a place high enough on a big party's departmental electoral list to have a realistic chance of election. As well, electoral campaign financing was readily enough available that it was easy for political entrepreneurs to build their profiles at public expense. Three months of nationwide, government-subsidized image building has to be very tempting.

Beyond the structure of incentives offered by the law, which will be described in more detail below, a further factor was at work in Nicaragua: the dissolution of the two main parties from 1990. The UNO's death was long foretold and surprised nobody. Once the alliance fractured, though, it was curious that the leaders of the several constituent parties forgot that what got them into power in 1990 was fusing into a grand electoral alliance. The schism in the FSLN was harder to predict, even though factions began to appear soon after 1990's loss. In any event, once splits occurred, it was probably inevitable that the emergent factions would want to test their wings and, in some cases, maybe teach their former compatriots a lesson. Without a set of rules to push them toward cooperation and possible coalitions, there was no reason for them not to go it alone.

The Administrative and Political Context

Nicaraguan elections—national, regional, and local—are administered by the CSE. This body has formal constitutional status; indeed, it is often called the "fourth branch" of government, as is common throughout Latin America. Due to its solid performance in 1984 and 1990, the CSE enjoyed a good reputation among Nicaraguans, though the most zealous anti-Sandinista ideologues never fully accepted that the council could be truly nonpartisan. As with any arm of government, the CSE depended on the national budget for its maintenance. In times of spending restraint it, along with other branches and departments, gets less money to do its job. This last factor gravely affected the CSE's performance in 1996.

The political climate prevailing in Nicaragua as the country entered its election year held substantial promise for critics of the Chamorro administration. Though the president had managed to keep the nation from falling into chaos and dictatorship, and though her economic policies had made hyperinflation a memory, combined instability, conflict between the branches of government, and economic stagnation left Nicaraguans again hungry for change. The main beneficiaries of this discontent were Managua's mayor Arnoldo Alemán and the rejuvenated PLC on the right, and Daniel Ortega and what remained of the FSLN on the left. However, the breakup of both the UNO and the Sandinistas complicated matters by leaving many able and ambitious politicians without allegiance to a large party.

More important than the lineup of electoral contestants was the certainty that the 1996 race would shape Nicaragua's political system for years to come. President Chamorro's victory, though a repudiation of the Sandinistas, could be viewed as an interim measure. The president's very lack of partisan affiliation meant that she would not leave a strong political legacy. The country had plainly shed its revolutionary Sandinista politics, but it had yet to define for itself a new identity. Whoever emerged the winner after 20 October would be well positioned to set Nicaragua's political path for the first part of the next century. A Sandinista victory could not restore the revolutionary status quo ante, but it would bring more expansive social policies and a foreign policy less aligned to Washington. A Liberal win promised not just economic continuity, but perhaps a renewed effort to eliminate the Sandinistas as a factor in Nicaraguan politics.

Electoral Machinery and Administration

None of Nicaragua's elections since 1984 were without administrative difficulties. In 1984, besides a general lack of experience, the CSE also ran into real problems when reports from outlying regions were reported far more slowly than anticipated. The 1990 race saw more political than administrative problems, but there were war zones where, as six years before, registrations could not be held and the vote itself was in jeopardy until the last moment. The presence of armed bands and a generally underdeveloped infrastructure combined to complicate the 1994 regional elections on the Atlantic coast. So there was no reason to believe that the 1996 general elections would not offer their own challenges. The novelty lay in the sources, nature, and gravity of the obstacles to administrative effectiveness.

Problems began during the constitutional conflict of 1995. The term of the CSE's directorate expired in June, before the National Assembly and the president had reached their final agreement. Although the resulting delay in naming a new council, which retained its president and vice president, was short, it did cause the CSE to effectively halt operations a little more than a year before the official start of the next campaign.

Much more serious was the dilemma that an amended Electoral Law presented the CSE. Passed in December 1995, within eleven months of the next elections, the reformed law would affect electoral administration in several ways. First, it added three races to the list of those to be decided on 20 October 1996. Mayors would now be directly elected by voters instead of by municipal councils; twenty of the National Assembly's ninety members would be elected at large—that is, on a national ticket—rather than from departmental lists; and Nicaragua's delegates to the Central American Parliament in Guatemala also had to be chosen. This translated to six simultaneous elections: president, departmental deputies, national deputies, members of the Central American Parliament, mayors, and municipal councils. As Nicaraguan elections use paper ballots, not voting machines, and since two dozen parties ran nationally, the actual ballot papers were almost a yard long.

A second complication arose from a new electoral map the law introduced. Where in 1990 there had been nine electoral divisions, there were now seventeen, corresponding to the revised departmental structure of the country. Accordingly, where before there were nine Departmental Electoral Councils (DECs), there were now seventeen. Moreover, where these DECs were once staffed by CSE appointees who were civil servants, their members would henceforth be named by political parties. Party nominees would also replace CSE employees at the 8,995 polling stations, or Junta Receptora de Votos (JRVs), in place for the elections.[11] The final selection would be in the hands of the CSE, or in the those of the DEC for JRVs, but it would have to make its assignments to reflect the array of parties in the country.[12]

Ostensibly, this provision for deprofessionalizing the electoral office was to counteract Sandinista influence. It is true that the president and the senior member of the CSE were Sandinista appointments who had served since before the 1984 election. It is also true that they had acted with admirable impartiality in the past, especially in 1990. Further, the division of the FSLN into warring camps meant that its capacity to influence the CSE's behavior was greatly reduced, even if electoral office officials had been receptive to its blandishments.

This suggests that another motive must have also been at work. The most plausible is a desire to extend the range of patronage appointments available outside the presidency. Being a member of a DEC is certainly a significant honor; serving as president of a JRV does bring some recognition and carries at least a small stipend,[13] never unimportant in a poor country. However, though the partisan logic was unassailable, the practical effect of the new rules was to make it necessary for the CSE to train an entirely new set of midlevel and front-line officials to run the 1996 elections.

The last new twist the CSE had to contend with was the possibility of a runoff election. Article 147 of the amended constitution provides that a second round of voting will be held to decide between the top two contenders if no candidate receives 45 percent of the vote. To accommodate this change, which again reflects sound political logic, the CSE would have to print new ballots, ensure that it has sufficient personnel to manage the vote, prepare the official publicity that explains the mechanics of voting, and find the money to pay for all this.[14] Between the new constitutional provisions and the reformed elections act, the CSE had a very full administrative plate.

Mariano Fiallos, who had been president of the CSE since its inception in 1983, was extremely troubled by these changes and by the fact that they were only passed on 5 December 1995. To signify his discontent, Fiallos resigned his position in early January 1996, but he was persuaded to remain to try to work changes in the law and to seek a larger budget for the council. Within a month, however, Fiallos carried through his earlier threat and resigned in protest. A few weeks later Rosa Marina Zelaya, who had been Fiallos's deputy and an official of the council since 1983, was elected president of the CSE by a unanimous vote of the National Assembly.[15]

Though not added at the last moment, there is a duty that the CSE shares with most electoral offices that had caused it some pain in the past: registering voters. Registration for both the 1984 and 1990 elections had been done specifically for those events, with all Nicaraguans over sixteen, the country's voting age, receiving a voter's card (*libreta cívica*) once they had been added to the list. Since 1990, the council had been charged with creating a permanent voters' list and assuring that every Nicaraguan citizen had an identity card (*cédula*). Once in place, the permanent list would make the CSE's work much lighter, but putting the list together was very difficult. War had destroyed civil registry offices in the northern and central parts of the country, and continuing violence in those areas made it impossible to reopen those that remained. Even where the records offices were intact, a casual attitude toward recording births, marriages, deaths, and movements from one place to another made the registries unreliable.[16] The result was that the list was not finished, nor the IDs distributed, in time for the 1996 elections.

Accordingly, the first big task the CSE faced was putting together another one-election voters' list. Ad hoc registration began in June in twenty-six municipalities[17] where violence had impeded earlier registration. On the first of two scheduled weekends of registration, an armed group kidnapped a USAID official sent to observe the process. Though she was released unharmed after two days, the incident gives a sense of the challenges surrounding Nicaragua's 1996 elections.

Less dangerous and dramatic, but posing a greater threat to the electoral process, was the CSE's constant shortage of money. For example, ad hoc registration was originally set for only two weekends, because there were not enough funds to mount it for longer. Though the money was eventually found to extend the registration process, the electoral authorities lived a penurious and precarious existence while the administration was repeatedly entreating donor countries to contribute the funds to mount a properly organized election.[18]

Beyond the problem of registering people in conflict zones, there were also difficulties in getting IDs to those already on the list. About one million of the country's 2,421,067 voters had *cédulas*, but another million could not get theirs in time to vote; they received *documentos supletorios*, temporary voters' cards, valid only for 1996. Finally, the roughly 352,000 people who registered in the ad hoc process also got a temporary document bearing the same name as the 1984 and 1990 voter's card: *libreta cívica*. Eventually, a fourth document *(constancia)* was added to serve as a last-minute voter's card for those who did not receive one of the more regular documents. Unfortunately, some potential voters never received any document and so were disenfranchised.

Though poverty and time constraints can account adequately for the problems in voter registration, the climate of distrust that marked Nicaraguan politics throughout President Chamorro's administration meant that every slipup was seen as a vile partisan plot. Politicians on the right insisted that Sandinistas dominated the CSE and were working to keep supporters of Mayor Alemán from voting. Sandinistas denounced decisions that they saw favoring "the Somocistas," the Liberal Alliance. There is no evidence that any of the shortcomings in the registration process favored one side over the other. Indeed, the only "party" to suffer from the registration was the CSE, whose hard-won reputation for efficiency and impartiality was being rapidly eroded.

A last and very taxing task handed the CSE was that of deciding whether a candidate should be disqualified. Constitutional amendments adopted in June 1995[19] established a set of criteria that a potential candidate had to meet before being allowed to run: (1) presidential candidates had to resign cabinet posts or mayoral offices a year prior to the elections; (2) no candidate could have renounced Nicaraguan citizenship to become a citizen of another country; and (3) no close relative of the sitting president could run to succeed the incumbent. Three presidential candidates failed the second test: Alvaro Robelo, Haroldo Montealegre, and Eden Pastora. Antonio Lacayo could not meet the third test. All those who were eventually disqualified claimed that the restrictions on their candidacies were unconstitutional, but the Supreme Court declined to decide their cases and threw the complaints back to the CSE. The council had no choice but to apply the existing law. However, the lack of transparency with which it dealt with the cases further harmed its image.

The Political Scene: Parties and Issues

Nicaragua's party system had undergone a strange evolution by mid-1996. A two-party system in 1990, at least in the division of the vote, the dissolution of the UNO, the fractionalization of the FSLN, and the emergence of the PLC as the strongest Liberal faction and putative leader of the right transformed the landscape. But some things had not changed. The Sandinistas were still bêtes noires of political conservatives regardless of party label, but they were weaker than at any time in the past eighteen years. The parties of the right were still squabbling among themselves to decide who should carry the anti-Sandinista banner. And the center remained a great swamp of unappealing reasonableness. The election of 1996 would have to define the country's party system "empirically," much as the 1990 vote had done.

Another thing that was unchanged from 1990 was the proliferation of parties. In the earlier race there were, besides the FSLN and the UNO alliance, nine independent parties, for a total of eleven. Out of all eleven, only the FSLN was a national party, as opposed to an ad hoc electoral alliance, with a permanent organization. The UNO once held some promise of being a conservative counterweight to the Sandinistas, but it fell prey to centrifugal tendencies. In 1996, there was again a profusion of parties and alliances in the national races (see Table 7.2), but this time two of them were large and permanently organized: Daniel Ortega's Sandinistas and Arnoldo Alemán's Constitutional Liberals. Though some of the remaining contenders had a well-known leader (Ramírez of the MRS), solid financial backing (the PNC led by Noel Vidaurre), or represented a new force in national politics (the CCN of Pastor Osorno), they end up fighting over the crumbs.

Table 7.2   Parties and Alliances Running Nationally, 1996
**   (in order of votes received in the election for national deputies)**

AL	Liberal Unity Party
FSLN	APC
CCN	PCN
Pronal	Nicaraguan Workers', Peasants', and
PNC	Professionals' Party
MRS	Democratic Action Party
PRN	National Renovation Movement
Unidad	PSN
PLI	Central American Integrationist Party
UNO 96	MAP[a]
Pan y Fuerza (Bread and Power)	Movement for Action for Renewal
ANC	Nicaraguan Democratic Alliance
National Justice Party	

a. Did not run a presidential candidate.

Four factors help explain why so many parties would fight an election dominated by a pair of heavyweights. We have already seen two of these. One was a politician's calculation that heading a small party furthers one's career more so than being even a senior member of a larger party; the other was the constitutional provision (Article 133) assuring an assembly seat to all losing presidential candidates who can garner roughly 1.1 percent of the national vote.[20]

The first of the two additional elements also refers to ease of election. Nicaraguan National Assembly seats are divided into two classes: the twenty elected nationally and the seventy elected departmentally. Both are elected by proportional representation, and the form used for the seventy regional seats comes very close to true proportionality.[21] This enhances the probability that a small party will win a seat, as seven of them did.[22] The second consideration is rooted in an analysis of the state of public opinion early in 1996. Alemán was regularly polling about 40 percent, but Ortega was showing no more than 23 percent support; those undecided accounted for about 20 percent of the responses.[23] Many small parties bet that the undecided vote would not go to the two front-runners. In the end, they lost their bet, but it was a reasonable gamble.

With about four months to go before Nicaraguans would cast their ballots, the election was turning into a two-horse race. By July, polls were showing a Sandinista recovery, being the choice of about 30 percent of decided voters, while the Liberals remained stuck at 40 percent.[24] Two things were clear from this. First, it was time for the Liberals to start worrying about not getting 45 percent of the votes in October and having to face a runoff. Second, this election was going to pit those who wanted "anybody but Daniel" against those supporting "anybody but Arnoldo."

What the Sandinistas did to woo those suspicious or fearful of Managua's former mayor was to adopt a mildly redistributionist platform that promised to respect property and provide a "government for everybody" (*un gobierno de todos*).[25] The growth of a managerial sector within the FSLN made its economic promises plausible, but to give it even more credibility the party named Juan Manuel Caldera, a non-Sandinista cattle rancher, its vice presidential candidate. Further, the party reached out to the Resistance, the ex-contras, promising that José Benito Bravo ("Comandante Mack"), a onetime contra commander and Somoza National Guard sergeant with a reputation for not respecting human rights, would become minister of the interior and control Nicaragua's police. Finally, the Sandinistas sought a rapprochement with the Church, pledging to negotiate with Cardinal Obando y Bravo appointments to the education, interior, and defense portfolios.

However, the Sandinistas could not go too far in conciliating nervous conservatives or they would risk losing their core constituency: Nicaragua's poor and marginalized. The party offered them a basket of programs and policies that most populist reformers would have found familiar. There were promises of credit to small producers in the countryside, increased social spending, and a commitment to honor the principles set out in late 1995 for the solution of the property question, a formula that protected poor people who had received land or houses from the revolutionary government.[26] A rather more progressive commitment the FSLN undertook was to name a woman to every second spot on the twenty-person national candidates list, as well as to assure that 30 percent of all candidacies, national and local, would go to women.

Counting more than the campaign promises, though, was the presence of Daniel Ortega. The *gallo enavajado* (gamecock with steel spurs) of 1990 may have given way to a more sober and statesmanlike image in 1996, but Daniel still represented the combative Sandinista Front of old to many in the popular classes. They remembered that it was Daniel who drove the moderates from the party and who had given speeches defending workers' rights during labor conflicts. That he had also cut deals with the Chamorro administration that might have hurt popular and working-class interests was forgotten or perhaps forgiven.

Opposing Daniel was Arnoldo. A populist himself, if a populist is a politician who can rouse the masses and get them on his side, Alemán had been the street-paving mayor of the capital from 1990 to 1995. To make the most of Alemán's image as a fixer and a doer, the Liberal Alliance declared, "*El cambio viene*" ("A change is coming"). Though at first blush this was a curious theme for a campaign where the incumbent could not run, the perceived lack of progress during the Chamorro years combined with Arnoldo's vigorous image to make it plausible.

But Alemán also attracted support because he was a determined foe of the Sandinistas. In the early 1990s, he joined with Vice President Godoy and National Assembly Deputy Alfredo César to lead the UNO radicals against both the FSLN and President Chamorro. Of more concern to some voters was Alemán's connection with the pre-1979 Somocista regime. His father had been an official in one of the Somoza governments, and the candidate himself worked hard at raising funds among the Nicaraguan and Cuban exile communities in Miami. It was reportedly the latter that gave him the greatest financial support, as the Nicaraguans found him too confrontational and worried about the rumors that he had ransacked Managua's coffers during his time in city hall.[27] Eventually Arnoldo calmed much of the upper class by taking the Conservative former president of COSEP, Enrique Bolaños, as his running mate. Though Bolaños shared Alemán's reputation as a scrapper who had often crossed swords with the Sandinistas, he was more obviously a member in good standing of the elite, hence someone they could trust.

The platform of the Liberal Alliance pledged to continue the general economic line set down by President Chamorro, namely, market-led growth and reliance on foreign assistance.[28] Though not figuring prominently in the public campaign, there was certainly an undertone of rumors in 1995 and 1996 that an Alemán government would not be kind to the segment of Nicaragua's business class that had prospered under Chamorro. Some sectors feared that he would even invite foreign capital to the country to compete with them. On the ever-critical property question, the AL promised titles to rural and urban poor but demanded that those who got big houses pay the full price for them. One might note here that Daniel Ortega lived in the house that had been expropriated from Alemán's campaign manager. The Liberals also indicated that they would change the property law passed in 1995 to no longer destine funds generated by privatizing public utilities to back bonds issued as compensation for property that could not be reclaimed. In its place the AL suggested that the international community find the U.S.$400 million needed to "buy peace," something in which donors evidenced no interest.

The Elections of 1996

The start of the official campaign on 2 August did not put an end to the CSE's administrative problems. Indeed, these only worsened as demands on the council's time and money grew as voting day approached. The campaign became increasingly a two-party straight fight, although the also-rans were loath to admit it, as Sandinista support grew to the point where a second round seemed likely and even an FSLN triumph was not implausible. With victory or defeat hanging in the balance, the Liberals and other anti-Sandinista interests turned up the heat under their rhetoric, assuring that it was a polarized Nicaragua that went to the polls on the third Sunday in October.

Machinery and Administration During the Campaign

For the 1996 election, the CSE, after negotiating a deal with the finance minister, agreed to allot an amount equivalent to 15 percent of its budget to finance party campaign costs. There remained, though, the question of who would get the money. Eventually it was decided that parties represented in the National Assembly would get a grant, but other parties would get a loan that would be waived if they won a seat. Because these funds were not available before the start of the official campaign, a number of smaller parties complained bitterly, sought successfully to amend the law setting the conditions under which repayment was necessary, and after the election tried to amend the law again to turn all state-supplied campaign funds into gifts.

Even more troublesome was the crisis that surrounded the printing of the ballots.[29] Nicaraguan election ballots are big and busy, and each of the six races run in 1996 required its own ballot. The ballots are big because there are lots of parties. They are busy, that is, they contain lots of information, because they have to bear not just the names of the candidates and parties, but also the symbols of all the parties in full color. This last provision is to assure that illiterates are able to vote. Moreover, in 1996, the presidential ballot and the mayoral ballot for Managua bore color photos of each candidate. Providing each of the roughly 2.4 million voters with ballots for all six elections meant printing more than 17 million individual ballots.

The CSE began in May to search for a contractor to print the ballots.

Two printers were considered for the job: INPASA and El Amanecer. INPASA won, even though its bid was over twice as high as the other, because it supposedly had better equipment. El Amanecer, the FSLN's company, complained to the controller general that INPASA only got the job because CSE president Rosa Marina Zelaya's husband, Jorge Samper, had an economic interest in INPASA. To settle the issue, the controller had to investigate. Though the charge against Samper was unfounded, other claims of political interference (e.g., that the controller was upset by a CSE decision that went against his party and that the MRS leader had argued vigorously against giving any work to an FSLN organization) are reportedly better grounded. An independent assessor was then brought in and recommended splitting the job between the two firms to ensure that the work was done on time. However, neither printer accepted that suggestion, and in the end the CSE stuck by INPASA.

Having the contract investigated set the printing job back even before it got started. INPASA, which was originally to deliver the ballots on 25 September, then made its own contributions to retarding the production of the election materials. Heavy rains led to fluctuations in the supply of electricity, which forced the company to shut down its delicate and expensive presses. Then there were difficulties in getting the parties to submit their lists of candidates on time and to settle on which photos of their presidential candidates they wanted to use.[30] This led the CSE to move the delivery date back to 10 October, but even that was insufficient. Some districts, for example, the department of Chontales, got their ballots the day before the elections. Others only received theirs late on election day itself, when the army delivered the ballots by helicopter.[31] Still others did not get enough, as the great rush resulted in miscounts. Overall, about half of the country's 8,995 JRVs opened late, thus closed late and reported late. Assessing the situation, OAS Secretary-General César Gaviria concluded that INPASA's failure to meet its contract combined with a complicated electoral format to produce grave problems.[32]

A final aspect of election management involves observers. Electoral observation by national and especially by foreign scrutineers has played an important role in contemporary democratic transitions. The outsiders have a particularly delicate and important role. On the one hand, they are seen as more knowledgeable about the proper conduct of elections, thus better able to detect anomalies. However, it is in their capacity as independent, disinterested observers, free to denounce irregularities wherever they occur, that they can make their most valuable contributions.

Although the 1996 elections were observed by fewer groups than those of 1990, there were still about 500 individual observers in attendance, a substantial presence. The OAS was the CSE's "designated" observer, but several others were officially "invited" observers. Further, there were groups sent by voluntary organizations, such as an international women's delegation. What was new this time was a domestic observer group, Etica y Transparencia (Ethics and Transparency [ET]). The development of such a group is important because it dispels the belief that only foreigners can assure that elections are honest. Moreover, it gives many citizens a crash course in electoral administration that raises the general level of sophistication about elections in a country. For a domestic observer group to work, however, people have to believe that it is nonpartisan. That was not easy to achieve in Nicaragua's polarized political setting.

ET was the object of distrust for several reasons. First, it depended heavily on U.S. groups for its inspiration and funding; and since its earliest patron had been the International Republican Institute, it acquired a conservative tinge that could not be erased in the public mind, even when the National Democratic Institute entered the project and sought greater ideological balance. A second problem facing ET grew out of its suspected ideological leanings. Parties of the center and left, above all the Sandinistas, were keen to limit its role. This attitude led the CSE to restrict the domestic observers' mandate. The worst moment for ET came when Alemán announced that the group's president, Emilio Alvarez Montalván, a conservative activist who enjoyed reasonably wide public confidence, would be foreign minister in an Alemán cabinet. Alvarez Montalván resigned immediately, but further doubts about ET's ability to be an independent agent were planted.

Some Notes on the Campaigns

I have witnessed every Nicaraguan national electoral campaign since the Sandinista revolution. Though that of 1996 was the worst from an administrative standpoint, it was the most technically polished of the three. Big outdoor rallies figured prominently in this campaign, but they were not the centerpieces they had been in 1984 or even 1990. Press, radio, and especially television advertising had become very slick; and parties that started out with very homespun ads grew increasingly sophisticated as the campaign progressed. This was also the most peaceful of the three campaigns: partisan polarization did not produce violence, even in the terribly tense days following the election when charges of fraud were aired by all sides. The key to the campaign, and what may have clinched a first-round victory for Alemán's Liberal Alliance, was the role of Cardinal Obando y Bravo. His Eminence is an extremely skilled politician, perhaps the best in the land, but he is also a man of conservative instincts who has developed a strong antipathy toward the Sandinistas. His instincts must have overridden his political judgment, for he openly supported Alemán.

Much of the politics of the campaign was driven by the Sandinistas' comeback in the public opinion polls. Trailing the AL by twelve points early in 1996, by October they had closed to within three (see Table 7.3). This put them within the pollsters' margin of error; hence, they could have been tied with the Liberals or, at worst, six points down. Behind the FSLN's surge lay their good campaign, a Liberal campaign that did not take off, and the defection of anti-Alemán voters from the rest of the pack.

Table 7.3   Voting Intention: Alemán Versus Ortega, 1995–1996

	Date of Poll				
	April 1995	Aug. 1995	April 1996	Aug. 1996	Sept. 1996
Alemán	39	35	33	34	41
Ortega	20	21	21	30	38

Sources: Butler et al., *Democracy,* p. 11; *El Semanario,* 18–24 October 1996, p. 6.
Note: All polls by CID-Gallup. Figures shown indicate percent of voters.

Closing the gap on the Liberals was a tribute to Ortega's political skill and flexibility. The FSLN that he led was the radical wing that had expelled its Centrists and seized control of the party newspaper, *Barricada,* less than two years earlier. Ortega himself had spent much of the last six years on the barricades spurring the militants on at the same time as he negotiated deals with the government that seriously compromised the political force of the left. It was he and his colleagues, who became known as the *Ortodoxos* (the Orthodox faction), who defended the hyperpresidentialist old constitution against legislative reformers. And Ortega's mansion, which became party headquarters, was a constant reminder of the *piñata.*

Ortega, however, succeeded in portraying himself and his party as moderates. The party's television ads were slick and understated. One showed people at work and kids playing, followed by a very brief shot of Daniel's face before cutting to the closing shot: a big *X* in box 12 on the ballot, the Sandinista list. The Sandinista hymn was replaced by Beethoven's "Ode to Joy," with suitably inoffensive lyrics replacing Schiller's poem. But not all Sandinista campaigning was so anodyne. In particular, Alemán's links to the Somozas, as well as his connections to domestic and foreign (Cuban American and Central American) big money got a lot of play.

Alemán's campaign stalled once he left city hall and no longer commanded the cement mixers and paving machines. His high command counseled a low-risk campaign. The early polls were good, and the FSLN seemed weak and divided, so the prudent course was not to offend people. However, Alemán's term as mayor had given him the image of a go-getter. He could not run the understated campaign that Doña Violeta had in 1990 without appearing to have exhausted his energy and ideas.

What started turning things around for both parties was an ad placed by the *confiscados*. Done in black and white and using many old newsreel clips, this ad was designed to bring back all the bad memories associated with the Sandinista era. There were shots of Daniel with Fidel Castro, scenes from the war, and pictures of the Sandinista leadership when they were the revolutionaries of the 1970s, not the impresarios or political chieftains of the 1990s. Only at the end were the sponsors of the advertisement identified.

At first, the CSE refused to let the ad run. Council president Rosa Marina Zelaya said: "It's one thing to recall history in an objective manner and it's quite another to use certain facts to lead people to faulty conclusions, and that's where the problem lies. . . . All of this incites violence and doesn't help the electoral process."[33] Eventually, though, it was allowed to air, and for the last week of the campaign, people were constantly reminded that the somber, cautious Daniel in the white shirt was also the brash Daniel in fatigues.

The *confiscados'* ad was an enormously effective bit of political propaganda, far more so than the *Plan Sombra* (Shadow Plan) that *La Prensa* printed in its 8 October edition.[34] The paper claimed to have obtained a leaked FSLN document that called for the creation of "control teams" (*equipos de control*). These would be the instruments for putting old, hardline Sandinistas in positions where they could reverse any decisions made by non-Sandinista ministers in a future Daniel Ortega government. It even had the old revolutionary closing: *Patria libre o morir!* (A free country or death!).

However, the most effective campaigner the Alemán team had turned out to be Cardinal Obando. Three things he did in the ordinary exercise of his religious duties were taken by many as being both overt condemnations of the Sandinistas and equally open endorsements of the Liberals. First, in his sermon the week before the election, the cardinal spoke of the danger of taking a viper to one's bosom, saying that rather than treating the beast compassionately you had to kill it before it killed you. It took little imagination to determine that the viper was Daniel Ortega, and on election day there was a massive campaign by email and cell phone declaring: "Be a patriot, kill the viper today."[35]

The second event took place on 17 October at a thanksgiving mass for President Chamorro. The lesson that day was read not by the Cardinal or by one of the president's children, but by Arnoldo Alemán. The next day Cardinal Obando publicly bestowed his blessing on the Liberal candidate.[36]

There was never any doubt about which side the cardinal favored, for Obando y Bravo had not enjoyed good relations with the FSLN since the earliest days of the revolution; but for him to remind people of that in a pointed manner so close to election day was a powerful message.

Election Day

Though much of the campaign period had been rainy, washing out roads in many areas, Sunday, 20 October, was fair and warm pretty much across the county. Blue skies did not, however, bring good luck. Because ballots arrived late, many JRVs opened late and had long lines of people waiting to vote throughout the day. Some JRVs did not open in their assigned spots, sending voters on a hunt for their poll.

Besides these systemic flaws, there were also minor problems arising at various JRVs.[37] At one poll, the members of the JRV had not folded the ballot papers sharply enough, and voters had trouble fitting them in the boxes, holding up other voters. The members quickly set about refolding the ballots so they would fit. At another poll, the ballot boxes were not attached firmly enough to their tables, again making it harder for citizens to cast their ballots and slowing down the process. A bit of masking tape, already on hand to seal the ballot boxes, did the trick. To help people cope with the long lines and hot sun, some JRV presidents asked voters to let the elderly, pregnant women, and women with children in tow to move to the front of the line. Where several JRVs were housed in the same building, a president might dispatch one of the volunteer Electoral Police to check to see that voters were in the right queue.

When the polls finally closed, and those that opened late also closed late to remain open for the eleven hours the law stipulated, a new batch of problems arose. Some were more annoying than grave (e.g., not having carbon paper to make copies of the official documents for all the JRV members and party poll watchers, which could mean copying everything a dozen times), but they all further retarded the process. At best, this left the JRV members tired, hungry, and more likely to make mistakes or cut corners. At worst, it opened the door for anybody who wanted to try his or her hand at electoral fraud.

Since perhaps May, when the first storm blew up over the ballot printing contract, politicians, mainly those associated with the Liberal Alliance, had been issuing dark warnings about Sandinista sympathizers working to keep good Liberals off the electoral rolls. When, during the last week of the campaign, there were obviously going to be problems getting electoral materials to all parts of the country, another wave of protest was unleashed from the same quarter.[38] International observers gave this aspect of the election great attention, seeing in it the seeds of potential conflict. In the end, though materials arrived very late at some places, there were very few reports of Nicaraguans being denied the right to exercise the franchise. The anomalies came after the votes were cast and counted at the JRVs.

Postelection Confusion and Controversy

Though all the international observers, except those with affinities to the FSLN, declared the elections free and fair immediately following the vote,[39] it soon became evident that there were many irregularities. The most common of these were misreported vote totals, but there were also missing ballots, as well as many delays in both the receipt of ballots at counting stations and the release of results. This created a very tense situation and generated a new set of administrative difficulties that had to be confronted before a winner could be declared. Why, though, was the postelection segment of the electoral process so problematic?

Remember that in 1996, for the first time since the Sandinista revolution, poll-level and departmental electoral officials were not civil servants, but rather party nominees. Add to this the fact that supporters of the Liberals had seen their party's lead in the polls drop from twenty points to nearly zero. Next, factor in a political climate that led partisans of both the AL and the FSLN to see plots against them everywhere.[40] Finally, bring in a long, hot, frustrating day, and there will be both a reason to try to pad the figures as well as the opportunity to do so.

According to the Electoral Law (Article 29.3), the president of each JRV is to send a telegram to the CSE with the vote counts. This is not the final and official count, but it is the document that the CSE uses to make announcements about the progress of the count. When the JRV president goes to the telegraph office to send the results, he or she is to be accompanied by any of the party poll watchers who wish to come. In some cases, presidents, disproportionately members of the Liberal Alliance, did not do this, but went alone and submitted altered results. To give just one example, *Barricada* reported that JRV 8100 in the town of Jinotega, where 223 of 230 registered voters cast ballots, gave the Liberals 1,085 votes and the Sandinistas none.[41] As no JRV could have more than 400 voters registered to vote in it, the chances of the ploy succeeding were exceedingly small.

The Sandinistas, who were already upset when Alemán claimed victory with only 2.58 percent of the polls reporting, declared that they would not recognize the provisional count based on the telegrams. Further, fourteen parties, including the FSLN, protested the conduct of the elections in Matagalpa, the second largest department in the country. When the Liberal president of Matagalpa's DEC, Alberto Blandón Baldizón, was found to have about 40,000 blank ballots stored in buildings belonging to his family, those fourteen parties set up a hue and cry. When bags of marked ballots were found dumped in various spots around Managua (in many cases because the counting centers that were to receive them either were not open or working very slowly) and grave discrepancies showed up in other departments, it became necessary to organize a formal recount, something not foreseen in the law.

To expedite matters, council officials and party scrutineers decided to do complete recounts only where the tally sheets attached to the bags containing the ballots showed arithmetical errors greater than ten.[42] If tally sheets and bags of votes could not be matched, the votes had to be annulled. This occurred in 14 percent of the JRVs in Managua and 11 percent of those in Matagalpa, and their entire results were thrown out. Though the Sandinistas asked that the elections in these two departments be annulled and rescheduled, the Electoral Law only permits this action when more than half the ballots are tainted (Article 175).

Multiple recounts take time, and it was only on 8 November, almost three weeks after the elections, that final presidential results were announced and Arnoldo Alemán declared the victor. Full results of all races were not available until 22 November, thirty-three days after Nicaraguans voted. The long delay led the president-elect to grumble that in any other country he would have been confirmed long before.[43] Though likely true, this misses the point that it is up to the loser to concede until all the votes are in and the recounts completed. And that the Sandinistas were not prepared to do.

There were good reasons for the FSLN to wait for the official results. First, there were enough instances of malfeasance and misfeasance to justify caution. Even though the presidency was out of Ortega's reach,[44] electoral irregularities plausibly could have cost the Sandinistas the chance to win 40 percent of the seats in the National Assembly, the number they needed to be able to block constitutional amendments. Had the FSLN been able to persuade the CSE to run the Managua and Matagalpa elections over, the party would have gotten a chance to pick up the two extra seats it needed from among the twenty-nine at stake.

The second of the Sandinistas' reasons had more to do with internal politics. In many places, a political leader who had lost two consecutive national elections, both times trailing his adversary by a margin of over thirteen points, would probably soon be out of a job. One way to assure that this history did not repeat itself within the FSLN was to impugn the elections, shifting blame from the party and its standard-bearer to the electoral authorities. Some of the smaller parties whose hopes were crushed by the Liberal-Sandinista avalanche that took 88 percent of the vote also adopted this reasoning when they voted in 1996's lame-duck legislative session to waive their obligation to pay back money advanced to them for their campaigns.

A Comment on the Results

Nicaragua's 1996 electoral results raise three questions for political analysts: (1) What let Arnoldo Alemán win so easily? (2) What can the FSLN do after two straight electoral defeats? (3) How significant is it that only eight incumbents were returned to the National Assembly? Though these are really questions that will be answerable only as the next national elections roll around in 2001, we can set out some lines of inquiry to pursue in the interim.

Though Alemán was saddled with a bad campaign that found its feet only after outside help arrived in the last few weeks of the push, he nevertheless commanded significant resources. To begin with, the PLC was well organized and did turn out the vote. Then there is the money that Alemán obviously had, reportedly brought in from Miami, Guatemala City, and San Salvador. Of course, the man himself was also important. Flamboyant, capable of attracting financing, and good on the hustings, Alemán was an asset to his campaign. All of this combined to make the PLC standard-bearer the hands-down choice of Nicaraguans who did not want the Sandinistas back.

Alemán's solid victory caused comment only because the Sandinistas made such a strong run during the last half of the campaign. Able to polarize the race into a two-party straight fight, Daniel Ortega and his followers had to be disappointed when only 38 percent of their fellow citizens preferred them to the former mayor of Managua. The results should raise many questions for the party that is Nicaragua's only obvious alternative to a long spell of Liberal governments. One thing that Sandinistas will have to ask themselves is how important the loss of the MRS was. Though Ramírez's forces carried only 1.3 percent of the vote, the FSLN might wonder if expelling its moderate wing sent voters off to other parties, possibly even to the PLC. But before the FSLN can decide whether to change its ideological posture and shift at least rhetorically to the right, it has to decide if it still wants Daniel Ortega as its leader. Daniel is plainly a skillful politician, but he is equally plainly anathema to many Nicaraguans. An Ortega-led Sandinista party, even one that had wholeheartedly abandoned the revolution to embrace reformism, would probably face an uphill fight at the polls.[45]

The last curious twist that the 1996 elections left Nicaragua was a ninety-three-member legislature with eighty-five freshmen. It seems reasonable to attribute the absence of successful incumbents to three factors. The first is the 1994 split in the FSLN that made the party recruit an essentially brand-new slate of candidates for the National Assembly. To that we can add the failure of the new parties formed by experienced politicians after the dissolution of both the Sandinistas and the UNO to convince voters that a vote for them was not wasted. Finally, the most successful party, the PLC, was an outsider that drew most of its candidates from beyond the ranks of deputies who served between 1990 and 1996. It seems unlikely that such circumstances would present themselves again in the future, so 2001 will probably see more incumbents returned.

Conclusion

The most obviously positive aspect of the troubled 1996 Nicaraguan elections is that they did not give rise to violence. Nicaraguans have decided that it is not worth fighting about who is going to rule them for the next five years. This suggests another hopeful element, namely, that Nicaraguans are confident that there will be another election in five years. Moving a bit further into the realm of speculation, it may even be that Nicaraguan citizens believe that there are constitutional and legal ways to thwart politicians who misuse their authority. In other words, to find the brightest spots in the electoral record of 1996, we must hypothesize that they send a positive message about an increasingly mature, tolerant, and democratic Nicaraguan political culture.

Beyond the equanimity with which Nicaraguans faced the jumble that started the night of 20 October, one can also count the preservation of a two-party system as a positive sign. In late 1995, there were not many political commentators in Nicaragua who would have wagered that the Sandinistas would record almost 40 percent of the presidential vote or that the Liberals would not get a majority in the house.[46] If the FSLN's poll figures in late 1995 (usually 23 percent) represent the party's bedrock supporters, then swinging a full 15 percent of the nation's voters to the Sandinista side was a notable, if insufficient, achievement.

In fact, the results of the election (Table 7.1) reveal another interesting trend. Once past the presidential race, support for the Liberal Alliance fell more sharply than did that for the Sandinistas. Perhaps this was a case of voters choosing Arnoldo over Daniel but returning to their favorite son or daughter once past the presidential ballot. In any event, this evidence of ticket splitting, limited though it was, leaves the smaller parties who won seats some hope for the future.

A list of the negative outcomes of the elections is longer and more concrete. It has to start with the politicization of the Electoral Law. Poll officials can properly be party nominees, as they are in other countries. It would be useful, though, to limit the right to suggest appointments to parties that attained some specified proportion of the vote in the last election. Electoral officials at the departmental level, however, should be professional civil servants. Not only can the latter be justifiably punished for partisan behavior, their presence should deter poll-level party appointees from attempting any electoral chicanery.

Related to this, in the future the National Assembly should discipline itself by setting and adhering to a date after which it will not touch the Electoral Law—say, two years before a general election. Doing this should assure that the CSE does not have to reorganize itself to apply a new law at the last moment. Unfortunately, the prospects of this happening seem dim. After the 1996 elections, Assembly president Cairo Manuel López declared to *Barricada* that the CSE was responsible for everything that went wrong.[47] It was not, he argued, the legislature's job to draft a law that permitted effective application. Perhaps that is why he and his colleagues ignored the repeated counsel of Mariano Fiallos, whose dozen years as president of the CSE should have taught him something about running elections, preferring to design something that promised more political plums. The executive can also be brought to book for irresponsibility, due to its niggardly and tardy funding of the council.

The CSE has its own lessons to learn. Chief among them is the need for transparency. Being scrupulously honest is not enough; one must also be perceived as such. More open procedures might have saved the CSE some embarrassment over ballot printing, and they certainly would have lessened the confusion that arose when the very last seat in the chamber was assigned to Jorge Samper of the Sandinista Reform Movement, the husband of the CSE's president.[48]

Important as all of the above are, they are outweighed by the alterations the elections brought to Nicaragua's political landscape. Carlos Fernando Chamorro called the results a blow to political diversity, because they produced two blocs built around populist caudillos, both with multiclass support ranging from the poor to the executive suite.[49] Their domination of national politics left no room for the sort of quietly negotiated politics that gets constitutional reform under way. Worse, as the Sandinistas refused to recognize the Liberals' victory, preferring to talk again about direct action against an illegitimate government, they gave the new administration every reason to ignore them and the 669,443 citizens who lined up behind the red-and-black standard of the FSLN and Daniel Ortega.

All this leads to a final question: Did the 1996 elections advance or retard democratic consolidation in Nicaragua? In the short run at least, they set the process back. They proved that reviving old fears and hatreds was good politics and showed that a certain amount of fraud, even if detected, would not bring crushing punishments. Most of all, the elections illustrated that Nicaragua had not progressed quite as far toward full constitutional democracy as many had hoped and believed. They demonstrated that the system still had many weaknesses, notably in the country's party system and its capacity for administrative oversight.

When Violeta Chamorro took her oath of office in April 1990, the parties were also weak, but at least the electoral side of the administration worked well. Furthermore, she came to power in a setting where betting everything that enough people would vote against the FSLN to get you elected was the best political game in town. More than six years later, though Nicaragua was in many ways a more pluralistic and tolerant place, these things had not changed.

Notes

1. Unlike the 1990 elections, not much is written on Nicaragua's 1996 vote. See, however, Jennifer L. McCoy and Shelley A. McConnell, "Nicaragua: Beyond the Revolution," *Current History* 98:107 (1997): 75–80; and Henry Patterson, "The 1996 Elections and Nicaragua's Fragile Transition," *Government and Opposition* 32:3 (1997): 380–398.

2. The 1984 election is reviewed in Chapter 1.

3. An analysis of the 1990 elections is found in Chapter 2.

4. Margaret E. Scranton, "Panama's First Post-Transition Election," *Journal of Interamerican Studies* 37:1 (1995): 69–100.

5. Arthur W. Turner, "Postauthoritarian Elections: Testing Expectations About 'First' Elections," *Comparative Political Studies* 26:3 (1993): 330–349.

6. Scranton, "Panama's First," p. 90; emphasis in original. Costa Rica is famous for its scrupulously honest elections, so "holding a Costa Rican election" implies meeting the highest standards of procedural probity and efficiency.

7. Ibid., p. 91.

8. The question of eternal vigilance over elections and the laws governing their administration is taken up by David Close, Andres Franco, and Andres Talero, "Strengthening Democracy in Latin America Through Electoral Reform," a report prepared for the Canadian Foundation for the Americas, 1997.

9. Turner, "Postauthoritarian Elections," pp. 341–343.

10. It is impossible to specify how many parties are enough to sustain democracy, other than to say that there must be at least two. Americans would likely endorse a two-party option, as would the British, even though their party system conforms more to a "two-party-plus" model where over 15 percent of the vote regularly goes to third parties. In the end, it is the pattern of politically salient social cleavages and the ability of political parties to encompass and represent them, modified by the electoral system and constitutional structures, that determine the number of serious, functional parties a political system needs to properly reflect the views of the electorate.

11. In some places, JRVs were split when final figures showed that some had registered more than the 400 voters regulations allowed. Even 400 voters per poll proved to be unmanageable in many instances, due to the lengthy ballots and tardy arrival of materials.

12. The Electoral Law specifies that no party may have more than one member on either a DEC (Article 16) or a JRV (Article 25).

13. The sums for poll-level workers were 40 cordobas for poll watchers (*fiscales*) and 80 cordobas for members. Though even a member got only about U.S.$10 for a long day's work, it must be remembered that the average Nicaraguan

would make only about U.S.$400 a year. To make the comparison meaningful, we would have to take one-fortieth of an average American income, U.S.$24,000, which would yield a U.S.$600 per day payment. Seen in this light, the patronage does not seem quite so unimportant.

14. Roberto Evertz, a senior official of the CSE, indicated that the council estimated that it would be impossible to organize runoffs in less than four or five weeks (interview, Managua, 23 November 1995). The Electoral Law states that the runoff must be held within forty-five days (Article 151).

15. *NNS,* 21–27 January 1996, p. 1; 11–16 February 1996, p. 2; and 3–9 March 1996, p. 5.

16. Evertz interview.

17. A Nicaraguan municipality *(municipio)* is similar to a U.S. county in size.

18. See, for example, *NNS,* 26 May–1 June 1996, p. 1, and 9–15 June 1996, p. 2.

19. See Chapter 6.

20. The relevant part of Article 133 specifies a number of votes equal or superior to the mean of the regional electoral quotas. As there are ninety seats, the mean national quota would be one-ninetieth, or 1.1 percent. I do not know of any suggestion to raise the quota to one-seventieth, or 1.4 percent, since only seventy seats were elected on a regional basis in 1996 (the other twenty being converted into national seats elected at large). Even if the latter figure were applied, it would make a very low threshold.

21. There is a good description of the Nicaraguan system of proportional representation, established by Articles 153 and 154 of the Electoral Law, in Judy Butler, David R. Dye, and Jack Spence, with George Vickers, *Democracy and Its Discontents: Nicaraguans Face the Election* (Cambridge, MA: Hemisphere Initiatives, 1996), pp. 36–40.

22. However, this is partly offset by Article 73.4 of the Electoral Law, which specifies that parties that do not win a seat lose their legal status.

23. *NNS,* 13–30 December 1995, p. 4, and 24–30 March 1996, p. 2.

24. *NNS,* 28 July–3 August 1996, p. 3.

25. Butler et al., *Democracy,* pp. 31–32; FSLN, *Plataforma Nacional* (Managua: FSLN, 1996).

26. See Chapter 6.

27. This section relies on Mark Caster, "The Return of Somocismo? The Rise of Arnoldo Alemán," *NACLA* 30:2 (September/October 1996): 6–9.

28. The AL's economic thinking is set out in a working paper of the PLC titled "Nicaragua: La nueva estrategia económica, 1997–2001." This was apparently not published; I got my copy from a Nicaraguan journalist friend. A brief look at the AL's economics is found in Butler et al., *Democracy,* pp. 29–30.

29. Except where otherwise noted, this section relies on Butler et al., *Democracy,* pp. 23–25, and on *NNS,* 4–10 August 1996, p. 1; 11–17 August 1996, p. 2; and 1–6 September 1996, pp. 1–2.

30. *Siete Dias,* 15–22 October 1996, pp. 8–9.

31. Besides helicopters, the CSE used 516 trucks, 263 light vehicles (cars and four-wheel drives), 2,310 animals—mostly mules, 91 boats, and 74 tractors to deliver materials to the JRVs and then to ferry them back to the counting centers. See *El Semanario,* 18–24 October 1996, p. 11.

32. *La Tribuna,* 22 October 1996, pp. 1A, 5A.

33. Quoted in *La Prensa,* 5 October 1996, p. 10.

34. *La Prensa,* 8 October 1996, p. 2.

35. The general manager of IBW Internet Gateway, whose server carried the "kill the viper" message, immediately wrote to the CSE distancing his firm from the action; see http://www.elecciones1996.org.ni/carta_zelaya.html (3 January 1997). The campaign was obviously aimed at the upper classes, presumably to assure that they voted enmasse for the Liberals.

36. There is a recounting of these episodes in Walter Lacayo Guerra, "La Historia se repite," *El Semanario,* 25–31 October 1996, p. 13.

37. The following is based on what I saw in the department of Chontales, where I was part of the Carter Center's observation team.

38. Sandinista complaints before the election were of a different order. They were upset that CSE disqualifications of presidential candidates and rulings on campaign ads systematically favored the AL.

39. An interesting criticism of the international observers is found in Judy Butler, "Observing the Observers," *Envio* 15:185–186 (December 1996–January 1997): 50–61. My own experience leads me to think that the observers concentrated most of their efforts on polling day problems that would arise from improper voters' lists or people without proper documents, the issues that had arisen during the six months leading up to the elections. With only about half the personnel they had available in 1990, the international observers were stretched too thinly to properly cover the counting process. In any event, the law makes no provision for observers to accompany JRV presidents to the telegraph office, the main source of the original problems, though well-briefed observers could have informed party poll watchers of their right to observe the dispatch of the telegram with the JRV's results. The domestic observers, Etica y Transparencia, however, did keep vigil, except where excluded by JRV presidents. Though their exclusion violated the Electoral Law (Article 27.7), it was perhaps to be expected in the heated atmosphere of this election.

40. A Liberal Alliance worker I talked to in Juigalpa, Chontales, the night before the election claimed that a CSE advertisement showing a mock ballot was actually an ad for the FSLN. To reach that conclusion, all you had to do was find an arrow pointing to the middle of the sample ballot for the presidential race. As the FSLN had box 12 of 23 it was in the middle, so the arrow had to be emphasizing the Sandinistas. The fact that the arrow had printed in it "Here are the ballots" seemed not to make any difference.

41. *Barricada,* 23 October 1996, pp. 4–5.

42. This section draws on Council of Freely Elected Heads of Government, *The Observation of the 1996 Nicaraguan Elections* (Atlanta, GA: Carter Center, Emory University, 1997), pp. 31–36.

43. *La Prensa,* 27 October 1996, p. 1.

44. Nevertheless, the FSLN did not challenge any mayoral or assembly races, only the presidential contest.

45. In March 1998, Daniel Ortega's problems grew immeasurably greater when his stepdaughter, Zoilamérica Narváez, accused him of having sexually and psychologically abused her for nineteen years, since she was eleven. Though some in the party have rallied round Daniel, even his most loyal lieutenants must realize that he is damaged goods and that some way has to found for him to make as dignified an exit from active politics as his difficult circumstances permit. To do otherwise is to hand the next election to the PLC even before campaigning starts. The *Nicaragua News Service* and the *Central America Report* covered the issue thoroughly throughout March and April 1998.

46. I spent most of November 1995 in Nicaragua and had many conversations

with politicians, activists, journalists, and ordinary citizens about the prospects for 1996. The general drift was not just that Alemán and his Liberals would win, but that they would bury the Sandinistas and everybody else, leaving no effective parliamentary opposition.

47. *Barricada,* 31 October 1996, pp. 1, 7.

48. The election of Samper was really the creation of Nicaragua's ultrafair and immensely complex system of proportional representation. Another lesson for both the CSE and the National Assembly is that a less technically attractive system that the public could more easily understand would strengthen Nicaraguan democracy.

49. *El Nuevo Diario,* 30 October 1996, p. 10.

8

Nicaragua's Continuing Transition

Though there has been a tendency on the part of students of contemporary democratic political change to assume that transitions are quick, one-off affairs and that the consolidation of a democratic regime follows relatively quickly, Nicaragua's experience points in a different direction. Its transition away from personalist dictatorship began before the country's rulers made any move toward constitutional government. The full embrace of constitutional democratic principles came even later. Instead of being marked by one dramatic shift, Nicaragua's transition toward constitutional democracy unquestionably began with the downfall of Somoza, but it certainly did not end until the constitutional reforms of 1995, if even then.

If transition is prolonged, logically, consolidation must take even longer. Samuel Huntington has suggested that democracy is consolidated when there have been two elections in which the incumbent loses. In India, the developing world's oldest democracy, this would have been 1980, thirty-three years after the establishment of democratic government there.[1] Though Nicaragua has seen opposition parties win in two consecutive elections, the incumbent was forbidden to run in the second of them.

Of course, logically, consolidation can hardly happen overnight. A useful reminder of this comes form Paul Christopher Manuel, who argues persuasively that it took fifteen years (1976–1991) to consolidate democracy in Portugal.[2] Citizens and politicians must learn the skills and attitudes appropriate to democratic governance, as well as mastering the running of new governmental machinery. Victor Pérez-Díaz goes a step further to suggest that constitutional democracy must become institutionalized after it has been consolidated.[3] Democracy is institutionalized when its methods and instruments have become not just the way politics is always carried out, but also the only acceptable, even imaginable, way to seek and attain political ends. Where violence or fraud still carry weight as legitimate and

203

useful tools for taking and exercising power, democracy cannot be consolidated, much less institutionalized. By those standards, Nicaragua clearly still has some way to go before ranking as a fully fledged and secure democracy.

Despite these reservations, and qualifications, one thing is certain: Nicaragua was a more democratic country at the end of 1996 that it had been twenty years before, when the Somozas ran the country. Whether it was more democratic than at the end of the Sandinista years is a question requiring a more nuanced answer.

In 1996, there was no war, and levels of armed conflict had declined dramatically since the middle of President Chamorro's term. There was no draft, so young men and their families did not have to worry about being conscripted and sent to fight a guerrilla war. Censorship had ended, and political tolerance, though still weak, was probably stronger than it had ever been in Nicaragua. Although the economy was far from prosperous, at least inflation had been controlled and the currency stabilized. The constitution ensured a greater balance of power between the executive and legislative branches. And a conservative government had recognized the legitimacy and social utility of property redistribution. All of these certainly contribute to democracy, even if they are not parts of the term's usual procedural definition that centers on electoral competition. Taken together, one can argue that these varied elements make the Chamorro years more democratic than the Sandinista period because society is generally more open and has come to understand the perils of excessively concentrated power.

Against this must be set a general skewing of the political system, economic structures, and social and cultural values away from the marginalized and back toward established elites. However much the verticalist tendencies of the FSLN militated against real participation in party and state affairs by the rank and file, the "logic of the majority" was still the Sandinistas' ideological lodestar. After 1990, the new state managers put other values ahead of giving the poor and weak the institutions and recognition they need to participate fully in modern society. In this light, the new regime ushered in with the new administration is less democratic because it is less determinedly egalitarian.

Further complicating any assessment of the status of democracy in Nicaragua in 1996 is the unclear status of citizen or group politics, the politics of civil society. On the one hand, organized labor showed itself unable to protect its members from the ravages of austerity politics. But on the other, groups able to adopt more decentralized structures, women and the community movement, had some successes.[4] Neither class of popular organization had good access to decisionmakers, so those who could exist on their own resources obviously stood a better chance of surviving and protecting their interests.

If we are to understand how democratization has proceeded in Nicaragua, as well as what challenges it still faces, we must consider the contributions of both post-Somocista regimes. They sought, and to some extent secured, different visions of democracy and based their administration of the country on distinctive governing philosophies. Each government wished to remake Nicaragua according to its conception of the good; each, that is, had a transformational project. So any realistic assessment of Nicaragua's transition toward and consolidation of democracy has to incorporate the achievements and failings of both the Chamorro presidency and her Sandinista predecessors.

The Complexity of Democracy

The first step is to recall that the two governments defined democracy in quite distinct ways. For the Sandinistas, democracy was not about counting heads or holding electoral raffles to see who was most popular. Their view was that of radical democrats through the ages: democracy is about equality—material, social, cultural. A democracy of this sort always aims to assure that privilege and wealth do not buy state power. It will not scruple to burden a former elite when that is what must be done to benefit the weak and excluded. This is a democracy of results, measured by equality of status.

To this generic democratic radicalism the FSLN added its own brand of Marxism. Sandinista thinking was catholic, combining Marxism with liberation theology,[5] Latin American anti-U.S. nationalism, and multiclass populism. This made its Marxism less rigorous and orthodox. That said, the FSLN remains even today a fundamentally Leninist organization, tightly controlled from the top; and until its defeat in 1990, it never renounced its objective of building socialism in Nicaragua.

What resulted was a public philosophy totally at odds with anything that had ever even been close to the seats of power in Nicaragua. The rich and privileged were no longer automatically to accede to positions of rule, as if by right. A traditionally deferential society officially became egalitarian. And the Sandinistas restructured political power to minimize the value of the resources that the old elites possessed. The revolution's goal was to turn Nicaragua upside down, to make the last first and the first last.

The Sandinistas did not propose a liberal, constitutional democracy. They wanted root and branch changes, and they wanted them immediately. Despite that, the FSLN still gave Nicaragua its first honest elections and was the first government to leave power voluntarily on losing the people's confidence. Moreover, the revolutionary government substantially strengthened the organs of representative democracy and created the first modern political party in the country's history. Perhaps in spite of itself, the Sandinista legacy to Nicaraguan democracy is rich and varied, far different from what Communist parties in the old Soviet bloc left their people.

Violeta Chamorro broke a new path for Nicaraguan democratic development. Committed to the canons of orthodox liberal democracy, she wanted to create an *estado de derecho,* a government where the rule of law prevailed. In the Anglo-American political tradition, the concept of the rule of law generally carries two meanings. On the one hand, it signifies equality before the law: the principle that rich and poor, popular and outcast, all receive equal and impartial justice. The other side of the rule of law is that it demands that the state obey its own laws: *raison d'état* does not justify breaking the law.[6]

Such a concept was unknown in the practice of governments in Nicaragua. Although she set her country on the right path, President Chamorro cannot be said to have seen the rule of law consolidated. There were too many plausible charges of corruption within her administration,[7] and the judiciary was too weak. But it is unrealistic to expect the rule of law, which took centuries to evolve in England, to take root in half a dozen years in Nicaragua just because a fairly elected president made it the goal of her administration.

There is, however, another sense in which the *estado de derecho* may be translated into English, namely, as meaning limited or constitutional government. Here the president's record is better. The state no longer censors the media, and its economic role is greatly reduced. In fact, economic liberalization was carried on rather successfully throughout the government's term. At the same time, however, the government's role in setting a politicized curriculum for the schools has hardly changed, even if the material itself is different.[8] Though this may simply be proof that the nightwatchman state has never been more than an unrealizable ideal, it also serves as a reminder that using the state to secure policy objectives is not the left's monopoly.

Beyond all the specific policies or constitutional forms and practices, what the Chamorro presidency promised was to refurbish democracy's image among those who feared the class-based Sandinista version. Democracy ceased being about social or economic equality and became a legal, constitutional phenomenon. Far more than under the Sandinistas, it would work through periodic elections, the legislature, and the courts. Thus defined, democracy is a political system in which a privileged minority can defend itself well. Yet we know that this was insufficient for the most conservative segments of Nicaraguan society.

For the displaced elites from the Somoza period, as well as for most of those whose property was taken by the revolutionary government for redistribution to society's historic underdogs, democracy meant getting back what had been theirs. This is really more about justice, being given one's due, than it is about democracy, selecting leaders and governing. Yet the two notions inevitably merged. Democracy meant elections that would take power from the revolutionaries, opening the way for justice, the return of properties, and the restoration of rightful social positions. Though the Chamorro government started off with fairly vigorous policies aimed at breaking the power of unions and securing the rapid restitution of or indemnification for seized properties, the instability that resulted caused the president to seek less dangerous paths.

Of course, it was precisely the administration's decision not to reestablish the status quo ante 1979 at all costs that converted erstwhile supporters into committed opponents.[9] The governing philosophy of this opposition, which became an ever-smaller rump over the years, was founded on two premises: punishing the Sandinistas and attaining enough power to shape the state as it wished. Though this faction was never strong enough to impose its will, it retained more than enough potency to make it impossible for the government to disregard its demands. And it made the formation of a democratic pact among all sectors of the political elite, the people and organizations with the capacity to influence government, unattainable.

Because of this, six and one-half years after President Chamorro's election, and seventeen years after the Somoza dictatorship fell, Nicaragua still lacked a democratic vision that united its people. Whatever his own preferences in the matter might be, when Arnoldo Alemán became president he received two distinct and as yet unintegrated streams of democratic thought. This dual legacy adds the Sandinista inheritance to that left by the Chamorro administration, but it has not merged them. To gauge the prospects for consolidating and institutionalizing democracy in Nicaragua, therefore, we need to identify what remained of the Sandinista revolution after half a dozen years out of power, as well as the democratic inheritance left by President Chamorro.

What Difference Did the Revolution Make?

After the Sandinistas lost power in 1990, commentators tried to assess how a decade of Sandinista revolutionary rule had affected Nicaragua. Even more, they wanted to know if defeat at the polls meant the death of the revolution. Carlos Vilas argues that the revolution irrevocably changed the country's political culture by transforming poor and passive subjects into active, demanding participants.[10] An alert, politicized majority cannot be subjugated. It will not surrender its political and legal rights. Complementing Vilas's cultural interpretation is a structural analysis offered by Christopher Clapham. After reviewing the legacies of socialist experiments in the Third World, he concludes that these broke forever the old patterns of rule and made possible more modern and democratic societies.[11] Both agree that a revolution should so change society that, whatever else might happen, the old regime can never return.

Both Vilas and Clapham also de-emphasize the impact of the actual policies of the revolution. Most likely this represents their calculation that many of these will be significantly modified by postrevolutionary governments, but many people would automatically connect the revolution with programs of universal education, enhanced rights for minorities and women, and land reform.[12] In fact, policies like these are the foundations for the cultural and structural changes that may be the longer-lasting legacies of the revolution. So, if the revolution was to have some continuing effect, it would necessarily leave traces of its presence in both politics and policies.

We should start by examining the status of Sandinista policies at the end of the Chamorro years, because these are the easiest things for a new government to change. The great project of socialist economic transformation was gone, as were many of the more redistributive social programs linked to the FSLN, such as expanded health care, better education for the poor, and subsidized utilities. The most obvious survivors were also the most controversial: land reform and the attendant redistribution of rural and urban property. The adoption of Law 209 in 1995[13] signified the Chamorro administration's acceptance of the social consequences of Sandinista property policy.

Enumerating the residual Sandinista influences on Nicaraguan politics begins with the continuing existence of the FSLN itself. Not only did the party play an important role in moderating the pace of change after 1990, it also performed respectably in the 1996 elections. However, splits in the party, a second decisive electoral defeat, and its refusal to acknowledge the results of the last election indicate that the Sandinistas may need to undergo a thorough restructuring if they are to remain a major force in national politics. Other political remnants of the revolutionary period are the now-tarnished electoral machinery, the parts of the constitution not amended in 1995, and a well-functioning modern legislature. Governmental machinery has to be considered because it affects how private interests get access to government, how public agendas are set, and both how and how well citizens hold governments accountable. The first five years of the Chamorro administration were spent substantially within Sandinista-designed institutions. Although many of these have since been changed, they were the mold into which President Chamorro's government was injected and developed.

Important though the above are, the most significant contribution of the FSLN to Nicaraguan democracy was its defeat of the Somozas. In the mid-1970s, the old regime showed no signs of reforming itself. Indeed, the tenacity with which Anastasio Somoza Debayle, the last of the clan to rule, clung to power demonstrates with absolute clarity that the regime was not for changing, save by force. To suggest that the Somozas would have eventually followed the Duvaliers, the Marcos, and a host of other dictators into retirement is simply anachronistic: had Washington not needed democratically elected allies to point up the supposed sins of the Sandinistas, the White House could well have continued tolerating its tyrannical allies as it had for so many years in the past.

In addition to these obvious reminders of Sandinista rule, there are three less visible legacies. First among these is tolerance for opposition. The FSLN allowed its legal opponents far more room than had any previous Nicaraguan government. The second is the participation of marginalized groups as ordinary actors in the political process. Unions and peasants were regular participants in national dialogues throughout the Chamorro years, something that would have been unthought of in pre-Sandinista days. Last, the country has a far more inclusive, participatory, and egalitarian political culture than prior to 1979. More people know they have rights and that government is supposed to answer to them for its actions. None of these guarantee perfect or perpetual democracy, but they do make it easier to build, expand, and sustain democracy.

President Chamorro and the State of Nicaraguan Democracy

In an ideal world Violeta Chamorro would have fully constitutionalized the Nicaraguan political order while maintaining the Sandinistas' social programs as peasants, women, and workers assumed active roles within the political system. Regrettably, none of these materialized under her presidency. What did happen was that the president proved that crises do not have to bring constitutional rule to an end, sustained the nation's level of tolerance for political opposition, gave Nicaragua a free press, and delivered a measure of economic stability. All of these are significant accomplishments, even if not exciting ones.

Against these positive achievements must be balanced the administration's failures. Those that most stand out relate to violence and ungovernability, economic stagnation, and the constitutional and institutional crisis that gripped Nicaragua from the start of the constitutional conflict through the general elections. Certainly President Chamorro was not responsible for all of these shortcomings. All the same, they have to be included here because they occurred during her term of office.

Throughout the Chamorro administration, the IEN conducted a number of surveys for the UNDP. These revealed a great deal about the perceptions of democracy at the grassroots and present an intriguing, if not always hopeful, picture.[14] For instance, where just over 40 percent of respondents in 1991 felt that the government represented their interests, by 1994, this had dropped to less than 10 percent.[15] All the same, in 1994, those who felt that the country was more democratic than before President Chamorro took office outnumbered those who felt there was less democracy in Nicaragua by 49 percent to 32 percent.[16]

The best explanation for this apparent inconsistency is the overwhelming consensus among Nicaraguans that they were living through simultaneous political (90 percent), social (95 percent), and economic (99 percent) crises.[17] Democracy has never automatically implied efficiency, but it is hard to imagine democracy working well in an air of constant, all-pervasive crisis. That atmosphere is too conducive to looking for shortcuts, evading public scrutiny, and offering miracles in lieu of hard work to construct the consensus on which democratic governability depends.

The IEN's studies also considered the country's political culture, the values and beliefs that citizens hold about how government should be run and politics conducted.

> The traditional political culture of Nicaragua is hegemonic, exclusive, and confrontational, with a high propensity toward violence. Political identity consists of a global orientation ("Conservative," Liberal," "Sandinista," "Social Christian") whose ideological content is more general than specific, and which in any case is less important than the networks of loyalties to individual leaders marked by relations of personalism and patronage. . . . [This political culture] was dominant in Latin America throughout the nineteenth century and in the early years of this century. . . . Today in Nicaragua there exist side by side with the traditional political culture elements of a pluralist political culture . . . as well as . . . a tendency toward community organization and participation that can be an additional element in the exercise of democracy.[18]

No political culture that is well rooted can be transformed overnight. The steps toward forming a democratic political culture under the Sandinistas were mostly aimed at empowering the historically disenfranchised majority, not at learning the ways of negotiation, of compromise, and that a satisfactory outcome need not leave your adversary prostrate. The Chamorro years promised, at their outset, to cultivate these attitudes of tolerance and reconciliation. Conditions, social, political, and economic alike, were not propitious, and the project had limited success. However, if Nicaraguans, political professionals above all, actually pay attention to what President Chamorro did, they will note that she used a series of alliances to preserve a consistently shaky administration. To do this she and her chief adjutant, Antonio Lacayo, could declare no one anathema but had to remember that today's foe is tomorrow's friend. To some this will look like opportunism, to others it is pragmatism; but if these practices become ingrained habits and not momentary strategies they should put Nicaraguan democracy on a firmer footing.

Further contributing to the reorientation of Nicaraguan political culture were the ad hoc alliances struck between the members of the former Resistance and the Sandinistas. These began early in the administration as UNAG, a group with strong Sandinista attachments, began working with those who were recently its enemies to better protect the interests of all small property owners in the Nicaraguan countryside. And though the FSLN's last-minute electoral pact with parts of the RN may have signaled desperation on both sides more than it did reconciliation, it did at least bring the Sandinistas mayoralties in former contra areas and put the old enemies on speaking terms.

Less positive auguries of a democratic future reside in the administration's failure to strengthen state institutions.[19] Strong institutions can take great conflicts and render them amenable to solution by turning them into routine problems. That is why official development agencies like USAID and nongovernmental organizations like the National Democratic Institute spend time and money on "democratic strengthening." Projects that fall under this rubric aim to make the ordinary governmental instruments of democracy (electoral systems, judiciaries, legislatures) run better, thus performing their functions within the democratic political system more efficiently.

With the possible exception of the National Assembly, and the qualification is necessary in light of its members' behavior during their last month in office in 1996,[20] and the office of the controller general, which was growing increasingly powerful and independent as the Chamorro administration drew to a close, Nicaragua's governmental machinery did not grow notably stronger between 1990 and 1996. An overdeveloped executive, which did little to devolve the power concentrated at the center by the Sandinistas, was the main cause.[21] The 1995 constitutional amendments may be the best guarantee that Nicaragua will start to evolve the structures of governance needed in a constitutional democracy, but we need to see how the legislature acts toward a strong president with ample support in the house before making a definitive judgment.

Though the foregoing are all significant factors in the construction of democracy, the greatest problem President Chamorro faced was a deeply divided political elite, unwilling and unable to come together to support her administration's policies. Thus the central question that the Chamorro administration poses to theorists and practitioners of democratization is that of the minimum level of consensus required to sustain constitutional democracy in a transitional polity. No sooner had Violeta Chamorro taken her oath of office than her own partisans were calling for her to resign. When she did not, they organized protests and sought to make the country so ungovernable that the people would demand her ouster. That failed, too, so the president's old electoral allies, the people who rode her coattails to office, staged a legislative coup. They were lucky, because President Chamorro did not imitate her Russian counterpart, Boris Yeltsin, and send the military against the insurgents; but they did not seem to appreciate this. Rather, they were soon back looking for ways to force the president out and put in one of their own (Virgilio Godoy and Alfredo César were usually at the top of the list). Were that not enough, the president had episodes of fierce opposition from the Sandinistas, though these alternated with periods of loyal support, and was faced down by a coalition of dissent Sandinistas and defectors from the UNO in the Assembly over changes to the constitution. Worst of all for this devout Catholic, Cardinal Obando abandoned her in favor of her radical conservative detractors.

Why did the government hold? First, the security forces did not desert the government. Though their loyalty was in question at first, especially when they were very slow to act against strikers in 1990, they did not turn against Chamorro. Whether this was due to a calculation that a coup against her would bring the far right to power and the U.S. Marines to the streets of Managua, or because the FSLN counseled against it, or even because the army believed it ought to act constitutionally, is immaterial. The president could not be overthrown by force.

Second, none of the president's foes had sufficient legitimacy and authority to mobilize a serious movement against her. Though the FSLN had the best-organized party in Nicaragua, it had been rejected by 60 percent of the voters. Moreover, it was still on Washington's blacklist. The UNO's right wing had more friends in the American capital, but they had less support among Nicaraguans than did the Sandinistas; that, after all, is why the U.S. embassy in Managua intimated in 1989 that Chamorro was the best candidate to lead the UNO. And not everyone in Washington would have welcomed the thought of swashbuckling conservatives creating so much chaos in Nicaragua that the United States would again have to turn its foreign policy attentions there.

Third, and finally, Chamorro and Lacayo were able to cobble together a succession of deals and pacts that let the government muddle through. Though it was Lacayo who put the deals together, Chamorro's image and demeanor certainly had to help buy the frequently beleaguered administration time and public sympathy. The Sandinistas also deserve a nod here for recognizing that their interests were best served by pressuring President Chamorro and not by destabilizing her. And we must also include the ordinary Nicaraguans who put up with ineffective government and were not swayed by promises of political panaceas.

What emerges from this mix is a sense that the minimal level of consensus required to sustain a constitutional democracy is low indeed. The security forces must not want to oust the elected government. The bulk of the citizenry must find the incumbents more attractive than any nondemocratic alternatives. By extension, then, if people conceive of their democratic government as "the worst except for all the others," to recall Winston Churchill, democracy can survive. Yet it need not thrive. If that happens, it can become a quasi democracy with elections and the proper governmental structures, but one that manages to keep uncomfortable issues off the agenda and critics of the status quo on the minority side of the aisle.

This essentially is where President Chamorro left Nicaragua's democracy when she became the second chief executive in the country's history to hand the reins of office on to an elected successor. Democracy was stronger simply for having survived and proving to Nicaraguans that crises could be ridden out without significant restraints on public liberties.[22] Failures, especially the slowness of economic recovery and the miscarried elections, may have raised doubts, but no one was offering more attractive alternatives. So the full consolidation of democracy was not achieved, and the process of transition would carry on under President Alemán.

Nicaragua and the Politics of Democratization

Consolidation and institutionalization are not the predetermined fate of any democratic experiment. But there are alternatives to regressing to authoritarianism and dictatorship. Two of the better known are "low-intensity democracy"(LID) and "delegative democracy" (DD). The former term is used by Barry Gill, Joel Rocamora, and Richard Wilson to describe an executive-centered, conservative-dominated government that depends on the military for its survival.[23] The authors see LID as the logical outcome of low-intensity conflict (LIC), an indirect form of military intervention practiced by the United States and the Republic of South Africa in the 1980s. The LID hypothesis assumes that the old regime was rightist authoritarian,[24] so that this nonparticipatory and status quo form of democracy is the best guarantee of conservative continuity.

Guillermo O'Donnell uses DD to describe a political system that is polyarchic[25] (i.e., permits competitive elections and free opposition) but is making no progress toward deepening and broadening democracy (i.e., including more people as participants and making more parts of society subject to democratic rules).[26] In practice, a DD is strongly executive-centered; in fact, its central premise is that winning an election gives the president carte blanche to act as he or she deems appropriate. But it differs from LID in that it need not rely on the military, or repression more generally, precisely because it leaves the opposition free to criticize and the courts able to act independently of executive influence. The president,

however, can ignore these "horizontal checks" on executive power, because
he or she has the people's mandate to act decisively. Despite this concentration of power, O'Donnell argues that DDs are not effective governments,
relying as they do so strongly on one person's inclinations.

Neither of these precisely describe Nicaragua as it was in 1996, though
the delegative democratic model would have fit very well before the 1995
constitutional amendments strengthened the National Assembly's hand. Yet
the underlying notion that democratizing countries can stray from the most
direct route to their declared objective, even slip backward, certainly does
apply to Nicaragua. Staying within the six years of the Chamorro administration, one can oppose the advances of democracy (ending the war, ending
censorship, bipartisan cooperation on some issues, greater equality between
the legislative and executive branches of government) to its declines (ineffective administration, poverty inhibiting participation by some sectors,
deactivation of popular movements). It would be easy to ask if the
improvements made to the constitution offset the effects of six years of
crisis-ridden administration that ended with a botched election and leave
the matter there, but then certain points would not be considered.

Nicaraguan politics between 1990 and 1996 produced two potential
roadblocks to the institutionalization of democracy that are not much discussed by analysts of democratization. To begin, there is the parties problem. In one sense, there is no problem because the elections of both 1990
and 1996 show that Nicaragua is functionally a two-party state. However,
the presence of twenty-two other national political organizations implies
that many in the country's political class do not want to acknowledge this
or collaborate with one another to create credible third- or fourth-party
alternatives. Although these vanity microparties have done no harm, if they
were to take votes from one of the two serious contenders and so bring the
other to power, the loser might be reluctant to accept the result. This problem can be resolved by changing the Electoral Law to set a minimum
national vote needed to enter the house, but the administration that carries
such a bill through will have to be ready either to buy off the affected interests or to be castigated as an enemy of democracy.

The other possible source of obstacles to eventual democratic consolidation lies in failing to create a governing consensus, or pact, among all relevant elites. Governing without a general accord leads to adopting one of
two equally problematic models of rule. The first sees one of these competing elites always able to win a large enough quota of power to be able to
impose its philosophy on the rest, though that can produce grave discord as
easily as grudging concurrence. Alternatively, nonconforming interests can
be excluded in the hope that they will wither and die, but the dangers inher-
ing in this approach were amply revealed during the Chamorro administra-

tion. Stable, consolidated, and institutionalized democracy demands finding bases for consensus.

Nicaragua's experience between 1990 and 1996 offers eloquent testimony to how difficult that quest can be. However, the history of the Chamorro years demonstrates that these problems need not result in some truncated version of democracy in the short term. Whether any country, let alone one as poor and riven by deeply felt political divisions as Nicaragua, can overcome them indefinitely is far more problematic.

Postscript: President Alemán's First Year

Originally I had not planned to include anything about the Alemán administration. However, as the new president proceeded through his first year in office, there were signs that President Arnoldo Alemán was following more closely in the footsteps of Violeta Chamorro than he or his backers would have predicted. Because the government is still in its early days and still defining itself, this section will be brief and will focus on the country's continuing high levels of political conflict and the property settlement that he and the Sandinistas worked out.

When it became evident that Alemán was a strong candidate for the presidency, about 1994, concerns began to be expressed that the democratic gains won since 1979 would be eroded. This was not because people expected the former Managua mayor to bring back the National Guard and the repressive apparatus of the Somoza dictatorship, but because he was a caudillo, through and through. Caudillos are not patient with processes of checks and balances. They want to do things their way. If Alemán won the presidency and enough seats in the assembly, he could amend the constitution to his heart's content and have the delegative democracy Professor O'Donnell described.

Though his Liberal Alliance won only forty-two of the fifty-six seats in the National Assembly needed to reform the constitution,[27] on winning office President Alemán still struck a radical pose.[28] To show how clean his new broom would sweep, he asked the Supreme Court to step down to let him appoint an entirely new judiciary. The president also stuck by his hard line on the property question and stood firm against university students' demands for a larger slice of the national budget. Alemán, however, also ran into an equally determined and perhaps even more radical Daniel Ortega.

The Sandinistas were upset about two things. The elections, which they felt were so flawed that the races in the departments of Managua and Matagalpa should have been rerun, lay at the heart of their discontent. They also afforded the FSLN a handy means of mobilizing its supporters (defending their rights in the face of electoral fraud) and a rationale for taking politics back into the streets (the untrustworthiness of the regular legal mechanisms). To these concerns was once again added the property question. Alemán had stressed during his campaign that the resolution to the issue reached in 1995 was unacceptable, as he did not want to dedicate the proceeds of the sale of the phone company to underwriting compensation bonds. More troubling for the Sandinistas and the thousands of ordinary Nicaraguans who had benefited from property redistribution was the place the *confiscados* had staked out in the new administration. They had been key players in the president's campaign, and they were claiming their reward.

Talks on the property question between the new administration and the Sandinistas began in February. These were high-level discussions led by one top negotiator for each side: Vice President Enrique Bolaños for the government and Joaquín Cuadra Chamorro, father of the military's chief of staff, for the Sandinistas. Nevertheless, they failed to make progress, and the talks were suspended after a month. Each side charged the other of bargaining in bad faith, and each was probably right.

While its leaders were negotiating, the *confiscado* rank and file was acting. There were several attempts to forcibly evict land reform beneficiaries from their holdings in March 1997, some resulting in injuries and deaths. Lower court judges were exacerbating the situation by issuing eviction notices, even where property had been legally transferred according to rules adopted during the Chamorro administration. This raised the stakes and brought the FSLN into fighting mode. At a meeting held with the country's Sandinista mayors in mid-March to address the worsening property scene, Daniel Ortega declared that "if the government and [its] deputies don't vote in favor of suspending the evictions, this will amount to a declaration of total war . . . and continued dialogue cannot be guaranteed."[29] Vice President Bolaños retorted that Ortega and the Sandinistas were provoking violence.

As is so often the case in Nicaragua, things got worse before getting better. A week of protest, including, as in 1979, the building of barricades in the streets, led by the Sandinistas tied the country up in April. Out of this came a resumption of talks between the FSLN and the government and a "National Dialogue" organized by the Alemán administration. But where it had been the right, notably COSEP, that had played the spoiler at such meetings in the past, this time it was the FSLN and its allies who assumed that role.[30] Daniel Ortega threw down the gauntlet: "We, the Sandinistas, will not allow a dictatorship like the Somoza dynasty to be established again, and we are prepared to fight in the same way [with arms] to avoid it, because Alemán has a dictator's soul."[31]

That was in late June. By late August, the Sandinistas and the Liberals in the National Assembly were working together to pass a moratorium on evictions from contested property. In September, they agreed on amendments to the Electoral Law that greatly benefited them as the two biggest parties.[32] Then, in a bipartisan act of enormous moment, the two dominant parties in the country hammered out a new property law. Though the measure did less to protect the poor than the 1995 law, it left most expropriated property in hands other than those of its original owners. As a result, the *confiscados* objected, got the backing of the Catholic Church, and vowed to seek help in Washington.

What happened to turn the bitterest of enemies into at least momentary allies was the realization that the economy would never recover while the property question remained unsettled and the country remained poised on the brink of civil war. As in 1990, Ortega was able to mobilize the Sandinistas' partisans and use them to make the government blink. Unlike seven years before, however, the government's legislative support seemed solid and the administration secure from external threats. To be sure, the Church, the *confiscados,* and Vice President Bolaños were apoplectic, but they were without obvious leaders in public life. Godoy and César are out of office, and Alemán is the president of the republic who helped engineer the passage of the act. President Alemán, widely regarded as a pragmatist with a keen understanding of power, had realized that it was easier to coexist with the FSLN than fight it.

How did the ordinary Nicaraguan feel about all this? A Gallup poll published in early December 1997 showed them giving Alemán and Ortega identical approval ratings: 38 percent favorable, 33 percent unfavorable. Their views of Violeta Barrios de Chamorro were 69 percent favorable, 18 percent unfavorable. Doña Violeta must have been pleased.

Notes

1. Costa Rica, Latin America's longest lived constitutional democracy, followed a somewhat different route. Though the incumbent party did not retain the presidency until its fifth try (1974), one party (the National Liberation Party) held the legislature from 1953 until 1990. Rules of thumb for judging when democracy is consolidated must be seen as being approximate and indicative, not precise and absolute.

2. Paul Christopher Manuel, *The Challenges of Democratic Consolidation in Portugal* (Westport, CT: Praeger Publishers, 1996).

3. Victor M. Pérez-Díaz, *The Return of Civil Society* (Cambridge, MA: Harvard University Press, 1993).

4. Erika Polakoff and Pierre Laramee, "Grass-Roots Organizations," in *Nicaragua Without Illusions,* ed. Thomas Walker (Wilmington, DE: Scholarly Resources , 1997), pp. 185–201; cf. Karen Kampwirth, "Confronting Adversity with

Experience: The Emergence of Feminism in Nicaragua," *Social Politics* 3:3 (1996): 136–158.

5. An important influence on reformist and radical social thought in Latin America from the time of the Latin American Bishops Conference in 1968 until the mid-1980s, liberation theology interpreted the Gospels so as to discover a "preferential option for the poor." It further sought to make laypersons (delegates of the Word) and organizations other than the formal institutions of the Catholic Church (Christian base communities) key elements in the spiritual and social life of a community. Though the movement that grew around this perspective had some presence in Nicaragua, it was strongest in Brazil, Peru, and El Salvador. During the papacy of John Paul II, liberation theology fell into official disrepute and carries little weight today.

6. That this principle is violated with alarming regularity in long-established constitutional democracies, not least the United States and Canada, does not diminish its importance.

7. In early April 1997, the Nicaraguan press broke a story suggesting that substantial fraud had occurred during the privatization of agricultural properties. These were allegedly sold to administration insiders and their cronies at knockdown prices, then resold at full market value. There were also charges that state-owned banks gave loans to the insiders that were never repaid. See *NNS,* 31 March–6 April 1997, pp. 1–2.

8. Robert F. Arnove, *Education as Contested Terrain* (Boulder, CO: Westview Press, 1997), pp. 57–128.

9. Among these decisions were the retention of General Ortega as chief of staff, the exclusion of UNO party chiefs from the cabinet, and the isolation of Vice President Godoy, besides those noted here.

10. Carlos Vilas, "What Went Wrong?" *NACLA* 24:1 (1990): 10–18.

11. Christopher Clapham, "The Collapse of Socialist Development in the Third World," *Third World Quarterly* 13:1 (1992): 13–26.

12. A poll done in Grenada *after* the October 1983 U.S. invasion showed that the things that people liked about the former revolutionary regime of Maurice Bishop were better education and health care and improved physical infrastructure. For details, see Eudine Barriteau and Roberta Clarke, "Grenadian Perceptions of the People's Revolutionary Government," *Social and Economic Studies* 38:3 (1989): 31–53.

13. This law was described in Chapter 6.

14. I shall refer to three of these IEN studies: "La Probelmática de la gobernabilidad en Nicaragua: Informe de investigación sobre la opinión pública nacional," December 1992; "La Gobernabilidad y el acuerdo nacional en Nicaragua: Investigación sobre la opinón pública nacional," January 1995; and "La Transición en Nicaragua: Gobernabilidad, cultura política y opinión pública," September 1995. I wish to thank the executive director of the IEN, Rodolfo Delgado, for making these materials available to me.

15. "La Transición," p. 6.

16. "La Gobernabilidad," p. 4.

17. Ibid., p. 5.

18. "La Problemática," pp. 43–44.

19. See David R. Dye, "Notes on the Nicaraguan Transition," in *Nicaragua's Search of Democratic Consensus: A Conference Report,* ed. Cynthia J. Aronson, Joseph S. Tulchin, and Bernice Romero, Woodrow Wilson International Center for Scholars, Latin American Program Working Papers Series, no. 213 (Washington, DC: Woodrow Wilson International Center for Scholars, 1995), pp. 1–26.

20. See Chapters 4 and 7.

21. It may be objected that the Chamorro government devolved substantial responsibilities on the country's municipalities. But whether this was a genuine devolution or simply a thinly disguised downloading of responsibilities on to a junior level of government remains an open question.

22. The only suspension of the constitution occurred in 1993, and that was limited to the zones of the country where conflict was actually taking place.

23. Barry Gill, Joel Rocamora, and Richard Wilson, "Low Intensity Democracy," in *Low Intensity Democracy,* ed. Barry Gill, Joel Rocamora, and Richard Wilson (London: Pluto Press, 1993), pp. 3–34.

24. This despite the fact that LIC was best known for its use against the revolutionary states of Nicaragua, Angola, and Mozambique.

25. "Polyarchy" was of course developed by Robert Dahl. The notion of broadening and deepening democracy comes from Carl Cohen.

26. Guillermo O'Donnell, "Delegative Democracy," *Journal of Democracy* 5:1 (1994): 55–69.

27. It takes a 60 percent majority in two consecutive annual sessions to pass a constitutional amendment, for example, to allow the incumbent president to succeed himself. There are ninety-three seats in the National Assembly, counting the three that went to losing presidential candidates who scored 1.1 percent of the national vote. Thus an amending majority is fifty-six votes.

28. The description of the first year of the Alemán administration comes from issues of *CAR* and *NNS* from December 1996 to December 1997, unless otherwise noted.

29. Quoted in *NNS,* 16–22 March 1997, p. 1.

30. In fact, those who did not attend the National Dialogue constituted a National Forum, chaired by veteran Conservative leader Miriam Argüello. Participants in the National Forum were diverse enough that they could be more accurately described as opponents of Alemán and the Liberals than allies of Ortega and the FSLN.

31. Quoted in *CAR,* 26 June 1997, p. 1.

32. The changes will apply to the March 1998 regional elections in the two autonomous regions of the Atlantic coast.

Abbreviations and Acronyms

AL	Liberal Alliance
ANC	National Conservative Action
APC	Popular Conservative Alliance
APT	Area of Workers' Property
CAR	*Central America Report*
CCF	Cooperative Commonwealth Federation (Canada's)
CNN	Nicaraguan Christian Way
CNRC	National Commission to Review Confiscations
CORNAP	National Public Sector Corporations/Corporacions Nacionales del Sector Público
COSEP	Superior Council of Private Enterprise
CSE	Supreme Electoral Council
CST	Sandinista Workers' Central
DD	delegative democracy
DEC(s)	Departmental Electoral Council(s)
DN	National Directorate/Comandantes of the Revolution
EC	European Community
ECLAC	Economic Commission for Latin America and the Caribbean/Comisión Económica para América Laina y el Caribe
EPS	Sandinista Popular Army/Ejercito Popular Sandinista
ESAF	Enhanced Structural Adjustment Facility
ET	Etica y Transparencia/Ethics and Transparency
FAO	Broad Opposition Front
FNT	National Workers' Front
FROC	Revolutionary Campesino Worker Front
FSLN	Sandinista National Liberation Front/Frente Sandinista de Liberación Nacional

GDP	gross domestic product
GPP	Prolonged People's War
HDI	Human Development Index
IADB	Inter-American Development Bank
IEN	Instituto de Estudios Nicaraguenses/Institute of Nicaraguan Studies
IFIs	international financial institutions
IMF	International Monetary Fund
JD	Junta Directiva (the executive committee of the National Assembly)
JGRN	Governing Junta for National Reconstruction
JRV(s)	*Junta Receptora de Voto(s)* (polling station[s])
LASA	Latin American Studies Association
LIC	low-intensity conflict
LID	low-intensity democracy
MAP	Marxist-Leninist Popular Action Movement
MPU	United People's Movement
MRS	Sandinista Reform Movement
MUR	Unified Revolution Movement
NNS	*Nicaragua News Service*
OAS	Organization of American States
OOT	Office of Territorial Reordering
PCN	Communist Party of Nicaragua
PLC	Liberal Constitutional Party/Partido Liberal Constitucional
PLI	Independent Liberal Party
PLN	Nationalist Liberal Party
PNC	National Conservative Party
PPSC	Popular Social Christian Party
PRN	Nicaraguan Resistance Party
PSC	Social Christian Party
PSN	Nicaraguan Socialist Party
PUSC	(Costa Rica's) Social Christian Unity Party
RN	Resistencia Nicaragüense/the Resistance
SAP(s)	structural adjustment program(s)
SOE(s)	state-owned enterprise(s)
TP	Proletarian Tendency
UDC	Christian Democratic Union
UNAG	National Union of Farmers and Ranchers
UNDP	United Nations Development Program
UNO	National Union of the Opposition
USAID	U.S. Agency for International Development

Bibliography

Acevedo Vogl, Adolfo Jose, *Nicaragua y el FMI: El pozo sin fondo del ajuste.* Managua: Latino Editores, 1993.

Aldrich, John, *Why Parties? The Origin and Transformation of Political Parties in America.* Chicago: University of Chicago Press, 1995.

Arnove, Robert F., *Education as Contested Terrain.* Boulder, CO: Westview Press, 1997.

Asamblea Nacional de Nicaragua (National Assembly of Nicaragua), *Memorial legislativa, 1994.* Managua: Editorial el Parlamento, 1994.

———, *Monexico,* various dates.

Avila, Ricardo, "Hunger Strike in Nicaragua," *Nicaragua Through Our Eyes* 3:4 (1988).

Babb, Florence, "After the Revolution: Neoliberal Policy and Gender in Nicaragua," *Latin American Perspectives* 23:1 (1996): 27–48.

Barricada, Managua, various dates.

Barrios de Chamorro, Violeta, with Sonia Cruz de Baltadano and Guido Fernandez, *Dreams of the Heart: The Autobiography of President Violeta Barrios de Chamorro of Nicaragua.* New York: Simon & Schuster, 1996.

Barriteau, Eudine, and Roberta Clarke, "Grenadian Perceptions of the People's Revolutionary Government," *Social and Economic Studies* 38:3 (1989): 31–53.

Bauer, Peter T., *Dissent or Development.* London: Weidenfeld & Nicolson, 1972.

———, *Reality and Rhetoric: Studies in the Economics of Development.* London: Weidenfeld & Nicolson, 1984.

Baylora, Enrique, ed., *Comparing New Democracies.* Boulder, CO: Westview Press, 1987.

Berman, Karl, *Under the Big Stick.* Boston: South End Press, 1986.

Bethel, Leslie, ed., *The Cambridge History of Latin America.* Cambridge: Cambridge University Press, various dates.

Binder, Leonard, James Coleman, Joseph LaPalombara, Lucien Pye, Sidney Verba and Myron Wiener, *Crises and Sequences in Political Development.* Princeton, NJ: Princeton University Press, 1971.

Biondi-Morra, Brizio N., *Revolucion y política alimentaria: Un análisis crítico de Nicaragua.* Mexico City: Siglo Ventiuno. 1990.

Black, George, *The Triumph of the People.* London: Zed Books, 1981.

Booth, John, *The End and the Beginning,* 2d. ed. Boulder, CO: Westview Press, 1988.

Brown, R. P C.,"IMF and Paris Club Debt Rescheduling," *Journal of International Development* 4 (1992): 291–313.

Bulmer-Thomas, Victor, *The Economic History of Latin America Since Independence.* Cambridge: Cambridge University Press, 1994.

Burns, E. Bradford, *Patriarch and Folk.* Cambridge, MA: Harvard University Press, 1991.

Butler, Judy, David R. Dye, and Jack Spence, with George Vickers, *Democracy and Its Discontents: Nicaraguans Face the Election.* Cambridge, MA: Hemisphere Initiatives, 1996.

Cajina, Roberto, *Transicion politica y reconversion militar en Nicaragua.* Managua: CRIES [Coordinadora Regional de Investigaciones Economicas y Sociales], 1997.

CAR (Central America Report), Guatemala City, Guatemala, various dates.

Cardoso, Eliana, and Ann Helwege, *Latin America's Economy.* Cambridge, MA: MIT Press, 1992.

Carothers, Thomas, *In the Name of Democracy.* Berkeley: University of California Press, 1991.

Carranza, Carlos, and Jose Chinchilla, "Ajuste estructural en Costa Rica, 1985–1993," *Los Pequenos paises de América Latina en la hora neoliberal,* coord., Gerónimo de Sierra. Caracas, Venezuela: Editorial Nueva Sociedad, 1994.

Carter Center, *Observing Nicaragua's Elections, 1989–1990: Report of the Council of Freely Elected Heads of Government.* Atlanta, GA: The Carter Center, Emory University, 1990.

Carter Center, Latin American and Caribbean Program,"Nicaraguan Property Disputes," report prepared for the United Nations Development Program, April 1995.

Caster, Mark, "The Return of Somocism? The Rise of Arnoldo Alemán," *NACLA* 30:2 (September/October 1996): 6–9.

Castillo, Ernesto, "The Problem of Property and Property Owners," *Envio* 16:196 (November 1997): 38–39.

Catalan Aravena, Oscar, "The Logic Behind the Stabilization Politics of the Chamorro Government in Nicaragua," in *Economic Maladjustment in Central America,* ed. Wim Pelupessy and John Weeks. London: Macmillan, 1993.

Chamorro, Pedro Joaquín, *Estripe Sangriente: Los Somozas.* Mexico City: Diógenes, 1979.

Christian, Shirley, *Revolution in the Family.* New York: Vintage Books, 1986.

Christian Science Monitor, various dates.

Clapham, Christopher, "The Collapse of Socialist Development in the Third World," *Third World Quarterly* 13:1 (1992): 13–26.

Close, David, "The Nicaraguan Election of 1984," *Electoral Studies* 5:2 (1985): 152–158.

———, *Nicaragua: Politics, Economics, and Society.* London: Pinter Publishers, 1988.

———, "Counterinsurgency in Nicaragua," *New Political Science,* nos. 18–19 (fall/winter 1990): 5–19.

———, "Central American Elections, 1989–90: Costa Rica, El Salvador, Honduras, Nicaragua, Panama," *Electoral Studies* 10:1 (1991): 60–76.

———, "Nicaragua: The Legislature as Seedbed of Conflict," in *Legislatures and the New Democracies in Latin America,* ed. David Close. Boulder, CO: Lynne Rienner Publishers, 1995.

Close, David, Andres Franco, and Andres Talero, "Strengthening Democracy in Latin America Through Electoral Reform," report prepared for the Canadian Foundation for the Americas, 1997.

Collins, Joe, *What Difference Could a Revolution Make?* San Francisco: Food First, 1982.

Conroy, Michael, "Economic Aggression as an Instrument of Low-Intensity Warfare," in *Reagan Versus the Sandinistas,* ed. Thomas Walker. Boulder, CO: Westview Press, 1987.

CORNAP (National Public Sector Corporations/Corporacions Nacionales del Sector Público), *Avance del proceso de privatización al 31 de diciembre de 1994.* Managua: CORNAP, 1995.

Cornelius, Wayne, "The Nicaraguan Elections of 1984: A Reassessment of the Domestic and International Significance," in *Elections and Democratization in Latin America, 1981–1985,* ed. Paul Drake and Eduardo Silva. San Diego: Center for Iberian and Latin American Studies, University of California at San Diego, 1986.

Cortés, Guillermo, *La lucha por el poder.* Managua: Editorial Vanguardia, 1990.

Council of Freely Elected Heads of Government, *The Observation of the 1996 Nicaraguan Elections.* Atlanta, GA: Carter Center, Emory University, 1997.

Dahl, Robert, "The Newer Democracies: From the Time of Triumph to the Time of Troubles," in *After Authoritarianism: Democracy or Disorder?* ed. Daniel N. Nelson. Westport, CT: Praeger Publishers, 1995.

De Castro, Sergio, interview, Managua, November 1985.

Delaney, Tomás, interview, Managua, November 1991.

Di Palma, Guiseppe, *To Craft Democracies.* Berkeley: University of California Press, 1990.

Dickerson, Mark, and Thomas Flanagan, *An Introduction to Government and Politics,* 4th ed. Scarborough, Ontario: Nelson Canada, 1994.

Dickey, Christopher, *With the Contras.* New York: Touchstone, 1987.

Diederich, Bernard, *Somoza.* New York: Dutton, 1981.

Dillon, Sam, *Commandos.* New York: Henry Holt, 1991.

Dodd, Thomas, *Managing Democracy in Central America.* New Brunswick, NJ: Transaction Publishers, 1992.

Dodson, Michael, and Laura O'Shaughnessy, *Nicaragua's Other Revolution.* Chapel Hill: University of North Carolina Press, 1990.

Doh Shull Shin, "On the Third Wave of Democratization," *World Politics* 47 (October 1994): 135–170.

Dunkerly, James, *Power in the Isthmus.* London: Verso, 1988.

Dye, David R., "Notes on the Nicaraguan Transition," in *Nicaragua's Search of Democratic Consensus: A Conference Report,* ed. Cynthia J. Aronson, Joseph S. Tulchin, and Bernice Romero. Woodrow Wilson International Center for Scholars Latin American Program Working Papers Series, no. 213. Washington, DC: Woodrow Wilson International Center for Scholars, 1995.

Dye, David, et al., *Contesting Everything, Winning Nothing.* Cambridge, MA: Hemisphere Initiatives, 1995.

Eckstein, Harry, and Ted Robert Gurr, *Patterns of Authority: A Structural Basis for Political Inquiry.* New York: Wiley, 1975.

ECLAC (Economic Commission for Latin America and the Caribbean Comisión Económica para América Latina y el Caribe), *Anuario Estadístico de América Latina y el Caribe, 1993.* New York: United Nations, 1993.

———, *Statistical Yearbook for Latin America and the Caribbean, 1994.* New York: United Nations, 1995.

El Nuevo Diario, Managua, various dates.

Enriquez, Laura, *Harvesting Change.* Chapel Hill: University of North Carolina Press, 1991.

Envio, Managua, various dates.

Ethier, Diane, ed., *Democratic Transition and Consolidation in Southern Europe, Latin America, and Southeast Asia.* London: Macmillan, 1990.

Evans, Trevor, coord., *La transformación neoliberal del sector público.* Managua: Latino Editores, 1995.

Evertz, Roberto, interview, Managua, November 1995.

Feigelbaum, Harvey B., and Jeffery R. Henig, "The Political Underpinnings of Privatization: A Typology," *World Politics* 46:2 (January 1994): 185–208.

Fernández Poncela, Anna M., "The Disrputions of Adjustment," *Latin American Perspectives* 23:1 (1996): 49–66.

Fonseca, Carlos, *Ideario político de Agusto Cesar Sandino.* Managua: Departamento de Propaganda y Educación Política del FSLN, 1984.

———, *Sandino: Guerrillero proletario.* Managua: Departamento de Propaganda y Educación Política del FSLN, 1984.

ISLN (Sandinista National Liberation Front/Frente Sandinista de Liberación Nacional), *Plataforma Nacional.* Managua: FSLN, 1996.

Gamble, Andrew, *The Free Economy and the Strong State.* London: Macmillan, 1987.

Gamez, José Dolres, *Historia de Nicaragua.* Managua: Banco de America, 1975 [1889].

Gilbert, Dennis, *Sandinistas.* Oxford: Blackwell, 1988.

Gill, Barry, Joel Rocamora, and Richard Wilson, "Low Intensity Democracy," in *Low Intensity Democracy,* ed. Barry Gill, Joel Rocamora, and Richard Wilson. London: Pluto Press, 1993.

González, Miguel, "Militares y civiles planearon asesinar al Rey y al presidente en el desfile de a Coruña de 1985," *El Pais,* electronic ed. (9 December 1997), at: http://www.elpais.es/p/d/19971209/espana/coruna.html.

Gorman, Stephen, "Power and Consolidation in the Nicaraguan Revolution," *Journal of Latin American Studies* 13:1 (1981): 133–149.

Guevara Carrión, Ricardo, y Javier Matus L., "Analysis de la situación actual de la tenencia de la tierra en Nicaragua," unpublished ms., April 1996.

———, "Avances en la solución al problema de la propriedad: Situación al 30 de septiembre de 1996," draft document, UNDP in Nicaragua, 1996.

Haggard, Stephen, and Robert Kaufman, eds., *The Politics of Economic Adjustment.* Princeton, NJ: Princeton University Press, 1992.

Hillman, Richard S., *Democracy for the Privileged: Crisis and Transition in Venezuela.* Boulder, CO: Lynne Rienner Publishers, 1994.

Hodges, Donald, *Ideological Foundations of the Nicaraguan Revolution.* Austin: University of Texas Press, 1986.

Huntington, Samuel, *The Third Wave.* Norman: University of Oklahoma Press, 1991.

IADB (Inter-American Development Bank), "Basic Socio-Economic Data," *Nicaragua: Statistics and Quantitative Data,* electronic ed. (15 September 1997), at: http://database.iadb.org/int/basicrep/banic/html.

IEN (Instituto de Estudios Nicaraguenses), *Encuesta socio-politica nacional, #1.* Managua: IEN, 1990.

———, "La Problemática de la gobernabilidad en Nicaragua: Informe de investigación sobre la opinión pública nacional," report, December 1992.

————, "La Gobernabilidad y el acuerdo nacional en Nicaragua: Investigación sobre la opinión pública nacional," report, January 1995.

————, "La Transición en Nicaragua: Gobernabilidad, cultura política y opinión pública," report, September 1995.

International Institute for Strategic Studies, *The Military Balance: 1991–92.* London: Brassey's, 1991.

Kampwirth, Karen,"Confronting Adversity with Experience: The Emergence of Feminism in Nicaragua," *Social Politics* 3:3 (1996): 136–158.

————, "The Mother of the Nicaraguans," *Latin American Perspectives* 23:1 (1996): 67–86.

Karl, Terry Lynn, "Petroleum and Political Pacts: The Transition to Democracy in Venezuela," *Latin American Research Review* 22:1 (1988): 63–94.

Karl, Terry Lynn, and Philippe Schmitter, "Modes of Transition in Latin America, Southern and Eastern Europe," *International Social Science Journal* 138 (May 1991): 268–284.

————, "Democratization Around the Globe: Opportunities and Risks," in *World Security: Challenges for a New Century,* 2d ed., ed. Michael T. Klare and Daniel C. Thomas. New York: St. Martin's Press, 1994.

Kaufmann, Daniel, and Paul Siegelbaum, "Privatization and Corruption in Transition Economies," *Journal of International Affairs* 50:2 (winter 1997): 419–458.

Killick, Tony, *A Reaction Too Far: Economic Theory and the Role of the State in Developing Countries.* London: Overseas Development Unit, 1989.

Kirk, John, *Politics and the Catholic Church in Nicaragua.* Gainesville: University Press of Florida, 1992.

Komisar, Lucy, *Corazon Aquino: The Story of a Revolution.* New York: George Braziller, 1987.

Kornbluth, Peter, *Nicaragua: The Price of Intervention.* Washington, DC: Institute for Policy Studies, 1987.

Landau, Saul, *Guerrilla Wars of Central America.* New York: St. Martin's Press, 1993.

LASA (Latin American Studies Association), "Report of the Latin American Studies Association Delegation to Observe the Nicaraguan General Election of November 4, 1984," *LASA Forum* 15:4 (1984): 9–43.

————, *Report of the LASA Delegation to Observe the Nicaraguan General Elections of February 25, 1990.* Pittsburgh, PA: LASA, 1990.

Leftwich, Adrian, "Governance, Democracy, and Development in the Third World," *Third World Quarterly* 14 (1993): 605.

Lichbach, Mark, "Regime Change: A Test of Structuralist and Functionalist Explanations," *Comparative Political Studies* 14 (1981): 49–73.

Macauley, Neil, *The Sandino Affair.* Durham, NC: Duke University Press, 1985.

Mainwaring, Scott, Guillermo O'Donnell, and J. Samuel Valenzuela, eds., *Issues in Democratic Consolidation.* Notre Dame, IN: University of Notre Dame Press, 1992.

Manuel, Paul Christopher, *The Challenges of Democratic Consolidation in Portugal.* Westport, CT: Praeger Publishers, 1996.

Marenco, Julio, interview, Managua, November 1995.

Martínez Cuenca, Alejandro, *Nicaragua: Una década de retos.* Managua: Editorial Nueva Nicaragua, 1990.

McCoy, Jennifer L., and Shelley A. McConnell, "Nicaragua: Beyond the Revolution," *Current History* 98:107 (1997): 75–80.

Merryman, John Henry, *The Civil Law Tradition*. Stanford, CA: Stanford University Press, 1969.

Merton, Robert, "The Unanticipated Consequences of Purposive Social Action," *American Sociological Review* 1 (1936): 894–904.

Mesoamerica, San José, Costa Rica, various dates.

Millett, Richard, *Guardians of the Dynasty*. Maryknoll, NY: Orbis Books, 1977.

Munro, Dana, *The U.S. and the Caribbean*. New York: Johnson Reprints, 1966 [1934].

———, *The Five Republics of Central America*. New York: Russell & Russell, 1967 [1918].

La Nacion, San José, Costa Rica, electronic ed. (various dates), at: http://www.nacion.co.cr.

Neira Cuadra, Oscar, coord., *ESAF: Condicionalidad y deuda*. Managua: CRIES [Coordinadora Regional de Investigaciones Economicas y Sociales] 1996.

Nelson, Joan, ed., *Economic Crisis and Policy Choice*. Princeton, NJ: Princeton University Press, 1990.

New York Times, various dates.

Nicaragua, Government of, *La Gaceta: Diario Oficial* (Nicaraguan Official Gazette), various dates.

Nicaragua, Government of, Ministerio de Gobernación, Policía Nacional, *Compendio estadístico: 1991–1995*. Managua: Policia Nacional, 1996.

NNS (Nicaragua News Service), Washington, DC, various dates.

Nolan, David, *The Ideology of the Sandinistas and the Nicaraguan Revolution*. Coral Gables, FL: Institute of Interamerican Studies, Graduate School of International Studies, University of Miami, 1984.

Notifax, Managua, electronic ed. (various dates), at :http://www.notifax.com.

Núñez, Eusebio, interview, Managua, 20 October 1995.

O'Donnell, Guillermo, "Delegative Democracy," *Journal of Democracy* 5:1 (1994): 55–69.

O'Donnell, Guillermo, Philippe Schmitter, and Laurence Whitehead, eds., *Transitions from Authoritarian Rule: Prospects for Democracy*. Baltimore: Johns Hopkins University Press, 1986.

Oquist, Paul, "The Sociopolitical Dynamics of the 1990 Nicaraguan Elections," in *The 1990 Elections in Nicaragua and Their Aftermath,* ed. Vanessa Castro and Gary Prevost. Lanham, MD: Rowman & Littlefield, 1992.

Ortega Saavedra, Humberto, *Nicaragua: Revolución y democracia*. Mexico City: Organización Editorial Mexicana, n.d.

Ortega, Marvin, interview, Managua, March 1990.

Pastor, Robert A., ed., *Democracy in the Americas: Stopping the Pendulum*. New York: Holmes & Meier, 1989.

Patterson, Henry, "The 1996 Elections and Nicaragua's Fragile Transition," *Government and Opposition* 32:3 (1997): 380–398.

Pérez-Díaz, Victor M., *The Return of Civil Society*. Cambridge, MA: Harvard University Press, 1993.

PLC (Liberal Constitutional Party/Partido Liberal Constitucional), "Nicaragua: La nueva estrategia económica, 1997–2001," unpublished document, n.d.

"La pobreza en Nicaragua," *El Observador Económico* 43 (July 1995): 24–28.

Polakoff, Erika, and Pierre Laramee, "Grass-Roots Organizations," in *Nicaragua Without Illusions,* ed. Thomas W. Walker. Wilmington, DE: Scholarly Resources, 1997.

Polanyi, Karl, *The Great Transformation*. Boston: Beacon Press, 1944.

La Prensa, Managua, various dates.

Prevost, Gary, "The FSLN," in *Nicaragua Without Illusions,* ed. Thomas Walker. Wilmington, DE: Scholarly Resources, 1997.

Przeworski, Adam, ed., *Sustainable Democracy.* Cambridge: Cambridge University Press, 1995.

Ramírez, Sergio, ed., *El pensamiento vivo de Sandino.* San José, Costa Rica: EDUCA [Editorial Universitaria Centroamericana], 1980.

Remmer, Karen, "The Sustainability of Political Democracy: Lessons from South America," *Comparative Political Studies* 29:6 (1996): 611–634.

Rieff, Alexis, "The Role of the Paris Club in Managing the Debt Problem," *Studies in International Finance, No. 161.* Princeton, NJ: International Finance Section Department, Princeton University, 1985.

Rizo, José, interview, Managua, 5 October 1995.

Robinson, William I., and Kent Norsworthy, *David and Goliath: The U.S. War Against Nicaragua.* New York: Monthly Review Press, 1987.

Robinson, William, *A Faustian Bargain.* Boulder, CO: Westview Press, 1993.

Ruchwarger, Gary, *The People in Power.* South Hadley, MA: Bergin & Garvey, 1987.

Rueschemeyer, Dietrich, Evelyne Huber Stephens, and John D. Stephens, *Capitalist Development and Democracy.* Chicago: University of Chicago Press, 1993.

Rustow, Dankwart, "Transitions to Democracy: Toward a Dynamic Model," *Comparative Politics* 2:3 (1970): 337–364.

Ryan, Phil, *The Fall and Rise of the Market in Sandinista Nicaragua.* Montreal: McGill-Queen's University Press, 1995.

Saldomando, Angel, *Nicaragua con el futuro en juego. Managua: CRIES, 1996.*

Saldomando, Angel, and Elvira Cuadra, *Los Problemas de la Pacificación en Nicaragua.* Documento de Trabajo No. 94/2. Managua: CRIES, 1994.

Scranton, Margaret E., "Panama's First Post-Transition Election," *Journal of Interamerican Studies* 37:1 (1995): 69–100.

Scroggs, William O., *Filibusters and Financiers.* New York: Macmilian, 1916.

Selser, Gregorio, *Sandino.* New York: Monthly Review Press, 1980.

El Semanario, Managua, various dates.

Sevigny, David, *The Paris Club: An Inside View.* Ottawa: North-South Institute, 1990.

Siete Dias, Managua, various dates.

Sklar, Holly, *Washington's War on Nicaragua.* Toronto: Between the Lines, 1988.

Smith, Stephen Kent, "Renovation and Orthodoxy: Debate and Transition Within the Sandinista National Liberation Front," *Latin American Perspectives* 24:2 (March 1997): 102–116.

Spalding, Rose, *Capitalists and Revolution in Nicaragua.* Chapel Hill: University of North Carolina Press, 1995.

Stahler-Sholk, Richard, "El ajuste neoliberal y sus alternativas: La repuesta del movimiento sindical en Nicaragua," *Revista Mexicana de Sociologia* 56:3 (1994): 3–21.

———, "Breaking the Mold: Economic Orthodoxy and the Politics of Resistance in Nicaragua," paper presented to the LASA congress, Washington, DC, 1995.

———, "The Dog That Didn't Bark: Labor Autonomy and Economic Adjustment in Nicaragua Under the Sandinista and UNO Governments," *Comparative Politics* 28:1 (1995): 77–101.

———, "Structural Adjustment and Resistance: The Political Economy of Nicaragua Under Chamorro," in *The Undermining of the Sandinista*

Revolution, ed. Gary Prevost and Harry E. Vanden. New York: St. Martin's Press, 1997.

Stanfield, J. David, "An Analysis of the Current Situation Regarding Land Tenure in Nicaragua," report prepared for the Swedish International Development Authority November 1994.

Stansifer, Charles, "José Santos Zelaya: A New Look at Nicaragua's Liberal Dictator," *Revista Interamericana* 7:4 (1977): 468–485.

Talbot, John M.,"The Struggle for Control of a Commodity Chain: Instant Coffee from Latin America," *Latin American Research Review* 32:2 (1997): 117–135.

Teplitz, Benjamin, "The Political and Economic Foundations of Modernization in Nicaragua: The Administration of José Santos Zelaya," unpublished Ph.D. diss., Howard University, Washington, DC, 1973.

Torres Rivas, Edelberto, *Sandino.* Mexico City: Katun, 1984.

La Tribuna, Managua, various dates.

Turner, Arthur W., "Postauthoritarian Elections: Testing Expectations About 'First' Elections," *Comparative Political Studies* 26:3 (1993): 330–349.

UNDP (United Nations Development Program), *Human Development Report, 1990.* New York: Oxford University Press, 1990.

———, "Contributions to the Analysis of the Nicaraguan Transition," report presented to the Consultative Group on Nicaragua, 1995.

———, *Human Development Report, 1996.* New York: Oxford University Press, 1996.

USAID (U.S. Agency for International Development), "Nicaragua: Selected Economic Data," *USAID, 1996: Latin American and the Caribbean Selected Economic and Social Data: Country Economic Data,* electronic ed. (8 August 1997), at: http://www.lanic.utexas.edu/la/region/aid/aid96/Country_Economic/niccen.html.

Vanden, Harry E., and Gary Prevost, *Democracy and Socialism in Sandinista Nicaragua.* Boulder, CO: Lynne Rienner Publishers, 1993.

Vernoy, Ronnie, "Starting All Over Again," unpublished Ph.D. diss., Agricultural University of Wageningen, Netherlands, 1992.

Vilas, Carlos, *State, Class, and Ethnicty in Nicaragua.* Boulder, CO: Lynne Rienner Publishers, 1989.

———, "What Went Wrong?" *NACLA* 24:1 (1990): 10–18.

———, "Family Affairs: Class, Lineage, and Politics in Contemporary Nicaragua," *Journal of Latin American Studies* 24:2 (1992): 309–344.

Walker, Thomas, *Nicaragua: Land of Sandino.* Boulder, CO: Westview Press, 1991.

———, ed., *Reagan Versus the Sandinistas.* Boulder, CO: Westview Press, 1987.

———, *Revolution and Counterrevolution in Nicaragua.* Boulder, CO: Westview Press, 1991.

———, *Nicaragua Without Illusions.* Wilmington, DE: Scholarly Resources, 1997.

Walter, Knut, *The Regime of Anastasio Somoza, 1936–1956.* Chapel Hill: University of North Carolina Press, 1993.

Watkins, Melville, "A Theory of Staples-led Growth," in *Approaches to Canadian Economic History,* ed. W. T. Easterbrook and M. H. Watkins. Toronto: McClelland & Stewart, 1967.

Weeks, John, "The Nicaraguan Stabilization Program of 1989," in *Economic Maladjustment in Central America,* ed. Wim Pelupessy and John Weeks. London: Macmillan, 1993.

Wiarda, Howard, *Iberia and Latin America: New Democracies, New Policies, New Models.* Lanham, MD: Rowman & Littlefield, 1996.

Williams, Gavin, "Why Structural Adjustment Is Necessary and Why It Doesn't Work," *Review of African Political Economy* 60 (1994): 214–225.

Williams, Philip, *The Catholic Church and Politics in Nicaragua and Costa Rica.* London: Macmillan, 1989.

Woodward, Ralph Lee, *Central America.* New York: Oxford University Press, 1973.

World Bank, *Social Indicators of Development, 1996.* Baltimore: Johns Hopkins University Press, 1996.

———, "Nicaragua: Poverty Assessment Summary," *Summary of Poverty Assessments Completed in Fiscal 1995,* electronic ed. (7 August 1997), at: http://www.worldbank.org/html/hcovp/povertyfy95pa.html.

———, *World Development Report, 1997.* New York: Oxford University Press, 1997.

World Health Organization and Pan-American Health Organization, "Datos basicos socioeconomicos: Nicaragua, 1996," *Datos Basicos Nicaragua,* electronic ed. (7 August 1997), at: http://www.ops.org.ni.

Zakuta, Leo, *The CCF: A Social Movement Becalmed.* Toronto: University of Toronto Press, 1964.

Zawadski, Cristobal, interview, San José, Costa Rica, 17 January 1990.

Zub, Roberto, *Protestanismo y elecciones en Nicaragua.* Managua: Ediciones Nicarao, 1993.

Index

About the Book

In 1990, Nicaraguans voted out the revolutionary Sandinista regime and replaced it with the conservative government of President Violeta Chamorro. Chamorro's term of office was marked by constitutional, economic, partisan, and social conflict, as her administration attempted to replace the revolutionary system with representative government and market economics.

Close examines these conflicts and assesses their impact on Nicaragua's political actors and governmental institutions. He concludes with an analysis of the 1996 Nicaraguan elections and with a provocative exploration of the impact of the revolution on Nicaragua today.

David Close is professor of political science at Memorial University of Newfoundland. His numerous publications include *Nicaragua: Politics, Economics, Society* and *Legislatures and the New Democracies in Latin America.*